WOMEN'S EMPLOYMENT AND THE CAPITALIST FAMILY

The current political interest in the position of women bears evidence to the growing recognition of the economic, social and, not least, electoral importance of women. Likewise, the establishment and development of Women's Studies as a serious and legitimate subject and the subsequent growth in literature examining the rapidly changing lives of women.

Women's Employment and the Capitalist Family critically assesses much of this literature and contributes to it by offering an explanation of women's labour-market participation. In particular, the book deals with the domestic labour debate, the role of patriarchy theory, gender and labour-market theory, periodising the capitalist family and the specific position of working women in the British economy. In order to explain the timing of women's increasing dependence on waged work the author necessarily draws upon demographic, and historical factors such as tracing the drive to mass consumption through factory production – itself logically associated with women entering the labour market. While the economic issues associated with women's work form the central focus of the book, it is necessary to consider the non-economic contributory factors. The book, therefore, takes on an interdisciplinary approach. Thus, although primarily a theoretical contribution, full use is made of historical and empirical material, both in illustrating the arguments and formulating them.

The work is written from a Marxist-Feminist perspective and although there is a tendency at present to discredit all things Marxist, the author argues convincingly that this approach offers a greater challenge to the orthodoxies within economics and sociology which have been largely untouched by so-called 'post-modernist' theories. Despite the theoretical stand-point, the book avoids technicalities and will be accessible to a wide, interdisciplinary audience.

Ben Fine is Director of the Centre for Economic Policy for South Africa in the Department of Economics at SOAS. He is the author of many books and articles on political economy and he has served as an economist for the Greater London Council, the National Union of Mineworkers and as a member of the ANC's Department of Economic Policy.

WOMEN'S EMPLOYMENT AND THE CAPITALIST FAMILY

Ben Fine

London and New York

First published 1992
by Routledge
11 New Fetter Lane, London EC4P 4EE

Simultaneously published in the USA and Canada
by Routledge
a division of Routledge, Chapman and Hall, Inc.
29 West 35th Street, New York, NY 10001

Typeset by Michael Mepham, Frome, Somerset
Printed in Great Britain by
Biddles Ltd, Guildford and King's Lynn

British Library Cataloguing in Publication Data
A catalogue record for this book is available from
the British Library.

Library of Congress Cataloging in Publication Data
Fine, Ben   Women's employment and the capitalist
family / Ben Fine
p.   cm.
Includes bibliographical references and index.
1. Civil society. I. Title.

CIP

ISBN 0–415–08334–6

CONTENTS

v

CONTENTS

PREFACE

This book has been written as a consequence of a research project, funded by the Leverhulme Trust, to study consumption norms and female labour-market participation. It is complemented by a volume, jointly authored with Ellen Leopold and shortly to appear, covering both a critique of the treatment of consumption across the social sciences and a more positive analysis of consumption based on the idea of 'systems of provision'. The research has also led to empirical estimation of consumption norms for different household types by use of data from the National Readership Survey and the General Household Survey. The writing up of these results is also soon to be completed.

Many, some unknown, have helped me during the preparation of this book. I wish to thank them all, but particularly Jan O'Brien whose comments and encouragement have led to vast improvements in presentation and content.

INTRODUCTION

OVERVIEW

Women's lives are currently changing rapidly across many different dimensions of their lives. Unsurprisingly, this has been accompanied by an equally dramatic growth of interest in women's studies, with a corresponding boom in the associated literature across its many constituent disciplines. This poses a formidable task to those seeking to add to this literature. Both theoretically and materially, the subject matter constitutes a shifting terrain, a target that potentially moves faster than an accurate aim can be taken at it. The relevant literature is not only broadly based by subject matter but also demanding of an interdisciplinary approach. For the latter, compartmentalisation of the different social sciences has meant the availability of few analytical precedents upon which to draw and the necessity for any one scholar to tread on theoretical territory that is both unfamiliar and intellectually intimidating.

Consequently, this book is offered tentatively as an exploratory contribution to the literature. It has been motivated by the wish to understand the growth of female labour-market participation in the post-war period. Whilst it has been written by an economist, its content has unavoidably strayed far beyond its original intent, both in the issues covered and in the methods of enquiry employed. Such broadening of scope has not always been evenly spread, with some important topics being neglected or even omitted altogether, whilst others are explored in great detail.

This is because of the wish to address major theoretical issues and both to explore and to illustrate their application by use of historical and empirical material. Hopefully, this will assist others

1

in examining other diverse issues, not directly or insufficiently addressed, such as stratification, racial divisions and the role of training. The book consists of four main chapters. Each of them is a partial survey of the subject under consideration and a summary of the results of each of these chapters will be provided later in this introduction.

It is worth beginning, however, by bringing some methodological issues to the fore. To a large extent, although this has been less true of economics than of other disciplines, academic debate over the changing position of women has involved a presumed confrontation between principles of feminism and Marxism. In some instances, the abstract and gender-neutral categories of Marxism have been perceived to have led to the neglect of women's oppression, as their application in practice has not moved beyond that neutrality. This has meant a male-oriented focus and a blindness to the exploitative relations between men and women. Also, it has been argued that the problems of Marxism from a feminist perspective run even deeper. Marxist categories preclude the study of women's oppression other than as an epiphenomenon, as part of the determined superstructure. The political proposition that women's liberation will be dependent upon, and won through, socialist revolution looks no more palatable in theory than it has proved in practice – whatever the relation between the actually (or previously) existing socialist countries and the ideals of Marxism.

This critical view of Marxism is often wedded to an analytical transformation in which feminism substitutes the categories of gender for those of class. Paradoxically, whilst the substance of Marxism is rejected, its analytical structure is retained, and the oppressive relations of the sexes are treated by analogy with those of exploitation between classes (just as 'Third Worldism' treats the relations between nations as exploitative). The idea is to privilege analytically the categories of gender where previously this had been the perogative of (gender-neutral) classes. From a feminist perspective, there are theoretical, empirical and political attractions for doing this. Analytically, an abstract understanding of (male) power can be appropriated – from which can be derived an understanding of women's oppression, and their struggle against it, across the various aspects of social relations and their ideological rationales. Empirically, the persistence of women's disadvantage through history to the present day is readily incorporated. And,

2

politically, prominence and priority is given to women's struggles for equality with men.

This discussion has highlighted, possibly caricatured, the division between fundamental Marxism and radical feminism. The differences may be too sharply drawn and, to a large extent, they have become outmoded for two very separate reasons. First, there have been analytical developments which fall into neither camp and which would be described as Marxist feminism. A synthesis is sought between the two extremes and an irreconcilable conflict between Marxism and feminism is denied. The intent of this book is to contribute to this tradition.

A second reason why the crude opposition between Marxism and feminism has become less prominent is because each of them, especially in the academic arena, has experienced an intellectual evolution with some features in common. Within social theory, the age of post-Xism is upon us, where X may be equal to structural, modern, Marx or many of the other tokens of earlier discredited approaches. This has led to much greater emphasis being placed upon discourse and interpretative analysis and a rejection as dogmatic of a belief in the persistence and pertinence of analysis by way of abstract structures, processes and underlying determinants.

These recent developments, perhaps best summarised by the term post-modernism, apply across a range of applications which are diverse both in content and approach. They tend to neglect material practices. More attention is paid to what we mean by power than to what it is and how it is exercised. This book is more old-fashioned in the sense of attempting to unravel the material determinants, the forces and relations in society, that have been associated with women's changing labour-market position, although ideological considerations have not been left aside. To some extent, this inevitably courts the accusation of being antediluvian, of being forced to wear the mantle of old-style fundamentalism – even though such accusations are certainly inappropriate by the standards of the previous confrontation between Marxism and feminism. Paradoxically, then, much of the analysis offered here might be considered more relevant as a challenge to the continuing orthodoxies within economics and sociology, where the empirical tradition and their theoretical foundations have remained relatively untouched by the social theory that has evolved out of and beyond Marxism and feminism.

This all necessarily sounds defensive, unsurprising in view of the ideological climate currently confronting Marxism – both from the right and from within the left. The stance adopted here can be put more positively through the assertion of a number of themes whose rationale will be found during the course of the presentation of the arguments. First, the priority of gender over class is rejected, together with the idea that gender theory can be satisfactorily constructed by analogy with class theory. Paradoxically, one of the principal objections to class theory is its insensitivity to gender and other sources of social differentiation. But exactly the same critique, other than for gender, would apply to the notion that men and women as such form classes. The 'class' of women is so fragmented by traditional class as well as other cleavages as to constitute too heterogeneous a category for unravelling the social structures and processes by which they are oppressed.

Second, none the less, there are structures and processes within society that systematically lead to the oppression of women. However, it does not follow that these must be understood, in the first instance, through categories of analysis that are explicitly endowed with a gender content. The use of notions such as capital and the state, and the power relations associated with them, does not preclude an understanding of the oppression of women.

Third, such an understanding can be developed once analysis itself is structured in correspondence to underlying economic and other determinants, and the social relations within which they operate or which they press to transform. Gender relations can be situated in relationship to the interaction between these processes, structures and relations.

Fourth, such interaction is historically contingent, and so the analysis must also contain a historical component. This implies that the typical subjects of gender studies, such as the family and the sexual division of labour, must themselves be analytically constructed historically and not be seen as transhistorical categories (or consequences or forms of sexual oppression).

Many might accept these themes as unobjectionable if a little vague. It is, however, surprising how often they are not all characteristic of gender analyses. In the second section to this chapter, the validity of this observation, and of the themes themselves, is illustrated by reference to the domestic labour debate. In particular, the debate proved unable to progress beyond the limited point of observing, from different perspectives within Marxism, that women are exploited through their position of taking primary responsibility for housework. More through the absences in its scope than through what it positively provides, a critical review of the domestic labour debate is the source of further, more specific, analytical themes that are taken up throughout the remainder of the book.

Briefly these are, first, that the value of labour power has to be more fully explored in its historical and social aspects and, thereby, be linked to a mode or system, and not just a level, of consumption. Second, economic pressures towards commodification of products of domestic labour must be set against (and not just added to), possibly weaker but significant, simultaneous pressures to expand domestic work. Third, a range of demographic influences must be incorporated and the analysis extended to include single women. Fourth, historical analysis must be linked to a periodisation of capitalism. Last, the family itself must not be accepted uncritically as an unproblematical, unshifting and basic building block – as if it were of identical status to capital and, thereby, subject to articulating incorporation and/or confrontation with it.

The rest of this section is devoted to an overview of the other chapters, in which the themes already presented will also be seen to be of continuing importance. Chapter 1 is concerned with patriarchy theory. Although motivated by feminism, it has had a strong influence on gender studies more generally, including more orthodox accounts as well as those with a Marxist leaning. But patriarchy theory has first risen and then fallen in prominence and popularity. Initially, it appeared to offer the key both in explaining women's oppression and in compensating for its analytical neglect in male-dominated and male-oriented social science. The study of the oppression of women by men could supplement pre-existing analyses by articulating the two together. This gave rise to an analytical dualism – as in capitalist patriarchy, for example. However, it soon was realised that the notion of patriarchy as an analytical theme, running through the entire course of history, failed to offer any substantive causal content, since any particular identification of male oppression of women was inevitably and simply reproduced as a descriptive instance of patriarchy.

Moreover, the dualism involved was difficult, if not impossible, to sustain, since the fundamental parameter of patriarchy, male dominance of women, cannot be specified separately from the context within which it operates. What, in short, is the point of forcibly extracting patriarchy as an abstract analytical tool if it can only be wielded in conjunction with the other determinants from which it has previously been (artificially) isolated? Consequently, patriarchy has generally been rejected as unacceptably ahistorical and often, even if in a heavily veiled disguise, as essentially depending upon some form of biological determinism or essentialism. For male dominance of women is taken for granted, even if not as a consequence of directly physical attributes. These criticisms apply equally to those analyses that develop a more complex structure of patriarchal domination than a simple dualism – and to those who reject patriarchy but either rely upon ideal types of male or female behaviour or simply translate an empirically observed inequality between men and women into a structured explanation of disadvantage, whether due to education, ideology or whatever.

A further methodological problem with patriarchy theory, although a strength in highlighting women's disadvantage, is that it tends to identify individual motivations and interests immediately with social structures and movements. To put it polemically, it is as if the slogan 'the personal is political' could constitute the foundation for social theory once the personal ranges over all areas of activity, whether economic, political, ideological or domestic. Despite these problems, it is argued here, however, that the rejection of patriarchy theory is premature. This view is based upon a distinction drawn between the methods of investigation and exposition and, essentially, between methods of description and explanation. Ahistorical analyses are inappropriate both in exposition and explanation, both of which have to be historically and socially specific. But description – how much women get to consume and how much they work, for example – and thereby investigation are both often heavily dependent upon ahistorical analyses. This, indeed, is precisely why patriarchy theory retains its attraction despite its methodological problems. The (ahistorical) parameters of disadvantage are just the ones with which we are liable to begin our *inquiry* into female oppression. But these results do have to be analytically reconstructed to move beyond description, to provide explanation and to eliminate ahistoricism. This approach is illustrated by reference to Marx's method of investigating history more generally, for which ahistorical categories, such as production and class, are almost *exclusively* employed in investigation.

Even if patriarchy theory does have a role in investigative analysis, its general antipathy to gender-neutral categories at the most abstract level of analysis is considered to be misplaced, in so far as they are essential to the understanding of female oppression at a more complex level. It may be appropriate, indeed essential, to confront the gender-neutral category of capital before attending to the sources of women's oppression under capitalism.

Chapter 2 examines theories of women in the labour-market drawn from economics and sociology. Patriarchy theory, when applied to this topic, suggests that capitalism creates a hierarchy of jobs which are then filled to the disadvantage of women. In this, male workers, in particular, play a crucial role in excluding women from jobs or in segregating them from men where this proves impossible. This theory is critically assessed and is found to neglect the role of employers and capitalist imperatives (although these are often seen as in conflict with patriarchy) as well as the historical record. The idea that women constitute a reserve army of labour is also found to be unsatisfactory, not least because it too is essentially a version of patriarchy theory, although not usually recognised as such, since the theory of capitalist accumulation is seen as systematically providing the inferior reserve army labour-market positions which, it is presumed, are filled by women. In short, these theories proceed unsatisfactorily by attempting to marry a gender-neutral Marxism, which creates an economic hierarchy, with a gendered explanation of occupancy of the better or lesser places within it. As such, it is an artifical articulation of the two lines of thought.

A review of theories of occupational segregation, labour-market participation and pay differentials again finds patriarchy theory to have been prominent but wanting. None the less, four different analytical approaches are uncovered – those that emphasise structures (such as between home and market), or processes (such as skilling and de-skilling through technological change and the associated discriminatory gendering of jobs), or simultaneity (the cumulative effect of disadvantage as measured by training, education, work experience, etc., as in orthodox human capital theory but still leaving an unexplained residual wage differential), and/or historical contingency (in which particular employment patterns are laid down and tend to be self-reproducing).

These four approaches form the basis for Chapter 3. But a simple synthesis is not sought between them. Rather, the subject matter is reconsidered by bringing together three intimately inter-related themes – first, that labour-market participation is governed by access to the means of production, and this needs to be understood both in the most abstract sense of capital's mono-polisation of the means of production as well as in the detailed ability to gain access to jobs as governed by the availability of transport, training, childcare, etc. In other words, the notion of access to the means of production is employed in an analytically rich context. It refers to underlying economic and social processes, as well as to their historically contingent interaction to give rise to specific and gendered labour-market structures and conditions.

A second theme is that women's labour-market participation has to be linked to the value of labour power. This is to be understood in its fullest sense, both as the labour time required to produce the wage goods that constitute the standard levels of consumption to reproduce the workforce *and* the (changing) dis-tribution of waged work across the family or household as a whole. Thus, the changing position of men and women (and children) in the labour-market reflects a much deeper relationship to standard Marxist concepts, such as the value of labour power. Whose labour does this value cover and how does it relate to the more general sexual division of labour and changing economic and social struc-tures?

These issues are addressed by the third theme, and this is perhaps the most innovative part of the book. It is to provide a particular understanding of the periodisation of the capitalist family by the way in which it is linked to the periodisation of capitalism into the three stages of *laissez-faire*, monopoly and state monopoly capitalism. Correspondingly, there is the formal, real and social subordination of the family. It is, however, argued that chronologically the two periodisations do not mesh with one another in a simple fashion. The transition from *laissez-faire* to monopoly capitalism is associated with legislation to protect the working class and, as such, tends to withdraw women (and chil-dren) from the workforce until such time as the fragility and size of the working class family has been eroded by the demographic transition which releases women from early death and frequent pregnancy.

Subsequently, the mass production associated with monopoly

capitalism can still enhance the viability of domestic labour even as it undermines it, so that the drive of (married) women into work to attain ever higher consumption levels continues to be tempered. With increasing state economic and social intervention, a wedge is driven between the value of labour power of the household and that of individual workers so that the housewife emerges as a worker in her own right, even if her access to employment remains unequal because of domestic responsibilities and other sources of disadvantage. Consequently, labour-market participation and wages and conditions for women remain disadvantageous but they become increasingly independent of the structured impact of responsibility for domestic labour. Factors such as labour-market legislation, training and childcare provision have become both possible and influential in determining women's labour-market position, both within and between countries, even if occupational segregation has remained deeply entrenched.

In Chapter 4 these arguments are illustrated by reference to women's position in the British labour-market. Two particular features are highlighted. First, that the British economy suffers from low wages, low investment and low productivity and an associated weakness of manufacturing, intensifying the trend to deindustrialisation. Consequently, women have been entering the labour market at a time of expanding services (and state employment) during which low wages have been compensating for poor economic performance.

Second, economic and social policy in the UK has been more concerned, respectively, with macroeconomic and welfare objectives than with enhancing workers' positions in the labour market – whether through commitment to high employment, (re)training or, especially for women's employment needs, childcare provision. As a result, the labour-market position of women has been particularly disadvantageous, not only in the low wages characteristic of the economy as a whole, but also in dependency upon even lower paid part-time work which neither develops nor utilises the skills that women workers have and, consequently, consolidates the weak position of the UK economy. Ultimately, the implication is that measures to enhance the labour-market position of women in the UK will have some, but limited, impact unless they are combined with measures to regenerate the economy as a whole.

Such is a brief and deceptively simple overview of the contents

9

of this book. Its substance is, however, much more demanding for a number of reasons. Its coverage, both by academic discipline and by topic is extremely wide, encompassing economics, sociology, demography and history – across issues as diverse as value theory, labour economics, marriage and fertility, etc., and use is also made of both theoretical and empirical material. In addition, the analysis is grounded in a Marxist approach, employed at an advanced level in terms of the understanding of value theory. However, some care has been taken to provide explanations of the concepts used where it is felt to be both appropriate and not too unwieldy. And the arguments are addressed to as wide an audience as possible and not just to those committed to Marxism (or my own interpretation of it). Hopefully, the difficulties of the text will reward rather than frustrate the conscientious reader.

BEYOND THE DOMESTIC LABOUR DEBATE

Little more than two decades ago, a debate was initiated over the significance of domestic labour or housework as the source of women's oppression. There is no doubt that this issue was perceived at times both analytically and politically as a means of exposing and conquering women's disadvantage. Equally certain is that within a decade or so, the debate was perceived to have failed and deserving of being set aside as quickly as it had been picked up. It is worth recording some of the commentary on this failure, as it brings to the fore some of the broader issues previously raised concerning the relationship between feminism and Marxism as it then was.

The most damning indictment of the debate has been provided by Molyneux:

It is nearly a decade since the first texts in the recent domestic labour debate appeared, and since then over fifty articles have been published on the subject of housework in the British and American socialist press alone . . . The theoretical work so far produced on domestic labour has not adequately addressed the problems . . . In particular, the attempt to produce a theory of the political economy of women . . . has been characterised by one or more of the following limitations: first by a tendency to economic reductionism; secondly, by a recourse to functionalist modes of argument in constructing the relationship between capitalism and domestic labour; and thirdly, by a narrow focus on the *labour* performed in the domestic sphere at the expense of theorising the wider familial/household context. This latter focus has led, among other things, to over-emphasising the importance for the male wage worker of the labour performed by the housewife, and to the virtual neglect of that performed on behalf of the next generation of workers in the work of rearing children. Thus only one aspect of domestic labour, arguably the least important, is given serious consideration in this debate, a deficiency not overcome by the occasional generic references in the literature to the housewife 'reproducing labour power'.[1]

> (Molyneux, 1979, pp. 3–4)

This suggests that Davidoff's (1976) satirical quotation from Mainardi (1971), intended to reveal the difficulty of getting housework to be taken seriously, might be better employed in closing the debate than in initiating it:

> Housework? Oh my God, how trivial can you get. A paper on housework.
>
> > (Davidoff, 1976, p. 121)

Other commentators have been equally scathing: :

> One of the most fruitful debates which feminism had started was the debate on domestic labour . . . this debate . . . degenerated into a more or less academic discourse.
>
> > Mies (1986, p. 31)

The academic theme is picked up more benevolently by Himmelweit, particularly in the context of value theory:

> Most of the skirmishes of the 'domestic labour debate' either degenerated into arguments about pure semantics, or, and often quite usefully, provided examples upon which the nascent Anglo-American interest in Marxism could refine its understanding and clarify disputes about the meaning of Marxist categories.
>
> > (Himmelweit, 1984a, p. 170)

Barrett is even more prepared to be generous:

> In charity, it should be seen in the context of a history of

11

INTRODUCTION

Marxist thought in which questions of gender relations and male dominance have long been ignored and marginalized.
(Barrett, 1980, p. 23)

For Kuhn and Wolpe:

Domestic labour was seized upon as the key to an historically concrete understanding of woman's oppression, in that housework could be thought as the central point at which women's specific subordination in capitalism is articulated.
(Kuhn and Wolpe, 1978, p. 199)

These quotations do shed considerable light on the origins and subsequent path of the domestic labour debate. First, in rooting out the source of women's oppression, the position of the house-wife was perceived to be central, and her performance of housework to be exploitative. Politically, there was the necessity of making housework visible and for it to be granted appropriate analytical status next to wage labour. Initially, this was done by raising the demand of wages for housework.[2] Subsequently, there developed the treatment of housework as a separate mode of production and, usually along with this, the idea that women constitute a separate class exploited by men.[3]

Certainly, these propositions were adequate in raising the political and analytical prominence of housework. But the arguments employed were often inconsistent with the prevailing under-standing of the pre-existing, usually Marxist, concepts. These were too readily and casually employed, concepts such as mode of production, and these usages were also torn out of their original contexts and purposes and rudely and crudely superimposed upon one another. Indeed, symptomatic of this was the extent to which women's exploitation was frequently explained by analogy with other modes of production. Delphy (1984, p. 70), for example, refers to men sacking their wives and to wives as being like slaves, partially working on their own account when going out to waged work: (p. 101). For Mies (1986, p. 110): 'the Little White Man also got his "colony", namely the family and a domesticated wife'. She goes on to say:

It is my thesis that these two processes of colonization and housewifization are closely and causally interlinked. Without the ongoing exploitation of external colonies . . . the estab-lishment of the 'internal colony', that is, a nuclear family and

12

a woman maintained by a male 'breadwinner', would not
have been possible.

(Mies, 1986, pp. 142–3)

A detailed review of the domestic labour debate is provided in the
Appendix, in which it will be seen that such analogies and affinities
drawn from existing theory remained at least implicit in much of
the more sophisticated and considered contributions that were
soon to follow upon first attempts to locate domestic labour theoretically.[4] The purpose here is more to summarise the debate in
order to bring out its lessons, whether positive or negative, for
developing an understanding of women's labour-market participation.

Necessarily, then, the debate was itself heavily influenced by the
intellectual milieu of its time. Within political economy, it was raw
material for the then most controversial issue of (Marxist) value
theory. Reconsideration of domestic labour and value theory
forms the main substance of the debate surveyed in the appendix.
But there were other influences at work also, which directed the
content and the course of the debate. Already mentioned has been
the connection with debates over what constitutes a mode of
production – and how these are 'articulated' with each other.[5]
Equally important was to become consideration of 'reproduction',
and this contained affinities with the emerging interest in the
theory of the state and how social stability or reproduction was to
be guaranteed, or not.[6]

What both of these issues had in common, and much of the
debate that was to follow, was to feel the influence of Althusserianism. Its structuralism, with various divisions between the
economic, political and ideological levels and between their associated practices, proved irresistible in the domestic labour debate
as with other areas of Marxist theory. The same applied to its
notion of contradiction as a displaced and focused crisis of these
practices on to one or other level in particular. Domestic labour,
for example, could be perceived as an original and fundamental
source of other forms of female oppression. What appeared as
unquestionable, and unquestioned, within the domestic labour
debate is the importance of an articulation between the two separate levels, of capital and the home, just as previously the
psychoanalytical basis for explaining women's oppression had

been overtly Althusserian in constituting a separate ideological level for sexism.[7]

Indeed, in retrospect, it appears as if the complex determinants of specifically women's oppression could be reduced to an abstract notion of domestic labour, itself unproblematically institutionalised within equally abstract notions of home and family or household. Casual, if critical, observation about daily life became elevated to the substance of high theory.

This explains why a major reason for the debate's demise is to be found in the limited scope of its analysis, its formalism and, it is to be suspected, the waning influence of Althusserianism and of the other issues that fuelled the debate. However, a re-examination of the debate serves the function of explaining not only why it should have been confined to so limited an empirical scope but also how this was supported by the methodologies employed. Consequently, it becomes possible to re-examine the domestic labour debate more positively than before and to situate it more satisfactorily and fully into the shifting determinants of women's working lives. For decline of interest in the domestic labour debate can hardly follow from a decrease in domestic labour's continuing importance nor in the tools used to analyse it, such as value and modes of (re)production, even if they have been inappropriately wielded in the past.

From within the debate itself, an early position was established in which domestic labour, predominantly, performed by women, became seen as exploitative of the wife by the husband. She is deemed to contribute surplus labour – more work than is matched by her level of consumption. This is so despite her work lying outside the labour-market within which, more noticably for Marxist theory at least, the male employee is exploited with the wage representing less in purchased consumption goods than labour contributed in the factory.

Who obtains the surplus labour of the housewife and how is it obtained? The most immediate beneficiary is taken to be the husband. But, so it is argued, he can be paid less by the capitalist in wages, without loss in overall level of consumption, as a consequence of the support provided by the wife's domestic labour. Consequently, it is concluded that surplus domestic labour supplied is in principle and in part able to be passed on to capitalists and appropriated as profit. Thus, domestic labour is an indirect source of profit, passed on through the husband's lower wage as a result of household provision. This stance, whilst acutely demonstrating the exploitation of domestic labour and even constituting women as a separate class within a separate housework mode of production, could not long survive the keen and sophisticated application of Marx's value theory to the distinction between unpaid domestic work and paid wage labour. As Scott succinctly puts it:

> In a word, it is not possible to add domestic labor time to waged labor time because one is concrete, individual labor and the other is abstract, homogenized, social labor; they are not the same sort of thing. And if we could add the two it would topple Marx's model; labor power would sell for *less* than its value instead of *at* its value if this unpaid component from outside commodity production were added to it.
>
> (Scott, 1984, p. 143)

In short, the analysis reached a point where it emphasised what domestic labour is *not*, even if in the most abstract terms of its being distinct from *value* as in Marx's political economy. Analysis might then have been expected to move forward to examine what domestic labour *is*. Instead, the debate took two different directions. First, in deference to the empirically unavoidable rise in female labour-market participation, especially of married women, attention was shifted to the dual exploitation of women's labour, at home and in paid work. It was more or less presumed that disadvantage in each of these was mutually reinforcing and self-explanatory. As Scott put it:

> The distinct character of women's poverty has two sources: women bear the major responsibility for childbearing; and women's income and economic mobility are limited further by occupational segregation, sexual discrimination and sexual harassment. The two are, of course, closely related.
>
> (Scott 1984, p. 23)

The second route taken by the debate, and not unrelated to the first, was to supplement the previously outlined, static structure of exploitation, now incorporating a duality of paid and unpaid work, with a dynamic account of the shifting incidence of work between home and factory. Almost inevitably, the analysis was based upon existing conventional wisdoms, buttressed by existing theory, in which the growing productivity of capital increasingly

15

encroached upon the viability and desirability of domestic production – thereby releasing the housewife from the home and making her available for paid work. The wife was to be swept out of the home by mass produced commodities (which she would herself produce as a wage-labourer).

Again, significantly, this approach had unconsciously avoided an examination of domestic labour itself, other than as something to be eroded – at least up to certain limits, these being, as a minimum, the biological reproduction of the workforce which could not be undertaken by capitalism without its reverting to slavery. As a result, the domestic labour debate may be seen to have reached a point beyond which it could not move. Its analysis essentially suggested that capitalism was moving to liberate women, at least to a large extent, by commercialising domestic activity and making wage labourers out of them. But this is precisely the sort of prediction that had been made some hundred years before by Marx and Engels and which had not been realised. The slow pace and extent of change could only be reconciled by appeal to the obstacles, if not barriers, in the way of the higher productivity of capitalism filtering its way into the home. And these obstacles could be tied to the theoretical insight that domestic labour is not value production and, hence, not susceptible to the free flow of competition and, by analogy, not subject to bankruptcy and redundancy.

To progress any further, the domestic labour debate needed to confront the two black boxes that it had failed to open and examine. The first is domestic labour itself, an extremely heterogeneous activity, open to interpretation either as an endless multiplicity of detailed tasks or, gathering these together, as a more abstract feature (of capitalism) centring on social reproduction. Each of these interpretations was prominent more by way of word than by deed. Particularly important was the neglect of childcare, although it straddles both detailed tasks, encompassing most aspects of housework, and social reproduction of the workforce. Yet, during the very brief passage of capitalism's history, the very nature of childhood has been transformed and the number of children and childbearing years has been drastically reduced even as women's lives have been substantially lengthened. The implications of these changes for women's working lives have been substantial but had not been confronted directly, if at all, by analysis based on the shifting relative productivity of domestic and capitalist production.

The second black box, unopened by the domestic labour debate, was the detailed examination of the shift as between domestic and *non*-domestic provision. Emphasis here indicates that the shift has not simply been between the household and capital. In the recent period, much of the shifting or expansion of provision has been through the state, itself equally aloof from the direct dictates of value production and competitive forces. In addition, increases in capitalist production across a wide range of products has, at times, had the effect of *enhancing*, and not undermining, the viability of domestic production (and has even led to earning money from the home), as in mass production of cheap domestic inputs, such as flour and textiles, quite apart from 'capital' equipment, such as baking tins, ovens and sewing machines. More recently, microwaves and other durables have increased the productivity of domestic labour.

This points to a tension in the tendencies created by mass production, which does not just create unimpeded and unambiguous trends. Further, the presumed obstacles to these tendencies have to be examined, not just taken for granted, since these (such as rapid urbanisation and housing shortages) may themselves create domestic opportunities outside capitalist production (as in the taking in of lodgers). Last, but by no means least, at the more abstract level, these issues suggest that it is inappropriate to take the family or household as an invariant analytical building block, undertaking more or less of the functions of social reproduction through domestic labour. The position and nature of the family has been transformed by the changes mentioned here.

Rather than confronting these problems, the domestic labour debate simply expired, with a flurry of often unflattering obituary notices. It was apparently incapable of incorporating the complexity of the issues involved. These are taken up here in the later chapters, just as they have been analysed in detail in contexts other than the domestic labour debate. Perhaps the latter's death is explained less by the questions it raised and more by its failure to embrace both theoretical and empirical material from a wider compass than could be provided by Marxist value theory alone.

Indeed, Marxist value theory is better seen as identifying the analytical problems associated with the role of domestic labour rather than as resolving them. These problems form analytical themes to be taken up in later chapters, especially Chapter 4. First, economic analysis of the relationship between domestic and wage labour cannot afford to be simplistic in the sense of adding up hours of work (of men and women) and comparing these with levels of consumption. Whilst empirically the commodification of domestic work has been predominant in the most recent period, this does not imply that what goes on in or out of the home can be read off from this as a simple trend. For, as has been seen, such changes as do occur are mediated by the pressure to raise living standards (and domestic labour) with the use of even more house-work to employ the commodities purchased. This may even be associated with capacity to earn income from the home, employing a sewing machine to serve own as well as others' (paid for) needs.

Second, it is necessary to identify the social and historical determinants of the value of labour power, in which this is seen as being complex rather than representing the wage for the job. There is the issue of who works and for how much, but this also relates to the income and reproduction of the household as a whole. Is each wage labourer separate or not as far as the wage and reproduction are concerned?

A rather different aspect of this issue concerns the consumption that makes up the normal standard of living. Elsewhere, Fine and Leopold (forthcoming) suggest that this requires an analysis of systems of provision for each distinguishable group of com-modities – as in the food, energy, transport and fashion systems, for example. Each of these will be structured differently through the processes of production, distribution and exchange, as well as in the cultural or other factors determining consumption patterns and levels of demand. Consequently, each will have a different history and dynamic – influenced, but not exclusively determined, by developments in production and the imperatives of profitability through cost reduction. So it is not simply a matter of how much is consumed of what but also of how it is provided both in and out of the home. And provision is not merely capitalist (mass) produc-tion nor individualised domestic labour. It comprises other activities (retailing, for example) which, along and in interaction with domestic labour and capitalist production, can be structured very differently from sector to sector.

Third, similar considerations apply to state 'systems of provi-sion' such as the education, health and social security systems.

These are not merely constituted as state expenditure, subject to simple manipulation in response to the business cycle, the needs of capital, or the balance of class forces in economic and political struggle (although these are important). Rather, these too are subject to differing structures and processes of provision, the more so for not being directly subordinate to the criterion of profitability.

Fourth, great emphasis must be placed upon demographic change. This is not only to be concerned with the traditional variables such as age of marriage and fertility. For these factors are, in turn, affected by and affect the position of single women in the labour-market. Otherwise, it is implicitly and unreasonably assumed that married women's labour-market position and single women's subsequent marriage and fertility are unrelated to each other (or the first totally determines the second).[8] Whilst it is only mildly surprising that the domestic labour debate should have paid such scant attention to single women (as opposed to its scandalous neglect of children), this cannot justify the proposition that the position of married women is the determinant of (all) women's labour-market position, as is implicitly assumed by focusing on the duality of women's housework (child care) and wage labour.

Fifth, how are these separate factors to be brought together and how are we to know that there are not others of which account should be taken? Molyneux (1979, pp. 23–5), for example, concludes her critique of the domestic labour debate by suggesting that the wage form, high levels of (female) unemployment, the sexual division of labour and the premium placed on women's reproductive role are the crucial determinants of women's work situation. It is not clear, however, how these factors should be articulated or whether they, and possibly others, should be seen as simultaneous, contradictory or independent of each other in their impact. On the other hand, Bryceson and Vuorela (1984) embark upon a process of identifying a number of separate theoretical entities, such as reproduction and production, and consider each of them as each lying at a high level of abstraction and subject to structural interaction, articulation and historical contingency. This could, however, lead to an ever-expanding configuration of abstract determinants.

Whatever the preferred methodology, it seems essential that a broader historical judgement be embraced, one associated with a periodisation of capitalism so that the mutual conditioning of the determining factors identified can be appropriately organised analytically. Thus, the conditions in which women are able to provide income from the household, as opposed to doing so through going out to work, belong to very different stages of development of capitalism.

Finally, it does seem necessary to adopt a more critical stance towards the terms of the domestic labour debate. For it must be recognised that the structural separation between the capitalist economy and the household is one which situates each at a highly abstract level. For the household, this may be inappropriate. As a concept, the household is both empirically immediate and heterogeneous. But, within the domestic labour debate, it is transported into the most abstract world in which it is either considered to produce value or not. As it were, the household (or family) assumes an abstract analytical status on a par with capital or value. Consequently, the household must more appropriately be analytically removed from its position as a fixed and abstract ideal – in which labour is reproduced and socialised, etc. – and become itself recognised as the complex outcome of many processes of which the sexual and social division of labour is but one. In particular, the correct notion that domestic labour is private and, therefore, not social like wage labour, should not lead to the simplistic conclusion of a more general separation between the 'public' and 'private' which supposedly coincides, respectively, with the economy and the state as opposed to the family.

For, as in reproduction, these notions are complex and embody many and varied determinants, not all of which conform to these simple dichotomies. Recognition of this is crucial in analysing what is after all perceived to be shifting boundaries between those nebulous territories that divide the public from the private, the family from society.[9] As Kamenka suggests:

> The conception of *anything* as private, as standing outside society or as prior to it, as unrelated to other people and of no concern to them, or as resting on the rights and claims of single persons . . . is a dangerous illusion, theoretically confused and vicious in its practical consequences.[10]
>
> (Kamenka, 1983, p. 274)

This is merely to serve renewed notice that the issues broached by the domestic labour debate cannot be resolved only on the basis of

20

economic analysis and its associated trends. In subsequent analysis, these critical observations will be more constructively employed, both to distinguish different stages of development of the otherwise undifferentiated family or household and to examine the shifting boundaries between female domestic and waged work. First, however, an assessment is made of the light that patriarchy theory can shed on these and other issues related to female employment.

1

ON PATRIARCHY

INTRODUCTION

The domestic labour debate can be seen as just one part of a much wider concern with the sources of women's oppression. Whilst focusing on the allocation and appropriation of women's labour, the analysis of domestic labour did raise other material issues, less those of an ideological nature: issues such as the relationship between capital and the family and between sex and class. However, these problems can be broached on a much broader front, so that women's position can be assessed on the basis of a wider range of explanatory factors and a correspondingly wider set of consequences than were encompassed by a calculus of labour time formed around domestic and wage employment alone.

Such are the expanded terms around which the notion of patriarchy has been debated and for which the significance of domestic labour figures more as a narrowly defined and special case. For whilst female oppression may be associated with, or even be perceived to be rooted in, exploitation of domestic labour, this can hardly be considered to be the sole index of women's inferior position. Where female disadvantage is identified more generally, it is readily categorised as an instance of patriarchy. The purpose of this chapter is to assess critically the contribution that can be made by patriarchy theory. In this introduction, the scene is set by presenting both a brief review of the way in which the patriarchy debate has evolved and some of the methodological issues that have been involved. As the material of the chapter is often abstract, and possibly unfamiliar, an overview of conclusions is also offered in the introduction to serve as an initial guide.

Interest in patriarchy necessarily follows a multidisciplinary and, potentially, an interdisciplinary approach, rather than being defined by political economy alone – as in the domestic labour debate. Consequently, the understanding of patriarchy has been dependent upon simultaneous but separate developments across the social sciences. But different treatments of patriarchy have had some elements in common. In particular, in discussing social theory in general – and not just patriarchy theory – Walby (1988b) has usefully suggested that gender analysis has gone through four stages, presumably as an academic response to the wave of feminism originating in the late 1960s. The first stage was to realise how much women had been neglected or excluded from studies altogether. In sociology, this has been especially noted in stratification theory, where the study of class relations had been, usually implicitly, confined to males.[1] Otherwise, women had been 'hidden from history'.[2] In models of the labour-market, it was assumed that typical jobs were those associated with men's careers, working conditions and conflicts.[3]

The second in Walby's stages is for this neglect of women to be used to expose theoretical and empirical fallacies which become glaringly transparent on the basis of the first stage. In the theory of class, it becomes possible to demand stratification for women and to question whether a wife adopts the class mantle of her husband, and it can even be proposed that women constitute a separate class. In history, the role of women in community and other struggles comes to the fore.[4] For labour-market theory, it is recognised that 'malestream' models are inappropriate for sweated labour, part-time work and for sectors where women form the majority of the workforce.

This opens the way for a third stage in the development of gender studies, one in which models or analyses of women are added on to those for men, to fill the gender vacuum that has been discovered alongside the orthodoxy. Here, there are separate models of women in the labour-market and separate histories and sociologies of women,[5] and an opening up of the 'private' as opposed to the 'public'.[6]

Finally, Walby points to the current stage of recognising, and attempting to move beyond, the unsatisfactory analytical creation of a dualism in the models of gender relations, one model for men which might have previously been presumed to have been sufficient despite having implicitly excluded women and, in reaction against this, a separate set of models for women. Consequently,

23

integration is sought between the two sorts of models so that the relative position and role of men and women are understood simultaneously and symbiotically. In political economy, for example, dual or segmented labour-market theory attempts to explain the *co-determination* of primary (male) *alongside* secondary (female) labour-markets.

This account of the evolution of women's studies, whilst insightful for much social theory, is undoubtedly too stylised and forced for general application. It is totally inappropriate, for example, for psychology and anthropology where, however satisfactorily and accurately, women have long occupied a central role. The same is obviously true for much of the content of cultural studies. Consequently, the impact of a new wave of feminism upon them has been entirely different. At the other extreme, orthodox economics has remained largely untouched theoretically by the influence of the women's movement. Despite these discomfitures, this periodisation of women's studies may be usefully employed in examining the debate over patriarchy.

The first stage of recognising the neglect of women's oppression is well-represented by Firestone (1970) although she is more well-known, not so much for placing patriarchy on the analytical agenda, as for explaining women's oppression by appeal to a biological (reproduction) reductionism. Her book opens:

Sex class is so deep as to be invisible.

(Firestone, 1970, p. 1)

This is followed by a diagram mapping out human history that sees patriarchy take over from matriarchy around the time of Greek civilisation and extending to the era of proletariat revolution (p. 6).

The second stage of recognising how analysis has been gender blind is a point of departure for the domestic labour debate for which the rejection of work as only being made up of (male) wage-labour is paramount. Similarly, the notion of the personal as political and the writing of women's history have been attempts to redress the absence of women from discourse and to incorporate them on the basis of a recognition of the power relations between men and women. Perhaps earliest and most prominent were the ideological/psychological, sexual and domestic situations of women as sources of oppression, explicitly acknowledged as patriarchy or not, but soon extended to wage work and welfarism and other areas of public and private life, with increasing focus on the access to, and nature of, jobs – as women's growing participation in employment became acknowledged.

The third stage, following on from the 'adding on' of women, can be seen as having collected together these disparate contributions, that pinpointed women's oppression, and to have forged them into a *common* thread of male domination running through history and society. From this, patriarchy emerges as an abstraction from the more concrete details of the variety of earlier studies and becomes an explanatory variable in its own right. As such, it gains an independent analytical status and stands beside non-gendered analytical frameworks, especially that of Marxism, based on gender-neutral concepts such as class and mode of production. This gives rise to what became known as dual systems theory. Gender complements non-gender analysis. In particular, dualism considers that patriarchy exists side by side with capitalism and, more generally, might even be considered as a mode of production or means of oppression that prevails thoughout the course of history, as an accompaniment to what are otherwise non-patriarchal relations.

Finally, the stage has been reached where the dissatisfaction with dualism has led most to reject patriarchy, since the separate components of dualism are perceived as no longer distinguishable from one another. Accordingly, the analysis of women's oppression is increasingly sought through uncovering the social construction and reconstruction of gender, both male and female together, in material and ideological life. Whilst some continue to cling to a pervasive role for patriarchy, this now seems less influential than reliance upon analysis of gender (re)construction through methods other than as an articulation of patriarchal and non-patriarchal relations, which is increasingly seen as an artificial and forced division.

Those, the minority view, who continue to support patriarchy do so by seeking a synthesis between it and capitalism or, in historical analysis, with some other mode of production. In the notion of capitalist patriarchy, for example, each of capitalism and patriarchy mutually conditions the other rather than the two simply existing side by side as separate systems – as in the purest form of dualism.

In what follows, attention will be focused on the last two stages described above – on dual systems theory and after – since the stages of neglect and blindness have been more instrumental in initiating debate than in exerting a lasting influence.[7] It will be found that patriarchy as a concept has generally been rejected, even though it briefly enjoyed favour within dual systems theory (as in capitalist patriarchy). The reason for this rejection has primarily been because of the inability of patriarchy to serve both as an underlying and abstract explanation of women's oppression through history and as an historically specific factor with a greater causal than descriptive content. In short, patriarchy will always appear to be an explanation where and when women are disadvantaged, but this is merely to (re)name what is already known rather than to explain why women's oppression is the way it is and why and how it changes.

Given that these stages of development of patriarchy theory have been raced through in a little over two decades, with a remarkably similar timing to the domestic labour debate, it is hardly surprising that much potential within the analysis should have been lost in the hurry to move forward. Two particular issues have been glossed over. The first concerns the role of gender-neutral concepts, such as capital and labour, etc. Those seeking to highlight the neglect of women and the prominence of male-oriented models were quick to point to the role of gender-neutral concepts in covering up female oppression and, more often than not, in excluding women altogether.

Patriarchy theory has been prominent in exposing such male bias and has provided a corrective in insisting upon the primacy of gender relations. But this has often been based upon a questionable presumption – that gender-neutral concepts, such as those within Marxism, necessarily preclude analysis of female oppression. In the work of Hartmann, for example, the dualism between capitalism and patriarchy can be seen in part as an attempt to compensate for the gender-neutrality of the one by the gender content of the other.

In the next section, however, it is argued, partly by reference to the work of Seccombe, that gender-neutrality of a concept, such as capital, does not pre-empt its ability to explore female oppression – just as, for example, class analysis does not forbid an understanding of fractions of classes nor, even if they are defined by economic criteria, the role of classes in politics or culture.

A second issue rushed past in the patriarchy debate has been the role of ahistorical categories of analysis. These, such as production, labour, consumption and (biological) sex, are quite rightly seen as inadequate to explain the historically and socially specific character of any period of whatever duration. Consequently, it has been all too easy to reject patriarchy theory since it relies upon the ahistorical (or transhistorical) notion of men's oppression of women.

From a Marxist point of view, this conclusion is too hasty. After all, concepts such as mode and relations of production, classes and exploitation are equally ahistorical. Yet, they have been employed to investigate and to uncover the historically specific nature of one society as opposed to another. Thus, drawing upon the work of Connell (1987), who critically evaluates theories of oppression which rely directly or indirectly on biological determinism – indirectly by associating (dis)advantage with (fe)male characteristics, even though these have not been explained – it is argued in the first section of this chapter that patriarchy is an important tool in investigating female oppression. It provides an important method of inquiry or investigation. As such, it yields an exploratory analysis whose results should be reconstructed for the purposes of exposition and explanation. For, otherwise, little would emerge other than a descriptive content (of men oppressing women), which would also be essentially ahistorical (women's oppression is explained by patriarchy).

In Hartmann's various analyses, the problems of gender-neutrality and of ahistorical concepts emerge and are dealt with extremely sharply, if unsatisfactorily. To caricature, dualism allows, for example, capitalism to provide the (gender-neutral) history and patriarchy to provide for female oppression. A more sophisticated but, consequently, less overt handling of these problems is provided by Walby, and this is assessed in the section after next. Her dualism between capitalism and patriarchy is further refined to allow for a complex structure of mutual conditioning between the two (and she, unlike Hartmann, tends to see patriarchy and capitalism as in conflict rather than as in harmony with one another, especially when it comes to control of women's labour). However, even though the dualism of patriarchy theory has been refined, the dependence of analysis upon an ahistorical thread of female oppression remains – the problem that has led many to reject patriarchy theory altogether.

Here, however, it is argued that this rejection of patriarchy is premature. This can be seen to be so by highlighting the distinction between the method of inquiry and the method of exposition and their respective relation to analysis of causation. The method of inquiry may legitimately begin with, and return to, ahistorical causal factors, such as patriarchy, even if exposition and causation should be historically rooted in the society under consideration. Finding those roots may well depend upon initial descriptive material of the type concerned with women's general disadvantage – how much they work, how much they consume, etc. Patriarchy theory is a good way of exploring, if not explaining, women's oppression.

But a strand can also be found in the literature that rejects patriarchy as a legitimate concept, only to reintroduce it surreptitiously and possibly unconsciously, by a theory of women's oppression comprised of three components – historical specificity, gender (re)construction, and the synthesis between different aspects and different types of female oppression. At such a general level, this appears to be unobjectionable. But it clearly carries the danger, as in the work of Walby, of re-admitting a more complex form of patriarchy theory, whether named as such, in which history and synthesis are employed as the magic wands to articulate the various sources of oppression identified (usually named as a gender rather than as a patriarchy theory).

Accordingly, to avoid this, explanations of the various sources of women's oppression, and their interrelationship, must remain complex and historically contingent and, consequently, not subject to a general theoretical determination. This is not, however, to argue that theory must give way to descriptive analysis, although this proves invaluable as the starting point for the creation of more abstract concepts. This is the intent of patriarchy theory when it extracts the underlying notion of sexual oppression as its theoretical starting point. Its difficulty, however, resides in translating such beginnings into historically specific causal explanations. In contrast, it is argued here that the appropriate theoretical tools for analysing and explaining women's oppression must, however, be historically specific – just as they are, for example, for analysing capitalism.

GENDER BLINDNESS AND AHISTORICAL ANALYSIS

In seeking explanations and rectifications for analytical gender blindness, an obvious starting point has proved to be the gender neutrality of the concepts traditionally employed (although it bears repeating that this does not apply to psychoanalysis, cultural studies and anthropology). In particular, for those working in relation to Marxism, it has been observed that concepts such as mode of production and, for political economy, value, capital, profit, etc., do not specifically address the issue of women's oppression. Hartmann states (her emphasis) that:

Marxist categories, like capital itself, are sex-blind.
(Hartmann, 1981, p. 11)

Whilst this gender neutrality is, in principle, equally applicable to both masculinity and femininity, it is far from symmetrical in its effective treatment of the sexes, since it draws a veil over the oppression of women by men. By analogy, neutrality before the market is a false equality as between rich and poor, precisely because their differences in income entail differences in access to benefits through the market. And, given in capitalist society, the greater power, prestige and public presence of men, conceptual neutrality almost inevitably leads to a preoccupation with models of men's lives, frequently represented as models of life in general. As it were, to put it more extremely, capital, value and mode of production are male views of the world despite, or even because of, their gender neutrality. Consequently, patriarchy theory seeks a corrective duality by adding itself to gender-neutral analysis – to redress the analytical balance as between the sexes and to expose their lack of balance in society. For Ward:

This discussion assumes that in general capitalism is gender blind, but in interaction with patriarchy or male dominance, the resulting system – capitalist patriarchy – uses gender as a basic category in the economic system.
(Ward, 1988, p. 18)

There are a number of problems with this approach. First, all concepts will be neutral as between certain divisions of the population in society if not as between others; and there is an issue of how the various divisions, and hence conflicts of interest, interrelate with one another (with much soul-searching over racism and sexism, in particular). As Scott puts it:

Theories of patriarchy do not show how gender inequality

structures all other inequalities or, indeed, *how*, gender affects those areas of life that do not seem to be connected to it.
(Scott, 1986, p. 1058–9)

Consequently, as all theory necessarily abstracts from some considerations, so it must be neutral with respect to them. Why should
the correction of the gender neutrality of concepts such as capital,
by the introduction of patriarchy, be analytically sufficient and
prior to the 'correction' of other biases? There are other divisions
than those by sex and class alone, most obviously as between
nations or globally between the First and Third Worlds, for which
it has also been plausibly claimed that one oppresses the other.
And, whether the division is between races, gender or nations,
these are far from simple two-dimensional categories (as is usually
assumed for gender relations, with closer attention to biological
rather than to social determinants of what in reality are a variety,
not a duality, of sexual orientations and characteristics).

In addition, there seems to be an error in assuming that gender
neutrality in basic concepts necessarily implies gender neglect or
blindness in their *subsequent* application. *Equality* before the market, for example, is the starting point for Marx's analysis of the
commodity form, from which he derives *inequality* in capitalist
relations of production and for which, to resume the earlier
analogy, inequality subsequently emerges as a consequence of the
differing, and by no means symmetrical, place of capital and
labour before the market.

However, whilst gender neutrality in basic concepts may not
preclude a subsequent uncovering of oppression, as the motivation for the notion of patriarchy reveals, the actual record of
analysis had been a poor one. Consequently, the option of specifically seeking out the independent sources of women's oppression
is extremely attractive, if possibly in conjunction with other gender-neutral analyses of other sources of (class) oppression. In
other words, it is arguable that societies should be scrutinised for
their gendered relations in initiating an analysis of them. But it
does not necessarily follow from this that gender must be explicitly
present in the *most* abstract concepts employed. For example,
feudal relations of servitude in general may be elaborated prior to,
but not preclude, the subsequent presentation of the respective
positions of men and women.

This point can be expressed in another way by distinguishing between the order of discovery or investigation and the order of exposition. It is more than plausible that an analysis of history in general, or of a particular historical era, should lead to a recognition of both the pervasive presence of women's oppression and, at the most abstract level, the need for expositional categories that are neutral with respect to this oppression.[8] An example, by analogy and distinct from gender relations, is clearly provided by Marx. His mode of investigation through the materialist conception of history led him to focus upon the forces, relations and modes of production and their associated classes. But, for *Capital*, he begins expositionally with none of these but with the simple commodity (from which class relations are then derived, with labour power as a commodity and capital as generating surplus value).[9]

A significant example of understanding patriarchy in this way is provided by Seccombe (1980a). His notion of the capitalist mode of production, for example, is predicated upon three properties that he believes he has established (and which are gender neutral). These are: the private household as the main location of daily reproduction of the ability to work; the ownership of accommodation by the regular wage-earner; and the dependence of the household both on domestic activity and the products bought with wage income.

Our own experience of capitalism associates these activities and functions closely with corresponding sex roles and stereotypes. But, for Seccombe, this is not logically necessary, and so correspondences between what is essential to reproduction under capitalism and gender relations cannot be derived from analysis of the (capitalist) mode of production. In particular, the nuclear family, the predominance of (household) property ownership by men and of domestic labour by women is not essential to the capitalist mode of production.

Accordingly, Seccombe constructs patriarchy as contingent upon the form taken by the capitalist mode of production:

> The concept of the capitalist mode of production is not sufficient to explain it. To simply derive patriarchal relations from this concept would be to seriously overreach its explanatory power and, in the process, to oversimplify and to

collapse into one the many determinations which comprise the concrete structures of capitalist societies.

(Seccombe, 1980a, p. 61)

Seccombe will be quoted at some length, despite some shortcomings (his analysis of patriarchy being unduly 'housebound').[10] However, his analysis neatly and remarkably illustrates the way in which a theory of patriarchy is potentially consistent with the expositional priority and neutrality accorded to the (capitalist) mode of production. As he puts it himself:

We are shifting from one level of analysis to another . . . From the sexless and epochal abstraction of the capitalist mode of production, we are moving toward the sexist and historically periodized concrete of developed capitalist societies. We are moving from the household, conceived as a necessary part of the capitalist mode of production, to the nuclear family, the predominant form for the recruitment to and maintenance of private households.

(Seccombe, 1980, p. 59)

Here, there is an important methodological recognition of the relation between more abstract, gender-neutral concepts and more complex, gendered analysis. Paradoxically, however, Seccombe also proceeds to define patriarchy on an ahistorical basis, that is independent of specific reference to the mode of production or otherwise defined period of history from which it is contingently drawn:

(a) effective possession of, entitlement to and ultimate disposal rights of the father/husband over the mother/wife and the resident children; (b) supervision of the labour of other family members; (c) conjugal rights of sexual access to and possession of one's spouse in marriage and custodial rights over children.

(Seccombe, 1980a, p. 63)

In practice, this apparently ahistorical definition is heavily loaded with a content that is drawn from bourgeois society – not least its emphasis upon the (nuclear) family, property and income. Seccombe depends upon the power of the father/husband over the mother/wife and children, including their labour, possessions and bodies (as in conjugal rights). Consequently, the work of Seccombe illustrates how fine the line can be drawn between abstract concepts that are historically contingent and those that are ahistorical generalisations. More usually in the literature, however, the idea of patriarchy has been more dependent upon ahistorical generalisation, and this been a source of criticism that has generally been accepted as valid.

This is especially so if it leads to the explanation of the oppression of women by men as resting upon biological determinism – even though the differences in our bodies cannot support such a heavy burden. Such criticism has been most powerfully posited by Connell (1987). His starting point is that biological difference is capable of explaining very little in gender differences. Yet this limited explanatory power is compensated for by exaggeration of gender differentiation in society, as if this were biological differentiation:

> There is, therefore, a logic to such paradoxes as the gross exaggeration of differences by the social practices of dress, adornment and the like. They are part of a continuing effort to sustain the social definition of gender, an effort that is necessary precisely *because the biological logic*, and the inert practice that responds to it, *cannot sustain the gender categories*.
> (Connell, 1987, p. 81)

Connell also explores the extent to which biological determinism is implicitly found in popular consciousness and practices: 'sex-role socialization proceeds with impressive unanimity along additive lines, tracing out the ways society improves on nature's handiwork in shaping little girls and little boys' (p. 73). Such ideology, that dresses are female and trousers are male in much the same way that there are biological differences between the sexes, has its counterpart in theoretical work. Connell refers explicitly to sex-role theory and categorical theory. For the former, the characteristics taken on by the two sexes – and not usually more than two except by way of deviancy – are left unexplained, even though they are known to have differed over time, and emphasis is placed upon how appropriate roles are learnt. For categorical theory, focus is upon what these differences are, leading to: 'descriptive literature on sex inequalities in income, education, occupation and health'.[11] Thus, whilst apparently moving away from a biological basis for explaining gender differences, this is an illusion; for identified differences between the sexes are just presumed to be male or female. In short:

> The main reason why it has been difficult to grasp the historicity of gender relations is the persistent assumption that a transhistorical structure is built into gender by the sexual dichotomy of bodies. This is the assumption that sex role theory finally falls back on, and most kinds of categoricalism too.
>
> (Connell, 1987, p. 64)

On the basis of his critique, Connell is able to propose a strong case for a historical and practical concept of gender relations. For, otherwise, they will tend to be surreptitiously explained by prior assumptions about differences between the sexes. As gender is constructed and reconstructed during the course of daily life and through history, this should be adequately reflected and reproduced analytically. For this reason, Connell is profoundly critical of ahistorical/biological notions of gender (and he roots these out from their hiding places). This would apply to such uses of patriarchy which, apart from biological factors, would be unable to explain, even if otherwise analytically acceptable, why men and women are not occupying one another's places in the gender hierarchy. It is a matter of explaining both gender relations and occupancy within them.

During the course of discussing Connell's contribution, a subtle but significant shift in emphasis has been effected. Whilst previously attention has been devoted to the methods of discovering and of elaborating the sources of women's oppression, Connell's concern has been more with causal factors. This is why for him history and practice assume an important role, rather than categoricalism and role-playing. It cannot be presumed that any of the lines of discovery, exposition and causation are coincident, although there will be a relationship between them. If, again, appeal can be made to Marx's theory, just as the commodity is the simplest concept for analysing the capitalist mode of production and is used to derive *capital* at a later stage of analysis, so capital is causally prior to commodity circulation and is used to explain it. By the same token, Marx's method for discovering these orders of exposition and causation are quite different. For the former:

> The general result at which I arrived and which, once won,

served as a guiding thread for my studies, can be briefly formulated as follows: In the social production of their life, men enter into definite relations that are indispensable and independent of their will, relations of production which correspond to a definite stage of development of their material productive forces. The sum total of these relations of production constitutes the economic structure of society, the real foundation, on which rises a legal and political superstructure and to which correspond definite forms of social consciousness. The mode of production of material life conditions the social, political and intellectual life process in general. It is not the consciousness of men that determines their being, but, on the contrary, their social being that determines their consciousness. At a certain stage of their development, the material productive forces of society come in conflict with the existing relations of production, or – what is but a legal expression for the same thing – with the property relations within which they have been working hitherto. From forms of development of the productive forces these relations turn into their fetters. Then begins an epoch of social revolution. With the change of the economic foundation the entire immense superstructure is more or less transformed. In considering such transformations a distinction should always be made between the material transformation of the economic conditions of production, which can be determined with the precision of natural science, and the legal, political, religious, aesthetic or philosophic – in short ideological forms in which men become conscious of this conflict and fight it out.

The purpose of reproducing at such length this well-known, by now even hackneyed, elaboration of Marx's method from the preface to *A Contribution to a Critique of Political Economy* is to highlight its total and exclusive reliance upon *ahistorical* concepts such as production, etc. It follows that there is some justification for those who argue that the gender neutrality of existing theory can be combated, as a method of investigation, by its confrontation with the ahistorical indices of women's oppression, as suggested by the notion of patriarchy.[12]

From this, two propositions follow. First, it is inappropriate to adopt a stance of wholesale rejection of gender-neutral categories such as capital, surplus value, class, production, etc., simply by virtue of the (false) belief that they preclude attention to women's oppression. Second, it is legitimate to employ ahistorical categories, including those associated with patriarchy, to uncover and provide a descriptive account of women's oppression. To move beyond this, however, to provide a causal content, separate categories drawn from the society under scrutiny have to be employed – within which the results of the preliminary descriptive investigation can be incorporated. Thus, resuming the analogy from above, for Marx, the expositional starting point for capital is the simple commodity, specifically extracted from, but not even unique to, bourgeois society. From its dissection, however, the anatomy of capital itself can be constructed and revealed.

There are, then, distinctions to be drawn between the method of investigation and both expositional and causal analysis; failure to do so tends to grant autonomy to patriarchy as a system of oppression. It is unduly endowed with expositional and causal priority. As Barrett observes of Millett, but with wider applicability:

> Her project is to establish a fundamental system of domination – patriarchy – that is analytically independent of the capitalist or any other mode of production. Millett's theory of patriarchy resembles that of Shulamith Firestone insofar as it gives not only analytic independence to male domination, but analytic *primacy*.
>
> (Barrett, 1908, p. 11)

Here, it suffices to add that analytic independence should be interpreted as being comprised of two components: one of investigation and one of exposition, for the first of which there is a rationale for patriarchy as an ahistorical category.[13]

If analytic independence is taken any further than this, it necessarily leads to dual-systems theory, for which Heidi Hartmann has been a leading exponent for patriarchy. Possibly caricaturing her position or, at least, extrapolating it from analysis of capitalism to earlier modes of production, she views the latter as defining positions within society and patriarchy as determining who shall fill them. As she puts it:

> Capitalist development creates the places for a hierarchy of workers, but traditional marxist categories cannot tell us who

will fill which places. Gender and racial hierarchies determine who fills the empty places. *Patriarchy is not simply
hierarchical organization*, but hierarchy in which *particular*
people fill *particular* places.

(Hartmann 1981, p. 18)

Young (1981) questions the dichotomy between patriarchy and
capitalism on logical grounds. Since the latter creates the positions
which men and women are to occupy, it appears that struggle
between the two over occupancy is superstructural or, at least,
heavily structurally determined and constrained, and patriarchy
is far from being an independent category through history. Otherwise, in so far as patriarchy does affect the evolution of specifically
capitalist structures, then its marriage with capital is more by way
of an integration from which it is impossible to extract distinct
patriarchal material relations. They cannot be defined, other than
ahistorically, except on the basis of categories drawn from capitalism and, hence, not independent of it.

Hartmann's position appears to derive from the incorporation
within patriarchy of all of those relations, particularly concerning
the material world of labour and property, through which women
are oppressed. Consequently, the (capitalist) mode of production
tends to be constructed abstractly and causally and as gender
neutral – since the investigative results of women's oppression are
assigned to patriarchy:

To recapitulate, we define patriarchy as a set of social relations which has a material base and in which there are
hierarchical relations between men and solidarity among
them which enable them to dominate women ... The crucial
elements of patriarchy as we *currently*, experience them are:
heterosexual marriage (and consequent homophobia), female childrearing and housework, women's economic
dependence on men (enforced by arrangements in the labor
market), the state, and numerous institutions based on social
relations among men.

(Hartmann, 1981, p. 18–19)

Indeed, the gender neutrality of capital tends to render it a force
for eliminating patriarchy – it seeks out the lowest paid (female)
worker after all – so that Hartmann considers patriarchy was
re-established/consolidated during the industrial revolution by

the exclusion of women from wage work (by male workers securing their labour-market position and their control of domestic labour), but that patriarchy is now once again under threat as women are entering the workforce. These issues will be discussed in greater detail in the next chapter. For the moment it suffices to observe that, for Hartmann, it appears that the analytical role assigned to capital is directly to mediate the conflict/cooperation between men over the exploitation of women:

> Patriarchy as a system of relations between men and women exists in capitalism, and that in capitalist societies a healthy and strong partnership exists between patriarchy and capitalism. Yet if one begins with the concept of patriarchy and an understanding of the capitalist mode of production, one recognizes immediately that the partnership of patriarchy and capital was not inevitable; men and capitalists often have conflicting interests, particularly over the use of women's labor power. Here is one way in which this conflict might manifest itself: the vast majority of men might want their women at home to personally service them. A smaller number of men, who are capitalists, might want most women (not their own) to work in the wage labor market. In examining the tensions of this conflict over women's labor power historically, we will be able to identify the material base of patriarchal relations in capitalist societies, as well as the basis for the partnership between capital and patriarchy.
>
> (Hartmann, 1981, p. 19)

There is, then, some tension in the work of Hartmann over the exact relationship between patriarchy and capitalism. At one level, the two work independently of each other, and the former serves to assign women to the disadvantaged positions provided by the latter. From this, it must follow that it is only uncomfortably that accommodation can be found either for the role of patriarchy in determining the material positions provided by capital or for the role of conflict between males within capitalism to advantage themselves from patriarchy. Such problems have led most to reject patriarchy theory.

RESTRUCTURING PATRIARCHY THEORY

The critique and rejection of Hartmann's dualism, on the

grounds that the separation between patriarchy and capitalism cannot be satisfactorily sustained, finds expression in mild form in the work of Walby (1990b) who, none the less, in positing what is probably the most developed and sophisticated material theory of patriarchy, remains committed to its incorporation within a dual system.[14] Walby's grounds for differing with Hartmann are that the latter is perceived as viewing the relationship between patriarchy and capitalism as being too harmonious and unchanging, although she may exaggerate this difference:

> Her [Hartmann's] analysis of the relations between capitalism and patriarchy overstates the degree of harmony between the two systems. The conflicts between the interests of capital in utilising cheap labour and those of patriarchy in restricting women to domestic labour or very limited forms of paid work is underestimated in her account.
>
> (Walby 1988a, p. 23)

Greater emphasis is placed by Walby (1990b) on 'the main basis of the tension between capitalism and patriarchy [which] is over the exploitation of women's labour' (p. 185).[15] Like Hartmann, then, she focuses upon the material oppression of women by men, particularly through the control of women's labour and, as such, sees herself as developing the details of, rather than breaking with, Hartmann's approach. She also anticipates charges of ahistoricism and essentialism by insisting upon a complex of historically moulded patriarchal structures. These mutually condition one another, as reinforcing or obstructing factors. They do so in different and potentially contingent ways, as well as relating similarly to the co-existing mode of production (although the discussion rarely departs from the capitalist mode of production and it is not always clear whether her analytical constructs are specific to it or are transhistorical). It is worth examining her arguments in some detail.

Her analytical starting point is an articulation of patriarchy with capitalism, reflecting commitment to *dualism*. As such, however, whilst firmly committed to patriarchy theory, her analysis is much less rigid than that of Hartmann and, thereby, more compromised in its analytical commitment to dualism. From here there is a movement to a 'lower level of abstraction', for which *six* different patriarchal structures are identified: the patriarchal mode of production (by which is meant domestic labour); wage labour; the role of the state; the incidence of male violence; the construction of sexuality; and the formation of cultural institutions (Walby, 1990b, p.20).

What is the status of this process of abstraction? It seems to have two properties. First is the categoricalism criticised by Connell, in which a number of different aspects of women's oppression are descriptively identified. These are then each simply translated into a causal structure. Such 'explanations' are tied to the more abstract concept of patriarchy which comprises them all. To put it pedantically: women are identified as unequal in the aspect X (education, for example); X is then seen as a structured disadvantage explaining inequality (the sexism of the educational system); and X, Y and Z and so on are seen as specific consequences of patriarchy in general.

Second, closely related to this categoricalism in Walby's abstraction is the way in which there is analytical movement from one simple level to more complex levels. For her, the move is from simple to more intensive form of detail, with the overall structure of patriarchy being subdivided into its six lower-level substructures. But this has been done in such a way that the original, higher level of abstraction appears to be rendered redundant. It is no more than its component parts. Its distinctiveness from the six substructures at the lower level lies only in its ahistorical content, at most useful perhaps in exploring oppression, but of no further use once the lower levels are embraced. Why not simply begin with these six substructures (with others potentially to be added also)? In what sense is patriarchy as a whole any greater than the sum of its individual parts?

From the six substructures, another lower level of abstraction is posited. This is in part derived from their interaction but also includes what might be termed a move to a more extensive level of detail. For this, account is taken of other determinants and effects, within which are included racial divisions which have not previously been incorporated. This begs the question of why these factors are not at the higher, if not highest level, and what are the criteria which determines what is to be included. Suppose, for the sake of argument, that racism and not sexism were the object of enquiry. Then, the same method would presumably locate six or so racist structures at the intermediate level and their gendered implications at least one stage lower. The priority of sex over race is not justified whether expositionally or causally and, one suspects that, if racism were under consideration, the dualism would begin with black and white and then give way to sexism at a lower level of abstraction. In short, the methodological content of Walby's abstraction is questionable, essentially asserting, rather than employing, higher and lower levels of analysis.

In addition, whilst detail is necessarily greater in moving from higher to lower levels, the causal relations between the simpler concepts (such as patriarchy) and the more complex (such as the sexual division of labour) is asserted rather than demonstrated. To some extent, causal content is provided within or across this analytical structure, when Walby suggests the potential availability of two distinct patriarchal strategies: one is the exclusion of women from the structures that men dominate, the other is women's segregation from men within these structures to hold them in positions of subordination. These strategies in turn follow on from the conflict between private and public forms of patriarchy respectively – the public forms emerging in response to capitalists' and women's conflict with men's private forms of control over women's labour and lives:

> The combined result of capitalist forces and feminist struggle have been previously responsible for the change from private towards public patriarchal exploitation of women's labour.[16]
>
> (Walby, 1990b, p. 59)

Walby's notion of patriarchy is, then, even in the form of this cursory précis, extremely complex. But its very complexity raises problems of consistency across its various parts. First, to return to earlier themes, the movement through levels of abstraction appears to be arbitrary, not only in the levels and structures of abstraction themselves, but also in the relations between discovery, exposition and causation. The initial movement through the six substructures is subsequently supplemented for historical purposes by a separate structural division between public and private as the site for 'patriarchal practices'. Further, this is causally related to strategic hypotheses concerning exclusion and segregation, whose status as systemic as opposed to subjective factors is unclear, as is their relation to the (sub)structural analysis. It must be suspected that empirical observation around the labour-market and political representation, in particular, are the source of a more general and abstract notion of a move from private to public patriarchy, with the latter persisting through segregation as exclusion fails. As Crompton observes:

> To establish that many men will gain an advantage from their relationships with women restates what is already known, rather than demonstrates the existence of a 'system' of patriarchy. In making this argument against the use of the concept of 'patriarchy', it must be stressed that the reality of male oppression is not being disputed, but rather the theoretical interpretation which should be placed upon it.[17]
>
> (Crompton, 1989b, p. 581)

Second, Walby's duality, like that of Hartmann, has become extremely one-sided, on the side of patriarchy. The theory of the capitalist mode of production has fallen away but for tendencies and obstacles to competition in the labour-market. Whilst there are six (or more) ways in which patriarchy is structured, the role of capital is not similarly structured. Instead, it is simply seen as a force undermining private patriarchy and attempting to appropriate the associated benefits from public patriarchy at the continuing expense of women.

Third, there are methodological problems with patriarchy theory as a *social* theory. The focus on the exercise of male power tends to lead to dependence upon the role and behaviour of individual men, even if grouped by common characteristics. This is rarely embraced absolutely but is approached through an even finer division of the (six or more) structures of sexist oppression – men as husbands, trade unionists, state officials, teachers, etc. There is an affinity between the behaviour of individual, or groups of, men in these roles and the more abstract concepts employed in defining patriarchy as an underlying social determinant. This, however, leaves unaddressed the origins of, and changes in, the social structures and processes by which men advantage themselves at the expense of women – even if their behaviour within these social relations is understandable.

To put this in a slightly different and more concrete way: if analysis is to be based on the priority of men as a group over women, then the formation and action of men, as men, as a coherent social force, despite their own differences, has to be identified and explained. In addition, even were this to have been done, there would still remain the issue of whether all, or sufficient numbers of, men have a sufficiently strong common interest for this to be formed and pursued in practice. To a large extent, these problems are handled by Walby through the complex interaction of the six structures of oppression and the strategies of exclusion and segregation across the public and private domains. But this is to displace the problems involved, not to resolve them. These issues will be taken up in later chapters. To anticipate and to exaggerate, patriarchy theory leads to a stance that trade unions, for example, are male organisations but that capital is surprisingly gender-neutral, or even a potential ally of female interests.

Fourth, reflecting these problems, Walby's analysis uneasily combines abstract with historical analysis. For the most abstract concepts with which she confronts capitalist patriarchy are ahistorical and are, consequently, simply projected directly on to their more specific empirical forms, as in the six structures and the private/public and exclusion/segregation dichotomies. Historical change thereby emerges as a complex but simultaneous, rather than causally structured, set of interactions across which the competing claims of public and private and women's demands are distributed.

Despite, or even because of, this, and the assignment of a secondary place to the ideology of gender, Walby's theory of the latter proves to be more sophisticated than its material basis:

> If we look at women's own expressed beliefs of the reasons they do certain things, not others, it appears as if cultural values are of overriding significance; however, the deeper question is what creates the structures that lead to these beliefs.
>
> (Walby, 1990b, p. 58)

Thus, whilst gender relations are seen as an articulation of discourse, power, sexuality, state, violence and work, the ideology of femininity and masculinity is allowed, in addition, a socially constructed history. It has to be made out of the raw materials of the articulation rather than being derived from the abstract principles of patriarchy. But such an articulation should also be used in the derivation of the material gender relations themselves and not just in their ideological accompaniments. Thus, gender relations are complex products of a system of economic and social relations, as suggested by Walby. Yet, in contrast to patriarchy theory, they are subject to reproduction and reconstruction only on the basis of their historically determined social forms, rather than their being

43

read off as the consequence of more abstract patriarchal and transhistorical determinants.

CONCLUDING REMARKS

Dissatisfaction with patriarchy has become the conventional wisdom, although it does persist as in the work of Walby and, as argued here, with justification as a mode of investigation. It has often been replaced, however, with analyses based on the notion of synthesis between complex structures and processes. Kuhn (1978), for example, seeks a synthesis between property and psychic relations as an explanation of capitalist patriarchy.[18] Dualism is also potentially explored on the basis of the relations between production (centred upon wage employment) and reproduction (centred upon non-employment relations, especially those ensuring the creation of an available and compliant workforce). How each of these is treated with regard to gender relations determines the extent to which they depend upon patriarchy theory, even though this is not initially taken as analytically and causally of the highest priority.

Connell (1987) rejects patriarchy theory altogether and proposes analysis based on the practical and historical interweaving between the three structures of division of labour, authority and 'cathexis'. Obviously, there is a danger here of simply reproducing in more or less complex form the six structures of patriarchy suggested by Walby, even if this is presented as distinct from patriarchy, it having been displaced by an articulation of structures which is both historically contingent and (re)formative of gendered relations. Rather, it is concluded here, that the analysis of women's oppression must depend theoretically and not just contingently upon the history of gendered relations. This will hopefully be illustrated in the subsequent analysis of women's employment.

2

WOMEN AND THE LABOUR-MARKET

INTRODUCTION

The debates on domestic labour and patriarchy both became of interest in their own right and, to some extent, their connection to women's paid employment was not always explicit and central. More generally, both economics and sociology have attempted to explain women's disadvantaged position within labour-markets. Three separate issues are fundamentally involved – the level of labour-market participation, occupational segregation and differentials in pay. At the most abstract level, sociology at times drew upon patriarchy theory to explain these features just as political economy employed the determining role of women's confinement to domestic labour. Both of these general explanations prove inadequate as matters of greater empirical and historical detail are broached. The theories had to become more refined.

For patriarchy theory, female disadvantage in the labour-market is further developed through its combination with some form of segmented labour-market (SLM) theory which defines places in the labour-market, to be filled to the benefit of men by virtue of their power over women – at the expense of, or even in collusion with, capital. This view is critically assessed in the first section of this chapter. In particular, such theory emphasises how men have excluded women from jobs or have segregated them into those that are lower paid. The idea that this was especially acute in the nineteenth century is critically questioned in the second section.

There are other theories that explain women's labour-market position by analytically providing them with a prior place to occupy. Such a use of the reserve army of labour is criticised in the third section, and labour process theory is discussed in the fourth

45

section. Some have argued that technology is gendered to exclude women from jobs that are (or are designated as) more skilled, and this is used to explain occupational segregation. It is concluded here, however, that such arguments tend to exaggerate the degree of control of the male workforce over the gendering of jobs.

Orthodox economics explores these issues completely differently, as discussed in the concluding section. Its starting point is that the market and the household allocate labour efficiently, equitably and harmoniously according to abilities and preferences, whether innate or acquired. Where this proves to be empirically unfounded, wage differentials between the sexes are either put down to tastes for discrimination or to structural impediments to the perfect workings of (pseudo-)market allocations. Starting with human capital theory, from which a residual level of discrimination generally still remains after correcting for employees' training and work experience, attention has more recently turned to the correlation between women's lower pay and their being married, especially with (breaks in work for) children. But, of course, to find that marriage and mothering is a labour-market disadvantage is not to explain why this is so.

Models within sociology tend to emphasise other factors and structures, and to break them down into greater detail, thus focusing on socialisation, training and recruitment (or pre-entry factors) and managerial organisation, career structures and mobility (or post-entry factors, especially in internal labour-markets). Models within economics, taking imperfections in the labour-market as their starting point, have been few and far between in application to the female labour-market. Rather, such imperfections are seen as the, usually unexplored, way of explaining departure from perfect competition, for which a residual of discrimination results.

Thus, patriarchy theory and the new household economics can be seen to be at two extremes, one emphasising structure and power, the other harmony, fluidity and efficiency. Other contributions have, often implicitly, attempted to forge a synthesis between the two extremes – as, for example, in the work of Gershuny and Miles (1983). Central here is the notion of shifting comparative advantage within different economic and social structures, each driven by technological imperatives. Thus, labour is allocated to different parts of the economy and household, and services in the modern period are increasingly being produced within the home with the aid of durables purchased – in part, through the wages of female labour, itself associated with reduced domestic labour. In the work of Crompton and her collaborators, a synthesis is sought between the various theories of others, but there is much more emphasis on structures than on processes.[1]

At the end of the day, this leaves us with a rich and complex bundle of analyses. It is rich in theoretical fragments, and it is complex in the range of variables employed and how they interact to give rise to empirical and historical detail. The problem arises of how this can all be systematically and coherently organised, a matter taken up in Chapter 3.

THE UNHAPPY MARRIAGE OF PATRIARCHY AND SEGMENTED LABOUR-MARKET THEORY

In an earlier paper (Fine, 1987), segmented labour-market (SLM) theory has been criticised on a number of theoretical and empirical grounds.[2] Most important, in breathtaking summary, SLM theory adopts a 'middle-range' methodological stance. In this, abstract determining factors such as laws of capitalist development, class conflict, the relations of reproduction, etc., serve both as underlying determinants and as the immediate reference for empirical observation. Consequently, SLM theory tends at one and the same time to be eclectic and to provide a structured narrative, or description, of labour-market segments rather than a causal explanation of them. In addition, the most sophisticated form of SLM theory, associated with the Cambridge school, tends to adopt a supply and demand framework. Admittedly, this eschews an equilibrium approach and constructs segmentation as a dynamic and conflictual process. None the less, the analysis depends upon the interaction of supply- and demand-side factors to structure the labour-markets and their associated wages and conditions.

SLM theory has proved attractive as a tool for analysing women's employment because of its general ability to differentiate between men's and women's positions in labour-markets. In the crudest and earliest versions of dual labour-market (DLM) theory, women and ethnic minorities were lumped together within the disadvantaged secondary sector. For the more sophisticated SLM theory with its overlapping and multiple segments, ground out by a multiplicity of supply and demand factors, greater discrimination can be made both within female employment and between it and other 'secondary' workers.[3]

Nevertheless, the limitations of SLM theory have been recognised at two levels. First, it operates as a more or less tautological device for classification of the variously identified labour-market segments, 'explaining' women's generally inferior position by their being women. Thus, Siltanen observes:

/ While dual labour-markets can possibly account for very general male/female differences, it does not address the differences in male and female wage labour within the secondary (or primary sector). The radical version does address these differences somewhat but relies on 'sexism' as an explanation. We do not, however, get an explanation of what sexism is or of how it is legitimated within the social practices of wage labour.

(Siltanen, 1981, p. 32)

Beechey also points to the limited nature of SLM theory as theory:[4]

The dual labour-market approach tends to be static and ahistorical, providing a loose classification rather than an explanation of the ways in which the labour process structures the organisation of work in particular historical circumstances; and further, that it fails to analyse the specificity of women's position because it ignores the importance of the sexual division of labour and the role of the family in structuring sexual inequality.

(Beechey, 1987, pp. 18–19)

Of course, it is easier to point to the role of the family, the sexual division of labour and the all-embracing effect of sexism in structuring women's inferiority in the labour-market than it is to unravel how they, and other factors, interact to yield the results that they do. What appears clear is that SLM theory tends to allow these processes to carry on outside the scope of its analysis so that, whatever labour-markets emerge and are identified, they can be explained by reference to their conformity with a loosely developed analysis of women's inferior social position – which serves the purpose of explaining their disadvantage within the labour-market.

At one extreme, this line of circular reasoning simply identifies women's low pay: for example, with their being confined to low-paying work, as in Barron and Norris (1976).[5] A much more sophisticated outcome results with the greater complexity of the empirical analysis. Dex (1987b) takes this to the limits of the available data in the British context. Drawing on the Women and Employment Survey,[6] she analyses segmentation in terms of mobility between different types of jobs – the original defining characteristic of segments from the internal labour-market theory of Doeringer and Piore (1971) – although this has tended to be replaced by different characteristics between segments, with their persistence presumed to imply lack of mobility. Dex finds that:

> The initial theories tended to put women into a single category along with blacks: that is, in the secondary sector. Women's occupational mobility was then restricted to movements between secondary sector jobs. The examination of women's lifetime occupational mobility . . . suggests that a more complex structure of market segments exists for women.
>
> (Dex, 1987b, p. 124)

Dex then identifies eight segments, one (teaching) for women within the (male) primary sector and the other seven within female employment, itself structured as primary and secondary, with further divisions according to manual/non-manual, skilled/semi-skilled, part-time/full-time work and special sectors (within the women's primary non-manual sector) for nursing and clerical work.[7] Further, Dex (1987b, p. 124) argues that: 'had a finer breakdown of occupational categories been available, a more detailed description of labour-market segments might well have been possible'.

This serves to confirm, in the context of women's employment, the more general critique of SLM theory in which the latter is seen as infinitely flexible and complex in the light of greater detail in empirical information. This then inspires a finer division of the labour-market into segments. Consequently, women's contribution to labour-market segmentation becomes richer the more we find out about the extent to which they are segmented. But this remains predominantly descriptive; it cannot explain segmentation other than by identifying what are presumably self-explanatory structures or segments. On the other hand, it is important to recognise the value of this empirical research for it has identified many of the features of female employment and how

49

they relate to women's wider role, such as childbearing. But these links have not only to be identified, but also to be explained.

This means entering the broader literature on women's economic role. Interestingly, Hartmann, as one of the leading proponents of patriarchy theory, is supportive of SLM analysis. This should not be surprising, since patriarchy and SLM theory have substantial methodological affinities, ones which allow them to be easily married, and each is ready to translate underlying determinants into proximate empirical effects. For patriarchy theory, it is a matter of identifying the manifestations of male power. Accordingly, the simplest form in which it can be combined with the world of labour is through a dual systems approach in which capital (or the demand-side for jobs) is complemented by a patriarchy (or supply-side) in which men fill all of the best places in the division of labour.

For Hartmann (1979a) and (1979b) capitalism combines the continuing historical power of men over women with the specific power relations of the capitalist mode of production. In this light, SLM theory (as a branch of Marxism) is attractive because it provides an explanation for the structure of employment, although it cannot determine who gets what job.

> Capitalist development creates the places for a hierarchy of workers, but traditional marxist categories cannot tell us who will fill which places.
>
> (Hartmann, 1979b, p. 13)

This is of particular importance in the case of women's disadvantage:

> Marx's theory of the development of capitalism is a theory of the development of 'empty places' . . . They give no clues about why *women* are subordinate to *men* inside and outside the family and why it is not the other way around. *Marxist categories, like capital itself, are sex-blind*. The categories of Marxism cannot tell us who will fills the 'empty places'.
>
> (Hartmann, 1979b, p. 13)

The categories of patriarchy are then required to fill the empty places left by Marxism: as, for example, provided by SLM theory.[8]

In Hartmann's initial work, then, a relatively simple model of labour-market segmentation emerges from combining together models of capitalism (to give places) and of patriarchy (to fill them).

A more sophisticated version emerges once account is taken of capitalist strategy to moderate the effects of, and adapt to, the demands of patriarchy through a flexible accommodation with pre-existing economic and social organisation (Hartmann, 1979b, p. 17). Male control of women's labour in the home is a potential obstacle to their being free to function for capital by filling low-paid jobs. Thus, supply-side factors in women's employment come into conflict with the demand-side factors. Capitalists and male workers have competing interests and, consequently, capital may seek to modify, to its advantage, the conditions under which (private) patriarchy operates. Here there is a parallel between the increasingly complex analysis of patriarchy and capitalism and the shift from the simpler versions of dual labour-market theory to the later models of more refined segmented labour-markets.

Significantly, in this context, Hartmann recognises that she has merely provided a descriptive account with little analytical content:

> Patriarchy as we have used it here remains more a descriptive term than an analytical one.
>
> (Hartmann, 1979b, p. 22)

It is able to describe women's inferior labour-market position, among other things, and to associate it with a potentially complex interaction of forces derived from its co-existence with capital. Again, with some difference in the variables considered, this is analogous to the structured, dynamic supply and demand model of SLM theory.

Consequently, it is hardly surprising that patriarchy as a category holds the same analytical ground as SLM theory, as a middle-range theory. In other words, it is applicable both at the most immediate level of analysis, in the individual workplace or home, and at the most abstract level of underlying historical determinants – so much so that, unlike the categories of capitalism, it threads its way throughout almost the entirety of history. And, like SLM theory, as empirical analysis becomes more detailed, so the simultaneous interplay of determining factors has to become more complex and more widely cast. Thus, in her later work especially, Hartmann (1987a), in a detailed study of employment within an insurance company, finds that the hierarchical places in employment are themselves determined by patriarchy and not just filled by it.[9]

Hartmann's contribution is important because of its simplicity, which highlights the analytical structure inolved in its purest form. Thus, although it is rejected by most on grounds of theoretical and empirical naivety, it does serve, even as it is modified or abandoned, to display the theoretical origins of more sophisticated versions of patriarchy in which there is posited a wider spread of factors uniting the supply- and demand-sides of the labour-market for women (and Hartmann's initial stance often remains at the core of theories of women's employment based on patriarchy).

This should be borne in mind when considering the analysis offered by Walby. Her model of patriarchy, as assessed in Chapter 1, is clearly more complex than that of Hartmann, drawing upon six structures of oppression. These are not, however, of equal importance and this leads to a triple divergence from Hartmann – through incorporating more explanatory factors, by shifting the emphasis between them, and through allowing for greater interdependence between the explanatory factors (Walby, 1990b, p. 40).[10] There then follows a list of eight additional factors – conflict between patriarchy and capitalism, historical variations in patriarchy, ethnicity, spatial variations, workplace effects, the role of the state, sexuality and violence, and a broader notion of patriarchy itself. Significantly, these easily translate into direct influences on the development of labour-markets.

However, emphasis is, shifted between the factors that Hartmann and Walby do share in common, by the latter's insistence upon the conflict between patriarchy and capitalism over the exploitation of women's labour and upon the co-existence of patriarchal relations *within* paid employment itself. This leads specifically to a reversal in causal emphasis. For Hartmann, women's inferior labour-market position is very much a reflection of the disadvantages with which they enter the labour-market as a consequence of patriarchal barriers imposed by men through their confining women, to a greater or lesser extent, to the sphere of domestic labour. Walby takes quite the opposite point of view, arguing that women are confined to domestic labour because of their poor opportunities in the labour-market:

> The causal link between labour-market and family goes largely (but not exclusively) in the reverse direction from that conventionally assumed; it goes from the labour-market to

family, not vice-versa, when we ask questions about causation at a structural level.[11]

(Walby, 1990b, p. 57)

For the new factors that Walby introduces, there is also a hierarchy of importance – with ideology, for example, being seen more as a supportive effect than as a primary cause. More generally, she suggests that patriarchy has been realised through a strategy of exclusion and then segregation, as it has moved from a private to a public form. This means that her non-economic factors tend to be secondary, either as effects or as supporting, articulated factors in the exclusion/segregation and private/public dynamic. This is fundamentally based upon a threefold conflict of interests between (male) capitalists, male workers and women. The capitalists attempt to release control of women's labour from male workers, thereby potentially forging an alliance with women to free them for wage rather than for domestic labour.

> The combined result of capitalist forces and feminist struggle have been primarily responsible for the change from private towards public patriarchal exploitation of women's labour.
>
> (Walby, 1990, p. 59)

However, a compromise of employment segregation between men and women may be reached between capital and male labour, with women being paid less and proving more vulnerable in paid employment. Whilst the joint pressure from capital and feminism is resolved by the move from private to public patriarchy and from a male strategy of exclusion to segregation (or seclusion), this does not in and of itself weaken the strength of patriarchy (Walby, 1985, p. 162). For her, patriarchy lowers the wages that women are paid, but this potentially means that they can undercut men in the labour-market, where men's private patriarchy cannot keep them out of employment altogether. Consequently, the incidence of female employment and unemployment, and of pay and conditions, is centred upon the capacity of organised labour 'simultaneously fighting upwards against capital and downwards against women', with public and private patriarchy forcing women into segregated jobs or back into the home, respectively. This is argued even in the absence of a theory of what determines the levels of employment and unemployment in the first place.

As discussed in the previous chapter, male interests are identified with organised labour; it is powerful even if compromised with the interests of capital. By contrast, Hartmann begins from a position of emphasising capitalism as a potential liberating force from what for Walby is merely the private form of patriarchy. Ultimately, this leads her to view increasing labour-market participation as men's second chance to allow women to enter the labour-market on equal terms, the first not having been accepted during the course of the nineteenth century. Consequently, equality before the (labour) market is potentially a revolutionary development:

> The more revolutionary aspect of the comparable worth strategy arises because it creates the possibility that women will be able to support themselves financially on equal terms with men. Such an eventuality would revolutionize gender relations and create the possiblility of true autonomy for women. Moreover, by raising issues about how women's work is valued, obvious parallels are drawn to the undervalued work women do in the home ... Such questions directly challenge patriarchal norms and patriarchal power bases.
>
> (Hartmann, 1987b, p. 56)

In fact, this is to embrace Walby's causal analytical stance: for, as capital frees women into the labour-market, so inequality there becomes the source of inequality elsewhere in society. However, Walby remains more sanguine about the prospects for women's liberation in the transition from private to public patriarchy. This, no doubt, reflects a different path by which her analysis has evolved. Her starting point has been patriarchy in employment (Walby, 1986, for example), from which she has derived the importance of exclusion followed by segregation. It is plausible to speculate that this then led to these very same concepts being generalised to the six structures of women's oppression – with, for example, greater labour-market participation reappearing as the transition from private to public forms of patriarchy. Not surprisingly, given that patriarchy has been identified initially with paid work, Walby (unlike Hartmann) is not going to look to its extension (as such) as a source of women's liberation. Walby closes her most recent book with the following words:

> The form of patriarchy in contemporary Britain is public rather than private. Women are no longer restricted to the

domestic hearth, but have the whole society in which to roam
and be exploited.

(Walby, 1990b, p. 201)

Despite these differences in intellectual origins and conclusions,
both Hartmann and Walby place great emphasis upon the role
played by male workers in controlling the labour-market and the
labour of women. For Hartmann, wives have at times been confined to the home to work for their husbands. For Walby, they are
excluded or secluded as potential competitors in the labour-market. Moreover, as capital's interests point to treating all labour
equally, male workers appear to be primarily responsible for
disadvantaging women through exclusion at the workplace and by
dominance within the home. As Hartmann and Markusen put it:

> While it could be historically true that during the nineteenth
> century in Britain women freely chose increased dependence
> on men within the home and even helped men to struggle
> for it we suggest that the weight of historical evidence sup-
> ports the alternative explanation that men forcibly excluded
> women from wage labour in order to maintain their domina-
> tion over women and women's labour.

(Hartmann and Markusen, 1980, p 90)

Similarly, for Walby, male workers were responsible for excluding
women from employment in pursuit of their own interests and at
the expense of both women and capital:

> The passage of the Factory Acts should be seen as the out-
> come of pressure from the male operatives and the Tory
> landed interest. The interests of the manufacturers and the
> women were defeated on this issue.

(Walby, 1986, p. 127)

Moreover, this role for the male worker is sustained, even with
different effects, as female labour-market participation is realised:

> Struggles over female employment have usually resulted in
> one of two outcomes: the exclusion of women from the area
> of employment in question; or the segregation of women into
> jobs which are separate from those of men and which are
> graded lower. Segregation is often the result of the struggle

55

when patriarchal forces have been insufficiently strong to exclude women altogether.

(Walby, 1986, p. 86)

It follows for both Hartmann and Walby that the economy has a history in which, at some early stage of capitalism, male wage labourers excluded women from paid employment (and have, to a greater or lesser extent, continued to do so), so that women have (re)entered wage employment at a later date, thereby freeing themselves from the shackles of private patriarchy. This is, however, a heavily disputed history.

THE PRESUMED PRIMITIVE EXCLUSION OF WOMEN

Essential to theories of employment based on patriarchy is the idea that, at some point historically, women were excluded from the labour-market and confined to domestic labour in the interests of male workers, even if this were against the interests of capital and is even now being eroded. This presumed moment in history raises a number of issues. First, what was the position of women prior to this process of exclusion? Second, when did it take place? Third, what were its causes?[12]

In general, the answers to these questions provide variations on the analysis offered by Hartmann (1981), for whom women were systematically excluded from paid work during the course of the nineteenth century, having previously been absorbed into factory work at the expense of men and men's control over them. Men responded by a successful strategy to remove women back to the home, thereby continuing to appropriate their labour in domestic services and minimising competition and downward pressure on their wages in the labour-market.[13] This view has some immediate empirical appeal, given the dip in female labour-market participation in the UK in the second half of the nineteenth century. But it does not stand up well to closer theoretical and empirical examination.

First, it raises problems of timing. For it is essential not to idealise nor to generalise the pre-nineteenth-century family as being relatively free of both gender inequality and a sexual division of labour. Indeed, it would be perverse for patriarchy theory to neglect considerations of men's earlier advantage under feudal and primitive capitalist relations. As Middleton observes of feudalism:

> Peasant women made, in numerous capacities, a significant contribution to the creation of that surplus which was expropriated by the feudal lord . . . In addition they made a varied and indispensable contribution to the economy of the peasant household not only through their domestic activities, but also by their work in the fields, the yard and the garden, and through their involvement in by-industries. In this labour they were rarely free agents for, while they may have achieved a fair degree of practical autonomy in their everyday routines, they were always bound to obey the directives of their head of household and, moreover, after the payment of feudal dues and taxes, the entire product of the household was at his disposal.[14]
>
> (Middleton, 1981, pp. 126–7)

Yet the industrial revolution of the eighteenth century was hardly a release of women from such oppression. As McDougall observed:

> The industrial revolution had a limited effect on most women's work. Although it created more paying jobs for women, it did not offer the majority paid employment; whilst it opened up a few 'masculine' trades like weaving, it restricted most women to sexually segregated industries; and if it drew a minority of women into factories (where they were better paid and worked shorter hours), it drew as many into sweated trades.[15]
>
> (McDougall, 1977, p. 268)

So it is questionable whether women benefited enormously from the increasing availability of waged work.

Second, certainly in the UK, the changes associated with the nineteenth century were themselves the consequences of a long period of capitalist development which, in addition, had its origins in agriculture. For all agricultural workers there was a fall in the security of stable year-round employment, with women suffering particularly from loss of seasonal work and from labour previously made possible through the availability of open fields prior to enclosure (Snell, 1985). Moreover, women's exclusion from trades associated with apprenticeships worsened during the nineteenth century but were far from free of gender bias prior to then. As Snell puts it:

> To avoid misinterpretation, I re-emphasise that the 'male' trades were indeed male dominated, but were not exclusively male as so often is supposed; that there did indeed exist opportunities for women to be apprenticed to these trades; and, in particular, that such opportunities were more notice-able before the nineteenth century.[16]
>
> (Snell, 1985, p. 311)

Third, it follows that women's changing labour-market position tended to evolve over a much longer period than is suggested by the chronology of nineteenth-century exclusion, with differing results by region and by sector of the economy. As Redclift notes:

> The differing paths of transition to capitalism give rise to varying forms of relationship between the family and the productive system, and that these themselves are influenced by the precise configuration of the local labour-market and its insertion in the national and international economy.[17]
>
> (Redclift, 1985, p. 110)

Jordan (1989) also points to the varying degree of employment of women by trade and by location in nineteenth-century Britain, and this is associated with the sex-typing of jobs and the ideology of domesticity as the sectoral and spatial composition of employment is transformed.[18]

In short, the exclusion hypothesis tends to concentrate a long and varied set of historical processes into the nineteenth century: these comprising the transition to capitalism, the industrial revolution and the impact of the factory system, together with presumed changes in the working class family. The reason for this condensation is because of the wish to explain low levels of female labour-market participation in the second half of the nineteenth century through the dual effects of (male) trade union action and discriminatory protective legislation.

Consequently, a number of studies have attempted to show how male-dominated trade unions successfully excluded women from employment or, secondarily, segregated them into lower paid jobs.[19] Generally, it has been considered sufficient to demonstrate that this was union policy and that women were excluded. A further implication is that this is typical of the economy as a whole.

But this is not sufficient. For it takes no account of other forces at work, not least those operating in the interests of capital, although these are often set aside by the assumption that they were gender-neutral, and even favourable to women's paid employment, in seeking lowest possible wage costs. It is necessary, then, to ask what are the conditions necessary for the trade union strategy to succeed. At the very least, it requires (male) labour to overcome the undercutting of male by female wages that would have been a major avenue for increased profits, especially when these through productivity increase would have been quite limited. In other words, for the exclusion hypothesis to hold, capitalists must have been overcome by, or have been complicit in, the male worker strategy. It is imperative, then, to examine the employers' stance and the strength and success with which it could be pursued.

If we suppose that one capitalist, employing female labour exclusively, set up a new plant to escape the attention of male trade unionists, then competitors would be undercut in wage costs and would be forced, or would have the incentive, to follow suit. The only proviso is that neither trade unions (nor husbands) must be sufficiently well-organised across the sector as a whole to be able to bring old or new 'rogue' employers of women to a halt.[20] Alternatively, for whatever reason, employers must collude, without breach to an agreed gender division of labour within their workplaces.

In some cases, trade unions were sufficiently strongly organised to exert the supposed effect – as in cotton spinning, where capitalists effectively subcontracted labour organisation to the senior male workforce who were organised industry-wide and exerted their hierarchical power over women and young workers.[21] But this is far from being generally so, and the overwhelming weight of the literature suggests that male trade unions could not exert such an influence on the gender division of labour. As Busfeld states:

> The ability of unions to deny women access to skill was limited by the extent to which they controlled employment conditions in their trade. A number of writers have argued that . . . most unions were not able to impose skill definitions

– and the consequent wage differentials – on employers who were determined to resist them.[22]

(Busfeld, 1988, p. 162)

Further evidence for the limited extent to which trade union exclusion was the decisive factor in the gender division of wage labour is that the growth of new industries in the absence of trade unions could still be associated with reliance upon male workers alone or predominantly.[23]

Nor is it clear that the weight of union policy was unambiguously and universally in favour of exclusion of women workers. What is generally agreed is that exclusion has been a policy where skills and crafts are under threat but then it is directed against all potential labour-market competitors and not just against women. In addition, a union policy open to female employment has at times been adopted, subject to their being admitted at the same wages and conditions as men.[24] Even if this is not achieved and women are excluded, this does not explain why women should be paid less in the sectors in which they are employed and where, by custom if not trade-union organisation, men have equally been excluded. It might even be argued on the grounds of market forces that the exclusion of women from male employment would tend to enhance their bargaining position as they are rendered a single supply to sex-segregated, *female* occupations. Indeed, it has been found that the division of men and women into different sectors of wage employment can be advantageous to both – by restricting labour-market competition and by providing two sources of income, one of which might suffice for subsistence when the other is lost through industrial action.[25]

These arguments, and their empirical counterpart in historical studies which show that trade unions did not have the strength to carry the burden of the hypothesis of exclusion, lead to a second line of attack in patriarchy theory – that exclusion was organised through protective legislation. For example, Huber argues:

> The movement for *protective* labor legislation stemmed from the desire of male workers to restrict the competition of women and children and from the humanitarian impulses of middle- and working-class reformers to protect women and children from the worst features of the industrial system.
>
> (Huber, 1982, p. 32)

Here, again, the evidence is open to a differing interpretation. At the opposite extreme to patriarchy theory, with its hostility to the working class family as it emerged in the nineteenth century, stands the analysis of Humphries (1977a), (1977b), (1981) and (1987). She sees the family as a haven against the economic and moral degradation of capitalist employment, through which a strategy of enhanced survival is strengthened by the withdrawal of women's labour to the home, the better for it to serve the family and to bolster the ideological and labour-market support for a male family wage.

It is not necessary here to enter into the debate over whether the family served primarily as an arena of liberation from capital or as one of female oppression or, as Sen (1980) suggests, some synthesis of the two. Suffice it to observe that such concepts of the family need to be developed further and less ahistorically. It is unsatisfactory to judge the family as good or bad depending on its balance of external and internal relations in the abstract. It is necessary to provide both an understanding of the complexity of the relationship between the family and capitalism and a recognition of how the family system is itself (re)constructed in response to economic and social forces in which the (re)division of domestic and waged labour itself plays a major part. In any case, there is considerable doubt concerning the view that the motives of men in supporting protective legislation were simply inspired by self-interest buttressed by an ideology of the domestic place of women. Coontz (1988, pp. 297–304) points to the differences between middle-class familial notions of female domesticity and its working-class counterpart of an ethic of justice for labour and a strategy for survival. Kessler-Harris suggests that:

> Neither protagonists nor critics ever lost sight of the possibility that legislation could both ameliorate the worst abuses against women and simultaneously confirm their status as a separate group of workers.
>
> (Kessler-Harris, 1982b, p. 213)

In short, as Creighton (1979) makes clear, the evolution of protective labour legislation was both motivated and caused by a number of factors which were by no means limited to the exclusion of female labour to enhance the labour-market position of men and patriarchal ideology to confine women to domesticity. Different interests were involved quite apart from the male control of female labour (men, after all, had an equal if not stronger wish to limit the length of their own working day). And different tactics were at work – possibly the goal of a wedge of legislation was easier to win around the working hours of women and children.[26] But this neither guaranteed its legislative triumph nor its effective implementation. As Brenner and Ramas conclude:

> Legislation did not have any determining effect on the structuring of job segregation by sex . . . it appears to have limited men's as well as women's hours. Insofar as this was the case, it could not have adversely affected women's chances for employment within the [textile] industry. Indeed, it was precisely because a sexual division of labour already existed in the textile industry, such that male, female and child labour were utterly interdependent, that the Ten Hours Bill could win the shortening of the working day for all through the limitation of female and child labour. Nor does this legislation appear to have resulted in any significant replacement of male for female labour, either within the industry as a whole or within particular sectors. In fact, the proportion of women to men in the textile industry continued to increase during the latter part of the nineteenth century. It is probable that the extension of protective legislation to other industries in the course of the second half of the 19th century also failed to affect the sexual division of labour.[27]
>
> (Brenner and Ramas, 1984, p. 41)

Further, the evidence from the United States is no less comforting to the hypothesis of exclusion, since most of the protective legislation discriminating against women had not found its way on to the statute book until well into the twentieth century – at a time when women were beginning to increase their labour-market participation once more, even if on the basis of predominantly segregated employment.[28]

Given that men as trade unionists and as citizens were not able to exert a strong influence to exclude women from employment, arguments in support of patriarchal exclusion tend to retreat to the terrain of ideological factors, in which the notion of women's role as housebound comes to the fore in forging a society-wide barrier to female employment.[29] Accordingly, capitalists are generally unwilling, so it is argued, to employ women workers, especially in those trades in which the nature of the work is perceived to be 'masculine', thereby otherwise distancing women from their feminine domesticity.[30] This is, however, to put the (ideological) cart before the (material) horse: for, while not denying some causal role for work gendering in employment segregation and exclusion, it does tend to be constructed after the event, and historical studies are liable to be self-selective (around the extension of domestic duties to the female labour-market), neglecting those cases in which women are employed in what are or have been male jobs by the norms of the day.

Even so, at this point, the emphasis of explanation has begun to shift from the role of (male) labour to the role of capital. Employers can also be seen as having an equally culpable ideology and as having compromised with labour's appropriation of female labour in the home. The terms of that compromise are given by capital conceding that it does not seek the minimum wage bill by treating men and women identically, with women proving cheaper. Here, though, there is a false premise – that sexist ideology, as it were, is shifting the distribution of employment and wages away from what would otherwise be a level playing field as between the sexes. But it is evident that the interests of capitalists might well be served by a hierarchy of employments, as indeed is experienced within exclusively male or female job structures, for reasons associated with recruitment and control of the workforce (through, to put it crudely, divide and rule). The overall size of the wage bill itself may well be lower with a divided workforce than with one that is paid a more uniform wage. It depends whether the levelling, on balance, is up or down. Obviously, in eliminating gender segregation in employment, trade unions would attempt to maintain the male rate for women, and employers would attempt to reduce the male to the female rate. There is no telling where the common wage rate would actually be fixed and whether it would be higher or lower than the weighted average of the previous rates.

This is not to embrace the theory of a hierarchy of job places in the labour-market as determined by capital, and a theory of patriarchy to fill them. But the notion of exclusion by male workers as elevating their interests at the expense of both women and capital, does, within this slightly more complex stance, come into question, once allowance is made for capitalists to pursue their own interests in minimising the wage bill or satisfying other labour-market objectives. At the very least, the role of capitalists does have to be considered. At one level, of their being curiously passive in the labour-market, this has been curiously neglected in so far as it is generally to be presumed that they are all or predominantly men. And as strong a case can be made against them as against male trade unionists, when the sex segregation of employment and inequality in working conditions is noted for new industries and those where trade unionists have been absent.

At another level, however, if it is argued that capital's ideology of domesticity is complicit with that of labour, it is – to be fair in judgement and symmetrical in analysis – incumbent upon those proposing exclusion by patriarchy to examine how women have been barred from the ownership and control of capitalist property. For surely female capitalists would have given women workers a fairer crack of the employment whip if it had been held in their hands?

Curiously, this issue was a major factor in Engels' discussion of the family. Reproduction of property relations depended for him upon some form of patrilineal inheritance, usually excluding women from ownership. With the working class itself rendered propertyless (of the means of production), it was presumed that women would become of more equal status as they became obliged to work for wages. This suggests, especially for the nineteenth century, that inequality in the labour-market as a consequence of patriarchy might be more usefully sought in the positions held by male capitalists as owners of the vast majority of property.

Here, of course, the evidence is clear and general, especially for the UK. For the middle-classes, female control and management of property and business declined in the nineteenth century, this having been supported by an ideology of domesticity. As Davidoff and Hall observe:

> It is evident that women's decision to enter the market depended on their control over family property . . . [but] the major identity of most middle-class women was undoubtedly familial rather than occupational, whatever *tasks* they were actually doing.
>
> (Davidoff and Hall, 1987, p. 314)

Moreover, this position was the legal inheritance from before, and not the consequence of, a surge of male exclusionism Creighton points out that:

> Married women . . . were subject to a series of incapacities

and disabilities which by the start of the nineteenth century had reduced them to a status little better than that of chattels of their husbands. To all intents and purposes they could not own or acquire property in their own right, and in the law of torts and of contract they were treated as mere appendages to their husbands. These disabilities gave rise to some doubts as to their capacity even to enter into binding contracts of service without the consent of their husbands, and as to whether or not they had any rights to the fruits of their labour independently of their husbands.

(Creighton, 1979, p. 15)

Holcombe (1983, p. 18) emphasises similar points, and places nineteenth-century agitation for reform of women's property law on an equal footing, and dovetailing with, agitation for female suffrage – even if it has been neglected in retrospect as being less important to female emancipation, possibly for having been more easily won.[31]

That such evidence should be neglected, even when so conducive to the cause of patriarchy theory – and interestingly, there is no room for property relations even in Walby's sixfold structural specification of patriarchy – is symptomatic of the wish to tie women's labour-market position to the male workers' strategies for exclusion and segregation and their oppression of women within the working-class home. However, for the nineteenth century, the major occupation for women was domestic service, and this remained so until at least the 1930s.[32] Although this may have been associated with an ideology of respectability, along with seamstressing, this can only have been so with considerable reservations, given the potential paths to poverty, illegitimacy and prostitution. It equally demonstrates how women's work did not, thereby, remain under the command of their fathers or husbands who must have preferred for their women, as did women themselves, to earn higher wages in more formal labour-market occupations.

The failure of most theories of exclusion for the nineteenth century even to consider the major occupation undertaken by women reflects a neglect of factors which are not even limited to theoretical and empirical nuances. In short, differences amongst women themselves, young and old, married or single,[33] and between their occupations as wage worker or keeper of a small or large household, and other determining factors in structuring labour-markets (such as the role played by capital) are simply collapsed into a single theme of male dominance through labour-market exclusion and segregation. In addition, where, as is generally the case, this is found to be wanting as an explanation, residual reliance is based upon patriachal ideology, variously distributed across different sectors of the population and their associated activities.

WOMEN AS A RESERVE ARMY OF LABOUR

The marriage of Marxism and patriarchy theory is one particular example of a more general approach that has emerged in women's studies. Clearly, the latter has been stimulated by the emergence of the women's movement and, in the academic arena, by the increasing participation of women in higher education where they remain disproportionately represented in the social sciences, other than economics. What it confronted, however, was an existing body of theory that had specifically excluded women or which had set them apart for a special analysis that tended to exclude men. Consequently, it was easiest in the first instance to tack on the issue of women to pre-existing theory. As Kuhn and Wolpe observe:

> There was a tendency to appropriate existing theory, first by pointing to its amnesia where women were concerned, and second, by attempting to insert the 'woman question' into existing work and hence to add to rather than to transform it.
>
> (Kuhn and Wolpe, 1978, p. 1)

Or, as McKee and O'Brien put it more bluntly:

> 'Taking gender seriously' has until recently meant taking *women* into account.
>
> (McKee and O'Brien, 1983, p. 147)

In the specific case of employment, this has led to different models of the labour-market for men than for women. Men are presumed to work and have a primary orientation towards work in what is termed a job model, whilst women are perceived to focus around the home as a wife/mother, examined in terms of a gender model, with tensions existing between the two roles in the combination of paid with unpaid work.[34] As Perkins notes, the result has been that:

> Approaches tend to provide over-simplistic accounts of women's work because they identify differences between men's and women's employment as the *only* feature of women's employment that requires or merits explanation . . . It is perhaps worth noting that the analysis of male employment never starts from, nor even takes into account, this difference.[35]

(Perkins, 1983, p. 16–17)

In orthodox economic analysis, treatment of the labour-market for women has been developed in the same way. A model previously developed for men alone (or, more exactly, for sexually undifferentiated labour supply and demand) has been modified to include variables for women, such as family composition. Whilst, in principle, household labour supply should be estimated jointly where men and women are both present, in practice, this is only done when women's employment is under scrutiny. In other words, the household is only considered relevant to employment when there is concern with women's employment.

One particular way in which women have been incorporated into pre-existing theory is through the Marxist theory of the reserve army of labour. In this theory, there is necessarily a pool of unemployed: partly a consequence of the accumulation of capital as labour is displaced from production by the introduction of high productivity machinery; partly a precondition as ever larger capitals need to draw upon reserves of labour. Marx distinguishes between different sections of the reserve army according to its origins – i.e. having been made unemployed recently (floating), the long-term unemployed (stagnant) and those not previously employed (latent).

The idea of women as making up a major share of this pool of unemployed or employables is usually based on a less sophisticated account than in Marx's own theory, merely seeing women being drawn in, or thrown out of, the labour-market in response to the rhythm of the business cycle and tight or slack labour-market conditions.[36] Women's disadvantaged position within labour-markets has led to a ready identification of them with the reserve army of labour, particularly as women were being drawn into employment over the post-war period. The approach has, however, been of limited use. For, apart from empirical anomalies – such as the high and increasing degree of attachment of women to the workforce over the current period and even during recession – the reserve army is derived from Marx's theory of accumulation and, as such, is gender-neutral. It is quite arbitrary to assign women to a pre-determined reserve army – and there is an obvious parallel with the version of patriarchy theory which assigns women to subordinate positions in a predetermined division of segmented wage labour. As Yanz and Smith argue:

> The gaps [in our thinking] will only grow larger if we continue to try and straightjacket the reality of women's experience into the concepts of women as a reserve army.[37]
>
> (Yanz and Smith, 1983, p. 105)

A further objection to the women as reserve army stems from the simple observation that, as women's wages are lower than men's and as women can be employed equally well in times of labour shortage as in times of labour surplus, so capitalists would prefer to substitute women for men on a *permanent* basis. Indeed, during a recession, when competition imposes cuts on the wage bill as a condition of competitive survival, the desire to employ cheaper women rather than more expensive men may be greater than at times of labour shortage.

This criticism of the reserve-army hypothesis gives rise to what is termed the substitution hypothesis, that women's labour-market participation may be enhanced by their displacing men through accepting lower levels of wages. It implies that women's share of employment in those sectors of the economy where it is operative will be increasing. It is complemented by a third hypothesis, concerning the compositional effect. This takes the gender shares of employment within each sector as given but recognises that the overall level of female labour-market participation will change if there is a shift in the composition of economic activity between those sectors that are more or less male/female intensive in employment – as has been the case in many advanced economies in recent times with the growth of (female) service sector employment at the expense of (male) manufacturing.

Humphries and Rubery (1988), for example, have conducted a statistical exercise to discover the relative importance of these three effects for UK employment as a whole – to see whether women have served as a buffer stock to employment levels as a whole (in which case the share of women's employment would rise and fall with the level of employment), or as a substitute for, or as a separate segment to, men's employment. Like other studies on a smaller scale, it is hardly surprising that they should find that the buffer and substitution hypotheses are not so important as the compositional effect. Milkman (1972), for example, points to the growing female labour force in the 1930s in the United States, despite high male unemployment, because of the growth of jobs stereotyped as associated with women. Collinson (1987) notes the growth of women's employment in the mail order business, again in the context of high male unemployment, but is less hasty in rejecting the reserve-army hypothesis since he recognises that the jobs concerned tend to be temporary, part-time and unskilled – features that might be associated with the reserve army. Mallier and Rosser suggest that different sectors of female employment will have diverse experience of the effects involved:

> Over the period 1951 to 1981 the demand for female labour has been subject to both substitution and cyclical effects. The relative strengths of these two effects have varied from industry to industry and over times. Occupational structure, organisational and technological changes, as well as variations in final product demand, have all played a part in determining the relative strengths of these two effects. Observation of aggregate employment change by industry over time can only identify which effect, if any, may have been dominant.
>
> (Mallier and Rosser, 1987, p. 485)

This is because, in part, women have been in jobs, especially in manufacturing, that are more stable over the cycle, having some greater affinity with fixed costs of production, as in running the office.

Whatever the empirical results, however, they cannot provide an explanation of women's labour-market position, for they are merely descriptive of those changes that are taking place. In particular, lack of change itself has to be explained, in so far as it represents continuing disadvantage for women in labour-markets. The reasons for this are not going to be transparent from the relative extent to which the three hypotheses are confirmed or not. These changes themselves, or lack of them, would still need to be explained. And, when change does take place in the structuring of employment, as in the shift from a job being predominantly for one sex to its being predominantly for the other, it can at most be charted by exploration of buffer, compositional or substitution hypotheses.

In seeking explanations for women's (changing) employment, an important starting point is occupational segregation, given the rejection of the reserve-army hypothesis, since the relative import-ance of the substitution and composition effects depend upon the relative stability of job segregation – and, in addition, segregation is perceived to be a major source of women's inequality in, not just of, employment.

OCCUPATIONAL SEGREGATION

Necessarily, there are affinities between theories of job segrega-tion and patriarchy theory, with the latter tending to explain the former by its assigning women to the lowest places in an exogen-ously (capitalistically) determined employment hierarchy. The creation of the job places has, however, tended to go unexplored within patriarchy theory, which is itself subject to analytical ero-sion – as the determination of the division of labour by task and by sex are no longer perceived to be independent of one another. Accordingly, the division between patriarchy theory and job-segregation theory more generally (and with the material covered here previously) is somewhat forced. It has, however, been made along the lines of whether either some theory of job structures or some theory of job allocation (other than male imposition) is present.

One such theory, inspired by the idea that women's lives are defined as much by paid work as by family and reproduction, is provided by the labour process literature derived from Marxist theory.[38] This has a number of components. One is the idea that work and the workplace is a terrain of conflict, as between capital and labour. A second is that capitalism has a tendency to deskill and degrade jobs as accumulation substitutes machinery for la-bour. A third, articulating the first two, is that the definition of skill is socially constructed – neither independent of, nor determined by, the requirements of the job itself – and dependent upon conflict and negotiation over what shall be defined as higher or lower grades. Fourth, each of these processes is gendered, creating both a sexual division of labour and of skills.

The literature on the labour process has been renewed following the major contribution by Braverman (1974). He has, however, been criticised for overemphasising the tendency to deskilling or, more exactly, for not combining it with tendencies to reskilling – as jobs are intensified through combination of tasks through machinery and through the use, control and maintenance of the machinery itself.[39] Also such regradings and their associated work are subject to conflict between capital and labour and are not simply imposed by one on the other. Nor are these processes gender-neutral, since skills are thereby socially constructed, both with a material component in the specific work to be done and with a partly, or substantially, separate assignation of grading to different work which will tend to denigrate women's as compared to men's work.[40]

It is important to recognise, then, a number of processes that are systematic results of capitalist production: there is the reconstruction of skills, involving both deskilling and reskilling; there is the (re)definition of skills as a social construct; and there is the gendering of work. Thus, as is the object of equal-worth claims, women may claim equal pay for work of equal worth by some criteria and objective assessment of job requirements. Conceptually distinct, women may be denied access to jobs which are, or which are designated as, more skilled. Segregation in work may reflect women doing more skilled work than men but being designated as less skilled, or it may be that they are denied access to jobs which are more highly skilled and valued, whether this be through discrimination in recruitment or in the gaining of skills and qualifications.

For example, in looking at the effects of office automation on clerical work, Carter (1987) criticises Braverman's deskilling hypothesis as being too simplistic.[41] It neglects how it has enabled some work to be enriched and designated as skilled even though it continues to be occupied by women. There are also a number of other issues involved apart from deskilling: how control is exerted; the level of 'detailed autonomy'; pay and career structures; etc. This approach is confirmed by Webster:

> What seemed significant to the quality of each secretarial labour process was not the replacement of typewriters by word processors, but the presence or absence of diverse

components in the work and the proportions of time spent on these.

(Webster, 1990, p. 43)

Consequently, the introduction of word processors does not necessarily serve simply to deskill secretarial work further – for the typist in the pool attains the highest level of tedium whatever machine is used. The impact has been more dependent on the nature and initial organisation of work – see Webster (1989) and (1990) – and more powerful machinery does not necessarily entail job degradation and deskilling.

Not surprisingly, male strategies of exclusion figure prominently in such analyses. But in moving beyond the simple assertion of male hegemony in the assignation of jobs, two further factors are brought into account. First, it is recognised that the division of labour is subject to restructuring as capital is accumulated and new methods of production, management and control are introduced. Second, some emphasis is given to the ideological role of gendering jobs, with the restructuring of the sexual division of labour depending upon, and interacting with, the pre-existing notions of masculinity and femininity in the allocation of jobs between the sexes.

At one extreme, where such ideological factors are given considerable emphasis, women's skills are taken for granted – as if there were almost a natural division between women's and men's work, whether this be associated with physical attributes such as strength, or socially constructed skills associated with masculinity and femininity. For the latter, there is a tendency to associate women's employment with their carrying over domestic duties into the labour-market. Thus, for Davies and Rosser:

A gendered job was one which capitalised on the qualities and capabilities a woman gained by virtue of having lived her life as a woman.[42]

(Davies and Rosser, 1986, p. 103)

More explicitly, for Probert:

Many female jobs tend to be extensions of housework, including cleaning, making food and clothing, or to be caring and nurturing occupations such as nursing and primary teaching.

(Probert, 1989, p. 73)

Similarly, certain areas of work are perceived to be assigned to men because of their externally given characteristics, particularly those associated with the masculinity of science, technology and machinery.[43] Rothschild (ed) (1983) shows how women's contribution to technology has been significant but systematically ignored because technology is identified with what men do, and, whilst it has improved and has become a major part of women's lives, it has not escaped such gendering. Moreover, Sarsby (1985), for example, argues that the ideology of deference to, and attendance upon, men (together with a primary commitment to the home) can lead women to accept a similar role in the workplace – in the pottery industry for Sarsby's study.[44]

It seems that not too much weight should be given to such ideological factors in explaining the sexual division of labour. To begin with, women have engaged in most types of work in different countries at different times, including the heaviest of tasks – especially in agriculture – and continue to do so most notably in the Third World today. Second, whilst women in the West have been crowded into a few female occupations, these are not completely common across all countries. Dentists, for example, are typically female in Denmark (see Reskin and Hartmann, 1986, p. 7). Also, certain jobs have clearly been transformed from male to female work, such as clerical services. Third, this then suggests that the gendering of jobs by ideology is more an effect than a cause, especially over the longer term.

Indeed, there are those who perceive the ideology of gender at work as being much more derivative, rationalising what has been brought about. As Garrison puts it:

> As each new job became filled by women, charming theories were developed by both sexes to explain why the feminine mind and nature were innately suited to the new occupation.
> (Garrison, 1983, p. 160)

And the charm may well be employed to maintain pay differentials between men and women with an associated gendering of the division of labour, the crossing of which leads to stigma and abuse. Murgatoyd states:

> In general, then, particular occupations become defined as 'men's work' or 'women's work', as a result of conflicts between employers seeking to employ women as low-wage

labour, and groups of male workers attempting to exclude women from particular sectors of employment in order to protect their own wage levels.

(Murgatoyd, 1982, p. 589)

What is indisputable is the close association between different sorts of jobs and gendering, especially where segregation is high. Williams observes:

Highly segregated occupations . . . take on the 'gendered' attributes associated with the sex of their work force. Secretaries (99 percent female), kindergarten and preschool teachers (98 percent female) and domestic workers (95 percent female) are all expected to be emotionally sensitive and nurturing, reflecting the 'feminine' qualities of the workers. Exhibiting stereotypically masculine qualities, engineers (96 percent male), airline pilots (99 percent male), and auto mechanics (99 percent male) are assumed to be emotionally reserved and detached, concerned more with the rational manipulation of things than with the caring and support of people.

(Williams, 1989, p. 2)

But what is less clear is the direction of causation between the two. In the case of the Marine Corps in the United States, the archetypal male occupation even within the armed forces,[45] there have been changes since the 1970s. It was estimated that enlisting women would save $10 billion per annum in wages, improve the quality of the recruits and save on recruitment expenses.[46] Subsequently, there has been recruitment of women and a dramatic change in ideology – with women prior to the Second World War, for example, being dishonourably dismissed from the Army Nurse Corps for either pregnancy or marriage.[47]

A rather different example is provided by the case of US flight attendants. As Rozen reports:

The first stewardesses were hired in 1930 . . . registered nurses until World War II . . . charming, smiling but serious young women in professional-looking uniforms helping passengers. In the early 1950s, however, the airlines began to change the stewardess image so that it lost its professional aspect and gained a sexual overtone with which the occupation was identified until the early 1970s.

(Rozen, 1987, p. 225)

Such employees were chosen for their prescribed physical attributes, were not allowed to marry and were retired between the ages of 28 and 32. However, with the growth of air traffic and aeroplane size, the ratio of attendants to pilots increased rapidly, and the latter were unable to sustain their 'craft' as the basis for superior bargaining power, as trade unions for airline staff strengthened; and, with the growth of the women's movement from the 1960s onward (and the Civil Rights Act 1964), women successfully challenged employment restrictions and moderated the sexuality and glamour components associated with their jobs (and paradoxically raised the proportion of male staff).[48] Average employment duration rose from 18 months to 6 years between 1960 and 1975.

Obviously, the military is a special case and, other than arguing that increasingly sophisticated technology of warfare renders it more amenable to stereotypical female employment, is not subject to systematic restructuring of the labour process in conjunction with the sexual division of labour. Similarly, whilst changing technology, in the form of bigger aircraft, had a part to play in the changing conditions of female employment on the airlines, both unionisation and wider political influences were also of importance. Together these two examples illustrate the complex and variable relationship between the work process and the ideological gendering of jobs.

However, specifically associated with the theory of the labour process is the idea that restructuring of skills as a consequence of automation, mechanisation or whatever, degrades and cheapens jobs so that they are abandoned by men and left to be occupied by women;[49] or, if there is some general upgrading of jobs, women will be driven out of them. On the other hand, if male jobs and skills are threatened in conjunction with mechanisation, they may agree to accept the changes only subject to the continuing exclusion of women – as Baron (1987), for example, suggests for the US printing industry. In the first case, there is segregation, in the second there is exclusion, but change in the gender division of labour is opened up through the stimulus of job restructuring.

Cynthia Cockburn, appealing to patriarchy theory, has been the strongest exponent of this view in the context of focusing

75

attention on the labour process and the gendering of work.[50] She suggests that:

> Two mechanisms are important in this respect. First, the exploitation by men of horizontal and vertical differentiation in the occupational structure; and, second, the active gendering of both people and jobs.
>
> (Cockburn, 1988, p. 33)

This is less an explanation and more an account of what has to be explained, although it is supplemented by the argument that men move out of jobs (and up) as they are occupied by women due to greater male bargaining power, and that men systematically devalue women's work by constructing it as non-technical and inessential.

Thus, Cockburn states:

> To understand the continuing technical job segregation by sex we cannot do without a concept of long-term organised male self-interest, of systematic male dominance.
>
> (Cockburn, 1986, p. 80)

Significantly, but not of necessity and not always by Cockburn, the notion of male dominance has been associated with the male working class as if they alone exercised power over the allocation of jobs and conditions and their gendering. The reason for this is that capital's interests are usually represented as lying in the breaking down of restrictions in the labour-market, although there is also the view of divide and rule whereby the overall wage bill is reduced by paying some (men) more than others (women). But this does not explain why the some are men and the others are women. Thus, the quote from Cockburn above is in response to her own question:

> Why, under pressure from capital . . . male workers reacted historically not by fighting for women's right to work and their right to equal pay but rather against both.
>
> (Cockburn, 1986, p. 80)

Patriarchy is seen then in terms of job exclusion and lower pay for women acting against the dull but liberalising forces of capitalism. Not surprisingly, reference to the role of employers is limited – to, for example, 'the prejudice that inhibits the personnel manager from appointing a woman technician'. A similar view is taken of the unequal roles of capital and labour in Bradley (1986, p. 54) where two conflicting drives are the competitive pressure on employers to cheapen their labour costs by introducing women and the determination of organised workers to retain traditional forms of employment. For Liff (1986, p. 88), the hypothesis of feminisation of the workforce 'towards a goal of a largely unskilled, unorganised, undifferentiated and cheap workforce' is contradicted by the facts because 'the theory has failed to take account of the ability of male workers to oppose such changes'.

There are a number of problems with this approach that relies on the patriarchy of male workers as being primary. First, as in the historical material discussed previously, both the extent and the effect of trade union policies of exclusion tend to be exaggerated. The example of newspaper printing offered by Cockburn (1983) is atypical, especially because of the strength of trade union organisation across the industry, the strength of unity with other unions (in distribution), the tied location (to London) and the (daily) perishability of the product.[51] Such examples readily offer themselves as case studies. Others do not, such as Savage's (1988) discovery that new industries developed in the non-union area of Slough in the inter-war period with sex segregation of the workforce along traditional lines.

Similarly, Milkman (1983) observes that the shares of female employment in auto and electrical engineering were quite different in the United States in the inter-war period, even though both were new industries and both were unionised. She explains the difference in terms of management strategy, in that wage-cutting was more important in the more labour-intensive electrical industry (and compelled the union to press for equal pay in response to feminization of the workforce). Thus, she suggests that:

> The prevailing idiom of sex-typing (of engineering as male) cannot be used to account for the actual boundaries between women's and men's work or for the difference in the degree of feminization in the two industries.
>
> (Milkman, 1983, p. 170)

She concludes that causation is in the opposite direction and that:

> Thus the relatively high labor intensity of electrical manufacturing and its reliance on piecework for managerial control over labor affected the sexual division of labor very

77

differently from the auto industry's use of the moving assembly line and the high wages to control labor.

(Milkman, 1983, p. 193)

Further, on one of the few studies to test, however crudely, for the idea that employers not employees determine sexual segregation, Bridges (1982) finds that capital intensity of production and market power, and not unionisation, prove most important. He argues that this is because the wage bill effects will be of less significance in the presence of these as they form a lower proportion of costs (although this does not necessarily diminish the incentive nor the compulsion to reduce wage costs). He concludes:

> The burden of proof lies with those asserting that the intransigence of privileged men is the main stumbling block to the integration of men's and women's work.[52]

(Bridges, 1982, p. 290)

The second problem for exclusion theory is in dealing with the overlaps between male and female employment since segregation is high but not absolute. Where men and women do work together there tends to be an evening out of conditions, so that men are relatively worse off in predominantly female occupations and women are better off in predominantly male occupations, especially in the professions. Thus, OEEC reports that:

> The cross-country survey revealed that in jobs with low earnings and low skills for manual and part-time workers, there exists little difference in remuneration between women and men. But, due to segregation, comparisons in certain sectors are virtually impossible.[53]

(OEEC, 1985, p. 87):

This is at least consistent with the idea that it is the character of the jobs that determines their associated disadvantages rather than simply because they are done by women.

The third problem for exclusion theory is that this conclusion is confirmed by the high association of the jobs done by women with the characteristics of lower pay whether for men or women. In particular, women are located in jobs and working conditions whose economic features and potential for trade union organisation are limited. Purcell (1984), for example, recognises that the employment situation of women is non-conducive to unionisation and militancy and suggests that differential militancy can be explained, not by females as compliant workers, but to a large extent by women's material situation of combining domestic and wage work (see Purcell, 1979). Wage work for women tends to be in fragmented workplaces, which renders both unionisation and industrial action that much more difficult.

For the period before 1918, Thom suggests that it is the extent of women's militancy that has to be explained rather than its lack, and she points to the significance of the level of union subscription rates for women going out to work to supplement poverty income:

> The question should thus be, not why did so few [women] organise but why did so many, against such odds?
>
> (Thom, 1986, p. 262)

On a similar theme, Tilly (1986) examines the conditions under which women might engage in collective, community action. She gives seven that are identical in principle, if not in strength, to those that might be found for men engaging in industrial action. Women were, in addition, more likely than not to engage in collective action around household consumer interests according to two other conditions which could not be found in the industrial relations scene. This suggests that there is no evidence as such for the lesser militancy of women, only that their circumstances differ from those of men.

> These conclusions do not differ very markedly from those that predict higher participation rates by men [in collective action]. The chief difference is the case of defense of household consumer interest. Women were much more likely than men to participate in such collective action. Responsibility for household consumption was rarely a primary concern of men in an industrial economy. A general theory about comparative propensity to participate in working-class collective action, whether strikes or food protest, informs about women, too. No special pyschological or gender-attribute explanation is needed to understand women's proportionately lower participation rates.
>
> (Tilly, 1986, p. 39)

The fourth problem with the exclusion theory is that it neglects, as has already been suggested, the role of employers. Essentially, they will be seeking to employ a section of the workforce on low wages and poor working conditions. As has been seen, women are amenable to this because of their weak material basis for organising against it. As the OECD observes, in the context of the growth of part-time employment:

> The development of part-time work in these countries seems to have been initiated by the employers. It has meant that they have been able to attract a supply of labour at lower hourly wages than would have been necessary if the workers were obliged to work a full day and arrange and pay for their school-age children.
>
> (OECD, 1980, p. 27)

Similarly, Coyle sees segregation as a strategy in the clothing industry to create a section of low-paid workers:

> Employers need a formally segregated workforce for as long as there is the possibility of comparability between low paid and high paid workers. Once rates have been set at low levels then segregation is not important.
>
> (Coyle, 1982, p. 22)

Siltanen (1986) reveals the deficiencies of gender construction (and hence job exclusion) as an explanation of occupational segregation and sex-typing of jobs in her study of postal workers and telephonists. She finds that 'the Post Office management used a strategy of employing women at lower rates as a cheap answer to shortages of male labour' (p. 104), with the union adopting the demand of equal pay and proving unsuccessful until 1955 when this was adopted by the Civil Service as a whole. Subsequently, until 1975, women have been used by management as temporary workers to get round the problem of equal pay. In the most recent times, however, Siltanen finds that a structure of employment has emerged in which a 'full' wage is earned in certain jobs (such as postal with overtime and night telephonists) as opposed to a 'component' wage as day telephonist. The allocation of men as well as women to these jobs depends on their household responsibilities in terms of, for example, the level of income required and whether there are alternative sources of household income.

Thus, women in component wage employment tend to be under twenty or over forty whilst the men are typically young and/or single. Women in full wage employment tend to be in their thirties with dependent children or above forty and widowed or divorced. It is income need that determines the pattern of recruitment, with the employer fully exploiting this to moderate wages for both segments. Jobs, then, are not just gendered, but structured according to the financial needs of employees, whether men or women.

On the basis of her study, Siltanen (1986) finds no inconsistency in male trade union support for equal pay and opposition to female employment, a conclusion drawn by Cockburn (1983) in her study of male compositors. For Siltanen recognises that female employment is a management strategy to reduce the wages of all, and a defensive strategy of equal pay is a second line of resistance to this. Cockburn, on the other hand, appears to find the inconsistency in the presence of patriarchy in the one instance and its absence in the other. Patriarchal men should fight for exclusion and lower pay for women, as is made explicit in the previous discussion of her work, in contrast to the results of her own study of the compositors and of Siltanen's for postal workers. The problem arises because of the neglect of decisive factors other than the role played by male trade unions, such as management strategy and, as in Siltanen's study, differential income needs.

In summary then, the reading of women's employment position as being heavily determined by male exclusion is only supported by a narrow reading of much trade union policy, and depends upon setting aside other influences such as management strategy and the economic and social situation of women so that union policy can falsely be considered decisive (usually against the wishes of capital). As Lewis argues:

> The conclusions reached as to what was suitable work for women differed from place to place and between social classes, but were largely *shared* by male workers, employers, government and women workers themselves. Employers did not proceed to engage women wholesale when male union control was weak despite their cheapness.
>
> (Lewis, 1984, pp. 172–3)

It must at least be recognised that had the unions been defeated in their policies of job exclusion, then employment would have become another female 'ghetto'. Considerations such as these lead Sen (1980) to distinguish between the short- and long-run effects of trade unions through exclusion, and to designate this as an exacerbating and secondary factor in determining women's employment position.

In short, theories of exclusion, even when synthesised with those of gender ideology, tend to experience difficulties when confronted with a wide range of theoretical and empirical evidence. This should not be surprising since they are liable to be successful in explaining an unchanging structure and gender division of labour which will tend, in the presence of trade unions, to confirm their approach – with union commitment to equal pay being seen as in their own male interest. If, however, major changes in the sexual division of labour are considered, problems more readily emerge. This is well-illustrated by clerical work.

It is commonplace that clerical work has been dramatically transformed from a male to a female trade in the passage from the nineteenth to the twentieth century. As McNally (1979, p. 25) reveals at the ideological level, whilst Alexandre Dumas advised of women, 'if they got one foot inside an office, they would lose every vestige of feminity', for males, *après le déluge*, this ideology was reversed with feminisation, 'born a man, died a clerk'.

How did this change in the sexual composition of the workforce come about? Note that for Walby (1986 and 1988), for example, it represents the triumph of capitalist cost-cutting over male trade union resistance. However, this explanation is rejected by Cohn (1985) in his detailed study of the feminisation of clerical work on the railways (Great Western Railway, GWR) and in the General Post Office (GPO). He concludes:

> Most unions have very little control over hiring decisions and only limited control over promotions and job assignments. Without such power, unions can contribute little to the process of occupational sex-typing, and gender decisions remain a matter of managerial prerogative.
>
> (Cohn, 1985, p. 20)

He begins, however, by observing that the GPO and the GWR introduced female clerks at very different rates. The GPO hired its first female clerk in 1870 and by the First World War had raised their share to 40 per cent. The GWR did not even hire female clerks until after the war, and even by the mid-1930s, when the GPO's share had risen to almost 50 per cent, its share remained well below 20 per cent.

Now, whilst clerical work was expanding at this time and the

GPO had five times the clerical intensity of labour as the GWR, Cohn rejects the argument that this, at least alone, explains the greater feminisation for the GPO and for clerical work more generally. For other jobs were newly expanding at that time without their employing women – although, in retrospect, we now tend to stereotype most of them as male. As Cohn notes:

> Between 1870 and 1930, however, employers also first began to hire accountants, life insurance salesmen, airline pilots, truck drivers, electricians, elevator operators, advertising consultants, radio announcers, and automobile mechanics. All of these jobs became overwhelmingly male. The expanding turn-of-the century supply of female labor does not seem to have had the same effect on every occupation that was created during the period. In fact, supply considerations seem to have very poor predictive power in explaining what types of jobs become male or female.
>
> (Cohn, 1985, p. 13)

Nor can cheapness alone explain the feminisation, for that would apply equally to the GPO and the GWR. Cohn does find considerable management opposition to the employment of women, much of it spurious,[54] and this is judged to be more important than the impact of unions:

> Unions played a negligible role in determining sextype. Consistently, management stonewalled union sex demands, denied them outright, or granted them in a form that deprived the concession of a substantive meaning. In some cases, this can be explained by union weakness, as was the case with the telegraphists of 1926. Even relatively strong unions, however, like the telegraphists of 1910, were unable to obtain significant concessions.
>
> (Cohn, 1985, p. 159)

Cohn finds that the evidence of women filling de-skilled jobs vacated by men to be mixed, since some jobs were monotonous and undemanding (such as filing) but others (such as typing) did require more dexterity and training. This is not to deny the presence of job segregation within clerical occupations, but again this seems to have been more the strategy of management. Women were regarded as a low-paid, uncareered workforce without pensions and subject to the dismissal of the marriage bar. Better jobs were reserved for males and were used to induce their cooperation with management and competition with each other – as in, for example, those jobs that did not require nightwork. Women were excluded from nightwork, not because of protective legislation nor because it was better paid, but because selection from nightwork became the route to a preferred career and promotion that did not require it. Cohn discusses this in terms of 'synthetic turnover' – forcing women into jobs without prospects so that they could be regularly replaced at low levels of pay.[55]

Cohn himself suggests that the relative pace of feminisation in the GPO as opposed to the GWR reflected the greater degree of capital-intensity of the latter and its lower composition of clerical as opposed to manual staff. Thus, the pressures to reduce clerical wage costs were that much greater in the GPO. This conclusion is readily interpreted within patriarchy theory, since feminisation can be seen as a proportionate response to the capitalist need to cut wage costs. This, however, neglects the extent to which it is the ideology of management which is the greatest barrier to women's employment, and that management, not male workers, structures labour-markets as between men and women to reduce wage costs. It is worth, then, contrasting Cohn's conclusions with those of Walby.

> The variations in segregation are a result of the relative strength of patriarchal and capitalist social forces at particularly crucial moments in the development of these areas of employment.
>
> (Walby, 1988a, p. 25)

For clerical workers in particular:

> Segregation was thus the outcome of a threefold division of interests between the employers, the male clerks, and the would-be women clerks. It can best be understood as the outcome of the articulation of patriarchal and capitalist interests and the compromise arrived at after struggle.
>
> (Walby, 1988a, p. 26)

Her view is that the male workers were insufficiently well-organised to prevent the entry of women but compromised through their own elevation to higher-level openings, so that women could fill the lower-level jobs. In engineering, by contrast, the unions are seen to be strong enough to exclude women altogether. Taking the two cases of clerical work and engineering together with that of textiles, Walby concludes:

> These varied historical outcomes show the importance of not simply considering the relative strength of only one or two social forces in understanding changes in the gender composition of paid work. It is rather the complex interaction of a number of factors which must be considered: employer demand for labour, which is crucially affected by the product market; trade unions, which are crucially differentiated by not only their overall strength, but also their policy towards gender relations; variations in the extent to which particular groups can mobilize the state; and the shifting relations between occupations due to changes in technology. Further, these interactions take place not only in sequence through time but also in spatially differentiated social and political contexts.
>
> (Walby, 1986, p. 201)

Interestingly, this conclusion is surely unexceptional and, significantly, stands apart from any dependence on patriarchy theory at all. If it were supplemented by a theory of the gendering of work, to which Walby assigns a second order effect, it would be compatible with the work of Cohn and of many others who reject patriarchy theory.

This points to the need for a more systematic analysis of the factors under consideration. First, there is the argument concerning male exclusion. Whilst this has focused on the motives of male trade unionists, attempting to enhance their labour-market position (and often treated in isolation from other factors), capitalists equally have an incentive to structure the labour-market to reduce wage costs. Similarly, each might have an incentive to demand equal wages and conditions for women: the one to forestall, the other to impose a lowering of wages.

Second, there is the process of work restructuring, deskilling and gendering. It cannot be presumed that the form this takes is predetermined, irrespective of the gender division of labour, since there is also reskilling and intensification of work to consider. Nor can it be presumed that women simply fill the jobs created at the bottom of the pile for, as the distinction between horizontal and vertical segregation illustrates, women will themselves be incorporated into a hierarchy of employment, relative to one another as well as to men.

Third, the occupational segregation of women's employment is dependent upon the conditions under which they enter the labour-market and these are, in general, different from those of men because of familial responsibilities and, more generally, sexual oppression in education, training, etc.

Fourth, the incidence of these factors is historically variable and equally so across different sectors of the economy as well as over time – most obviously, for example, in those employed by the state as opposed to those employed by private capital.

Fifth, the ideological counterpart to these material factors is complex. As the latter change and bring the sexual division of labour under pressure, so the notions of femininity/masculinity may serve as an obstacle to such changes, where previously they were a support. Thus ideology may change without significant material change in occupational segregation and vice versa. It thus makes little sense to attempt to disentangle cause and effect in the division of labour and the gendering of work. Clearly, in wage employment, whose structures tend to be stable over extended periods, the ideological gendering of work is liable to conform to the gender division of labour and appear to be its cause.

Finally, whilst many have recognised that the division of labour is gendered as a historical process and cannot simply be read off as an abstract consequence either of capitalist development or of male power or some combination of the two, such history has usually been narrowly confined to particular sectors, times or localities of the workforce. Thus, the redefinition of the material and ideological content of gender can be seen in detail to depend upon its pre-existing character as well as the forces that act upon it. This historical analysis, however, also needs to be more broadly defined, as will be argued in the next chapter by reference to the periodisation of capitalism.

ECONOMICS AND WOMEN'S EMPLOYMENT

In general, in economic theory as in sociology, models of the labour-market have traditionally paid no attention to the gender division of labour. Both the theory and, as often, the empirical exercises have focused exclusively upon male workers, usually full-time and predominantly in manufacturing industry. Unlike sociology, however, economics has responded to the growing importance of women in the labour-market by doing little more than extending its existing analysis, as if it were only accidental and of no significance that previous models had been totally independent of consideration of the sexual division of labour. There has been, for example, no emergence of a concept such as patriarchy to be debated as a potential explanation for women's inferior labour-market position.[56]

The reason for this is that whilst economics develops an analysis of equilibrium supply and demand through the mechanism of the market, the principles of doing so are perceived to be sufficiently elastic to extend to most, if not all, areas of life. Individuals are taken to be maximisers of exogenously given utility functions – through least-cost production and trading in activities in which they enjoy a comparative advantage. Thus, Becker sets himself the task of using:

> the assumptions of maximizing behavior, stable preferences, and equilibrium in implicit or explicit markets to provide a systematic analysis of the family.
>
> (Becker, 1981, p. ix)

It seems to be axiomatic that as much as possible should be explained on this basis, although why this should be so is never made clear (other than that it conforms to the orthodoxy of neoclassical economics).[57]

The main principle by which analysis is extended to non-market relations is by treating them as if they were governed by the (neoclassical concept of the) market. Accordingly, marriage is seen as a contract in which it is implicitly agreed to exhange certain goods and services between husband and wife (income for domestic duties). It is possible, of course, in doing this to see such pseudo-markets as imperfect: in terms of information available; honesty of, and commitment to, contracts; and uneven distribution of economic power. And children can be counted as if they were consumption goods which incur a cost to maintain (in time and money), but which might even ultimately yield a return to parents in later life in care and support.

In this way, economic theory can be employed to analyse whether individuals work or not, how much they consume and save and how many children they have and when. But England and Farkas point to a major empirical problem – that certain features of women's lives, especially those of concern to feminism, have been much more stable than others:

> The assignment of child rearing and housework to women, the sex segregation of jobs, and the sex gap in pay have been much more resistant to change than fertility, the double standard of sexual morality, female employment, or the volume of housework that is performed.
>
> (England and Farkas, 1986, p. 4)

At times, neoclassical economics, and Becker in particular, has displayed considerable ingenuity in dealing with these problems. At other times, however, the analysis has ventured little beyond tautology.

Consider female labour-market participation. As wage levels rise over time, it is argued that either a wife is attracted out to work by the higher income to be earned or that the household may be satisfied with the higher income of the male earner. The first of these effects is called price (or substitution) effect of the higher female wage and the second is the income effect of the higher male wage. Accordingly, women work as the one is greater or not than the other. As England and Farkas observe:

> The price effect (the female's wage rate opportunity cost of childbearing) has become stronger over time and is now more decisive than the income effect of husband's wages.
>
> (England and Farkas, 1986, p. 82)

This is, however, sheer tautology. For whatever happens, it can be argued that the extent to which women work or not can be 'explained' by the relative weight of price and income effects. It is also worth noting that these effects are theoretically constructed on the basis of fixed preferences, even though they are being applied to different individuals and populations over time.

Implicit so far, then, has been the assumption that men and women, respectively, begin from a division of labour – with men advantaged in the labour-market and women in the home. This is usually taken to be a consequence of exogenously given biological differences. On this basis, because of the initial impetus to speciali-sation in the division of labour, men are liable to accrue even greater returns than women from investment in human capital – that is, in education and training, etc. Consequently, women are endowed, more as a matter of efficient choice than of natural abilities, with lower qualifications over their lifetimes. Marginal differences in initial labouring characteristics are, thereby, heavily compounded – as put most strongly by Fuchs:

> Even a relatively small amount of initial labor market discrimination can have greatly magnified effects if it discourages women from making human capital investments, weakens their attachments to the labor force, and provides economic incentives for the family to place priority on the husband's career.[58]
>
> (Fuchs, 1988, p. 44)

This still leaves unexplained why women with equal qualifications to those of men should be paid less than them. Becker argues that women's prior commitment is to the home and, consequently, because of the long and hard hours of housework, women are less able and willing to work so intensely in the labour-market and, hence, are less well rewarded there. It can also be argued that as women's wages rise and they go out to work and accumulate human capital, so the gains from 'trade' between men and women become less pronounced. This implies that the gains from (marriage) partnerships become less and less secure, thereby explaining the increased breakdown of marriage.

Finally, there is the matter of children. Here, Becker argues that the relative cost of quantities of children has increased, since the wage forgone by women in attending to children will have risen. With women's time becoming more expensive, it becomes preferable to have fewer, higher quality children. Thus, Becker argues:

> The growth in the earning power of women during the last hundred years in developed countries is a major cause of both the large increase in labor force participation of married women and the large decline in fertility.
>
> (Becker, 1981, p. 98)

Less time need be spent with children, but this can be compensated for by showering expenditure upon them from the extra wages earned, and there can still be income left over to buy other consumption goods as well.

The neoclassical theory does have certain strengths. First, it focuses upon economic motives, where they might otherwise have been absented, and brings these to the fore (even if unsatisfactorily) in analysing issues such as family formation. Second, such incursions forge a connection between three separate areas – female labour-market participation, family formation, and inequality in pay and employment. Taken as a whole, however, the neoclassical theory, especially as associated with Becker, is like a leaking boat – scarcely afloat in a sea infested with the sharks of theoretical and empirical anomalies.

Consequently, it has usually been felt to be more appropriate to compartmentalise the issues involved with an assumption, sometimes implicit, that there are some structural constraints in operation. This might be on the grounds of a sociology of difference between the sexes or even by reference to the microeconomic theory of segmentation, as in the theory of screening – for which, uncertain information about potential employees leads to the stereotyping of men as more capable than women.

In the case of explaining pay relativities between men and women, focus has been upon the different characteristics that they bring to the labour-market, differences in human capital and stability in, and commitment to, work. It is argued that, once these are taken into account, then the fact that men are paid more than women will be seen to be an illusion – women and men with the same human capital will be paid the same wages. Whilst the techniques for exploring this are simple enough in principle, it has led to a number of competing models and assessments. A recent review of these is provided by Dex (1988a); see also Chiplin and Sloane (1976) – from which Figure 2.1 is taken, illustrating different potential models.

These differences derive from, first, some judgements about what factors constitute the normally functioning (male) labour-market. The more factors taken into account, the more likely it is that the empirical measure of discrimination will be reduced, since what are considered positive labour-market attributes are generally more characteristic of men. None the less, most studies establish empirically the existence of a degree of residual discrimination inexplicable in terms of labour-market characteristics alone and, thus, due by default to gender differences alone.

Second, even if there were agreement over what factors to include in modelling discrimination, some judgement has to be made about how they have an impact upon discrimination directly and indirectly through their interaction with each other. In other words, the model has to be structured. For example, it is generally recognised that large-scale firms usually pay higher wages than small-scale. Equally, those with a higher density of trade union membership tend to pay more. A triangular relationship between these factors, however, is a consequence of the strong correlation between trade union membership and large-scale firms. So, in deciding to what extent trade unions raise wages (or relativities against non-unionists), account has to be taken of direct effects, through trade union membership itself, and indirect effects due to the presence of large-scale firms in raising trade union membership (quite apart from the direct effect of the large firm on wages).

The example given in the previous paragraph makes no reference to the relative position of male and female workers. But exactly the same sorts of considerations apply. Women tend to work for smaller firms and in industries that are less unionised. This is a structured source of lower wages in conjunction with any direct discrimination involved. Again, how these, other and more complex structures of causation are modelled has an effect on how the level of discrimination is understood and measured. This is illustrated in Figure 2.1 by the diagram of potential influences taken from Chiplin and Sloane (1976).

Thus, Joshi (1990), for example, employs a model in which the effects of gender are analysed, together with motherhood, part- and full-time work and other, more traditional, labour-market variables such as education and experience. This disentangles the effects on relative pay over time, distinguishing the impact of motherhood (as such and through lost work experience) and gender. It is found that the level of pure discrimination has varied over time both for mothers and for non-mothers. Levels of discrimination have been much more severe for part-time as opposed to full-time women workers.[59]

As empirical studies for human capital, when restricted to differences in education and training alone, do not explain wage differences sufficiently, attention has also been focused on the effects of work experience. It is argued that because women take breaks from work, they fall behind men in on-the-job training. Consequently, they will be paid less and also choose to work in those sectors in which work experience and investment in human capital are less important. They have a comparative advantage in doing so; this, then, also explains a degree of occupational segregation.

Such a view has been associated with Polachek (1979).

91

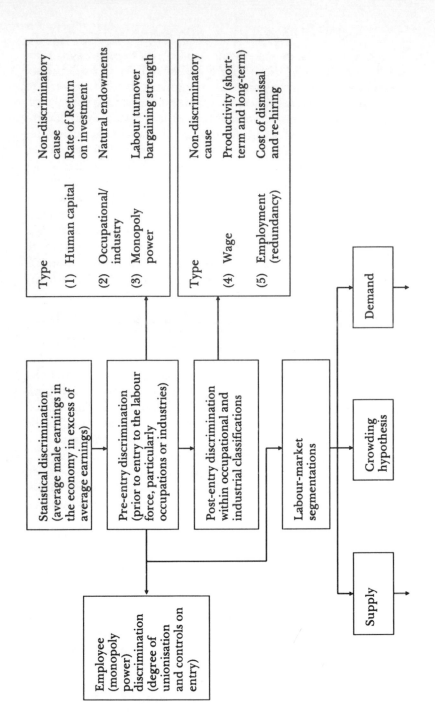

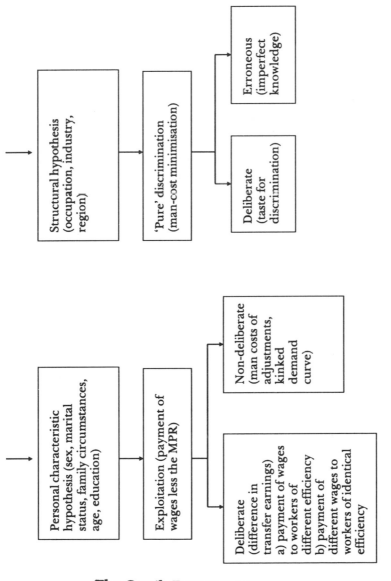

Figure 2.1 Components of discrimination
   Source: Chiplin and Sloane (1976)

However, as England (1982) observes, this suggests quite incorrectly that women should be penalised more in terms of relative wages if they are working in predominantly male occupations and that women without breaks in work should be more likely to be found in such occupations.[60] However, in estimating wage levels and differentials, work experience does prove to be empirically significant, so that part of women's lower pay is associated with their taking breaks from work to have children.

Generally, then, two important conclusions can be drawn from the studies that attempt to explain male-female wage differentials on the basis of individual workers' labour-market characteristics. As Gunderson's findings reveal:

> From the various studies, the following generalizations emerge regarding sex differences.
>
> 1 The greater the number of variables used to control for differences in productivity-related factors, the smaller the productivity-adjusted wage gap relative to the unadjusted gap.
> 2 Even when they use extensive lists of control variables most studies do find *some* residual wage gap that they attribute to discrimination. When the gap is closed to zero that usually results from the inclusion of variables whose values themselves may reflect discrimination.
>
> (Gunderson, 1989, p. 51)

This leads to a very unpalatable state of affairs. At one level, the model is estimated and leaves a residual difference between men's and women's pay which is then taken to be the consequence of discrimination against women, whether this be due to employers' tastes for, or sociological and economic structures of, prejudice. As Mincer, a leading neoclassical economist, puts it: 'the residual should be viewed as "a measure of our ignorance".'[61]Madden puts it thus:

> No statistical study has been able to explain the major part of the sex-wage differential by differences in productivity. No analytical model has demonstrated convincingly how sex discrimination in the labor market can persist.
>
> (Madden, 1985, p. 76)

Similarly, Gregory and Daly (1990) find that human capital models perform reasonably well in explaining variations of wages around the average for each sex within each country, but they are incapable of explaining why there are wage differentials between the sexes and why this differential is so different as between countries. They prefer to bridge these explanatory gaps by appeal to differences in institutional factors (Gregory *et al.*, 1989).

The very lack of an explanation of the residual differential even in this narrow statistical sense also means at a more fundamental level that any conclusions drawn from the estimates remain dubious. For they depend upon the unexplained and unidentified part of wage disparity associated with discrimination remaining unchanged and not interacting with the variables that do explain some degree of wage differential. To give a specifc example, it has been observed that if women (and men) were redistributed across sectors of the economy so that each is proportionally represented in each sector (thus moving women from low-paying female into higher-paying male sectors and vice versa), then there would be some elimination of pay differentials but the major part would still remain. This is because women are paid less than men within each sector of the economy (as well as being concentrated in the lower-paying sectors), reflecting inequality through occupational segregation: that is, statistically, horizontal pay differentials across sectors are less important than vertical differentials within sectors. Some then might conclude that it is more important to attack the issue of inequality of pay within sectors than between them. For example, Dex notes that:

> Giving women the same pay as men in a particular occupation, while leaving their occupational distribution unchanged, does more to remove the pay differential between men and women than redistributing women between occupations in the same proportions as men, but leaving their pay at its existing level in the occupational categories.[62]
>
> (Dex, 1988b, p. 146)

This is, however, highly dependent upon *ceteris paribus* assumptions; for major shifts in occupational segregation, that such remedies would require, would be impossible without fundamental changes across all the determinants of women's labour-market position. As Bergmann observes:

Some observers of the labor market have been led by this

undoubted mathematical truth to the mistaken belief that occupational segregation is of little harm to women and that ending it is of little concern. Such a view is incorrect because it ignores the causal connection between occupational segregation and the assignment of wage rates to jobs by the market.[63]

(Bergman, 1986, p. 137)

Thus, the idea that horizontal segregation is relatively unimportant tends to depend upon models in which relative wages are determined by a set of what are considered simultaneous but independent explanatory variables. But this is not satisfactory in so far as such variables as make up human capital, for example, are interrelated with each other and with the missing variables that make up residual discrimination. These variables cannot be changed independently of one another.[64]

More recently, attention has turned to the effect of marriage, and especially the presence of children, upon wage relativities – that is, over and above the effect on presumed loss of earnings because of lost human capital in the form of work experience. On top of this are the earnings lost while out of employment altogether and whilst in part-time employment (to make provision for childcare, especially for pre-school children). This is pay lost for being out of the labour-market. But it is also associated with lower pay on returning to work than would have been earned if there had been continuous employment. Moreover men earn more, but women do not, as a result of being married and, presumably, supported in their careers and daily lives by their wives – and not vice versa.[65]

Interestingly, the sources of disadvantage in female pay appear to have turned full analytical circle over the past twenty years. Initially, emphasis in the domestic labour debate came to be placed on the inhibiting impact of the dual burden of domestic and waged work. Subsequently, through patriarchy theory, especially as in Walby's work, attention turned to the disadvantages in work through exclusion and segregation. Currently, however, in response to the observed importance of married women, with and without children, to increased labour-market participation, a focus has been found for the role of domestic labour once more, most notably in the mother's responsibility for pre-school childcare. Thus, Joshi (1987), who has pioneered calculations of this sort, estimates that the loss of earnings from being a mother, through lost hours of work and lost work experience, are roughly equivalent to those of being discriminated against as a woman in the labour-market.[66]

In short, wage equations have taken labour-market characteristics of men and women and used them to estimate the level of residual discrimination – which remains unexplained. A different exercise takes relative wage rates as given, and, together with a selection of other variables, attempts to explain both fertility and labour-market participation on this basis. Thus, Sprague concludes that:

> Fertility and participation rates are substantially affected by male and female earnings and education. Vacancies, real interest rates and 'stocks' of children are also important explanatory variables . . . Education and the availability of jobs may be thought of as longer-term trends leading to increased labour-force attachment of women, whereas income variables such as real interest rates and male and female earnings determine the least-costly times to start childbearing.
>
> (Sprague, 1988, p. 696–7)

More generally, reviewing a mixture of studies, Joshi (1985) draws a number of conclusions;[67] for example: that once allowance is made for the presence and age of a youngest child, additional children have little impact on their mother working or not; through part-time employment, women lose a further 20 per cent of hours of work over and above the immediate loss due to leaving the labour-market to have children; this is itself associated with worse pay and conditions; there is an incentive for women to delay and compress their childbearing years, especially if their jobs are associated with rapid pay increase whilst they are in their twenties; marriage as such no longer appears to affect labour-market participation once the presence of children and availability of income is taken into account; but part-time work is more likely, as is work at all, the higher are female wages and the lower male wages.[68] Joshi concludes:

> Women's employment in post-war Britain had adapted as much to their reproductive role as has their reproductive behaviour to changes in their role in the economy.

This serves to reinforce the conclusion, not only that domestic labour is an important determinant of women's economic position, but that fertility and childcare are most important within it.

3

GENDER AND ACCESS TO THE MEANS OF PRODUCTION

INTRODUCTION

This chapter begins in the first section with a broad outline of four different approaches that have been used to analyse women's employment – methods based on structuralism, simultaneity, processes (or economic and social practices), and historical specificity. After examining each of these, they are brought together in discussing the value and reproduction of labour power – who works, for how long and for what reward. This, in turn, suggests that the family or household is subject to distinct changes of structure. These are identified in the following three sections through a periodisation of the capitalist family.

Before that, the first section closes by linking the issue of (women's) employment to the notion of access to the means of production. Some may find this section, and its preoccupation with Marxist theory, to be unduly abstract and may wish to proceed straight to the next section. It is argued that access to employment differs between modes of production, but also within them, both over time and as between different sections of the workforce. Clearly, men's and women's access to labour-markets is socially and historically very different as a consequence of their differing responsibilities for, and roles in, domestic labour and childbearing. Consequently, it is argued that the demographic transition, which has witnessed a reduction in childbearing, has not only freed women from domestic labour both absolutely and relatively, it has also seen them entering labour markets on terms and conditions less exclusively influenced by such continuing disadvantage. In particular, the character of the economy, and its labour-market and welfare conditions, have assumed a much greater importance, especially through the economic and social interventions of the state. In Chapter 4 this is illustrated by reference to the labour-market situation of women in the UK.

STRUCTURE, SIMULTANEITY, PROCESS AND CONTINGENCY

From the earlier review of some of the approaches to women's employment, a number of different methodological stances can be discerned. It is worth identifying and examining these individually, although it is important to recognise that any particular contribution will embody a methodological hybrid even if one 'gene' may be dominant within it.

First, theories of patriarchy inevitably depend upon a form of *structural* analysis in which men as a socioeconomic group oppress women (and, usually, patriarchy is structurally combined with other modes of production). But structural approaches are by no means confined to patriarchy theory, although alternatives almost always rely upon some form of gender discrimination (patriarchy in disguise?) to explain why women occupy inferior positions in hierarchical structures. Also, as the domestic labour debate illustrates, the structural divisions between paid and unpaid work, between the labour-market and the home, between production and reproduction, and between the private and the public spheres, play a crucial role in the specification of women's disadvantaged labour-market position.

However, structural analysis can be taken much further and to a more concrete and detailed level. In the case of the operation of the labour-market itself, a division can be made between pre- and post-entry factors. For the former, emphasis is upon the structural disadvantage that women suffer prior to their attempting to gain employment – whether it be in education, training, their prior commitment to domestic duties, or in the structured bias experienced in recruitment practices. For post-entry factors, a common focus is upon the operation of internal labour-markets and/or the internal organisation of firms. It is generally agreed that career structures disadvantage women so that they are confined to lower paying jobs – explicit in the case of marriage bars, no less significant in personnel management.[1] Thus, Heritage reports:

As late as 1975, on application forms for the Midland Bank,

only male entrants were asked: 'Do you undertake to study and make every effort to pass the Diploma Examinations of the Institute of Bankers?'

(Heritage, 1983, p. 134)

The presumption was that female workers would be confined to lower paying and careerless duties, through their allocation to the clerical side of banking. Similarly, Hacker (1990), following Kanter (1982), points to the neglect of how the internal organisation of firms channels men and women into different careers on the basis of sex differences that are more apparent than real.[2] For until the mid-1970s, 'writings on organisational change ignored sex as an important analytic variable' (Hacker, 1990, p. 47).

Jacobs (1989b) has possibly taken furthest the case for a structural approach to women's disadvantage in the labour-market. He argues that women face a 'revolving door' in pursuing their employment prospects. No sooner do they overcome one obstacle, or find an opening into the world of male advantage, than the door revolves and another obstacle swings into place – or provides for renewed disadvantage. In adopting this view he mounts some telling criticisms of other analyses and, of necessity, implies that simple reforms cannot overcome women's disadvantage. For those who believe that educational inequality is a key factor, he observes:

Men have not maintained an overall educational advantage over women the way whites have over blacks and the way the wealthy have over the poor.

(Jacobs, 1989b, p. 43)

In short, Jacobs emphasises structure after structure of social control that impedes women's labour-market progress at every stage so that to overcome one barrier is to face another:

The thesis advanced here is that sex segregation is maintained by a lifelong system of social control.

(Jacobs, 1989b, p. 48)

In support for this view, he examines empirically the extent to which individually women are able permanently to overcome occupational segregation. Whilst, in the United States at least, particularly in the professions, there has been some decline in occupational segregation since the 1970s, individual women are

101

just as likely to move into a male-stylised job as to move out of one – so to overcome the barriers of disadvantage is not permanently to enter the promised land of male employment prospects:

> For women occupation changers, the chances of ending up in a given sex-type category are virtually independent of the sex-type category in which the women started.
>
> (Jacobs, 1989b, p. 164)

In emphasising a revolving door of social control, Jacobs is particularly critical of the idea that women's labour-market inequality is the consequence of *cumulative* disadvantage. He emphasises much more the obstacles faced in the present as opposed to those that have been inherited and stored up from the past, such as education and work experience. True, females at an early age are, for example, discouraged from entering into technical subjects and training but, whether they do or do not, their ability to enter and *sustain* a technical career remains circumscribed. Indeed, Jacobs stresses the extent to which there is a limited correspondence between women's employment intentions and actual outcomes, especially as far as sex-typed occupations are concerned, and that women's labour aspirations are adaptable in the light of labour-market opportunities.[3]

In short, sex-stereotyping by a life-time of socialisation is not considered so significant by Jacobs as current forms of social control. As such, his structural emphasis on the revolving doors of opportunities in female employment implicitly involves the rejection of an alternative approach to women's employment – what might be termed the *simultaneous* approach. It is most obvious in the case of human capital theory and its associated empirical estimates. It simply explains women's labour-market position by reference to the aggregate impact of (less favourable) labour-market characteristics. There is little or no structure to the analysis, just a weighted aggregation of simultaneous influences. It is as if you get more or less points (i.e. pay) for skill, work experience, for being male or female (the residual discrimination) or, for what is often the same thing, taking primary domestic responsibility, or not, for a child, husband or elderly relative. As previously remarked, it is a moot point the extent to which this provides an explanation as opposed to a particular form of description of women's labour-market position.

A third approach, other than structural or simultaneous, is to emphasise *processes*. Here, for example, technical change is seen as an engine for generating low-paid jobs for women. Similarly, deindustrialisation is a process drawing women into the labour-market to occupy 'service' jobs that have been traditionally designated as female. More generally, the sexual division of labour is understood as a system of gendering, as in the labour process literature, in which there is conflict between capital and labour, and between men and women, over job control and allocation. In addition, there is a strong ideological component in stereotyping jobs as male or female. And, as productivity increases under capitalism and as household activities are displaced through commodification, then, from a variety of theoretical points of view, women are increasingly drawn into the labour-market.

Finally, there is a *historical* dimension to the analysis of women's labour-market position and this cuts across each of the other aspects. For example, it is commonplace to stress the inertia associated with the sexual division of labour; that once labour-market conditions or structures are laid down, it is difficult for them to be changed. This is in part due to the ideological content of sex-stereotyping – jobs, education, skills and patterns of behaviour become sharply distinguished as male or female. But also change is slow and impeded because of the need for adjustment in behaviour in moving from one generation to another since, for example, labour-market outcomes are affected by patterns of marriage and childbearing. Also, once women are paid less than men, it becomes rational for them to specialise in domestic labour and to forgo work experience and training, thereby reproducing sex-stereotyping and disadvantage. For such reasons, and the imperatives around the labour-market when industries are established or radically restructured, Milkman (1983) for example, argues that occupational segregation should be explored historically sector by sector to discover how, at points of major change, long-standing patterns of employment have been established. By analogy, it is as if the sexual division of labour is laid down like the system of nation-states – each can embark upon its own internal development but fundamental change between them only occurs periodically.

By the same token, however, it follows that the processes that reproduce these patterns must be revealed: stability as well as rapid periods of change both have to be explained – like, as Sherlock Holmes would have it, the dog that did not bark in the night. Even if we identify a stable pattern of inequality in employment as between men and women, and are able to discover the historical point at which it was created, this does not suffice analytically. It is also necessary to uncover what processes, structures and simultaneous factors sustain this situation and, by implication, what would bring it to change. For otherwise, when change does occur, as in a switch of stereotyping in employment or changing female labour-market participation, this can only be analysed in retrospect as the occasion on which a new sexual division of labour was established and cast in stone.

In short, it is important to root out the historical origins of a sexual division of labour. But, then, it does not suffice to rely upon self-sustaining inertia. It is also necessary to explain how a sexual division of labour is reproduced. In this context, it is also important to recognise the reproduction of gendering in employment as a contradictory process, reflecting tensions in material practices – conflicts over who does what job, how and for what pay – as well as in the ideological reconstruction of stereotyping: what exactly is a female education, training or job. History, with contingent outcomes, has to play a role.

This fourfold division of approaches to gender and the labour-market, as between structure, process, simultaneity and history, is both rough-and-ready and illustrative. It raises the issue of how their insights can be collectively employed whilst retaining coherence and compatibility between them. The approach adopted here is based upon three components that cut across these four approaches. The first concerns the value of labour power. For Marx this was determined by the socially necessary labour time required to produce the consumption bundle that was sufficient to reproduce the labourer. This, even narrowly interpreted as a consumption norm, is historically and socially determined. As such this raises more questions than it answers. A proper starting point, however, is that for Marx the value of labour power is the consequence of an exchange between capital and labour, confronting each other as the two major economic classes. It is not simply the wage earned on the labour-market by one individual as opposed to another.

The exchange of labour power between the two classes involves, in the first instance, the presentation of the labourer at the workplace for a definite period of time. Of course, the workplace could be the home, as in the putting-out or sweated system associated with homeworking.[4] But this serves to illustrate that the labour offered to capital in return for the value of labour power is not fixed in terms of who does it (and where and how much). Marx is clear on this in so far as he sees the extension of wage labour to women and children in the nineteenth century as an increase in the amount of labour performed in return for a given value of labour power. The work is spread over the family, possibly together with the addition of overtime, so that the value of labour power is a more complex concept than the wage rate or earnings of the typical worker.

In this light, of course, there is an indeterminancy not only in who performs the labour but also in the relationship between the value of labour power and the value of wages. As interpreted here, the value of labour power is the norm for the working class as a whole, established through conditions of production and consumption. But the value of wages is both variable for the class as a whole – in terms of the vagaries of supply and demand on the labour-market and in the markets for consumption goods, and in the balance of distributional conflict – and variable in the levels of wages paid to individuals and to individual sections of the workforce. Clearly, the relationship between the value of wages and the value of labour power is a complex one, bridging both the vagaries of the market and, more fundamentally, the relationships *within* the working class as producers and as consumers.

This complexity is illustrated by the debate over the family wage.[5] The family wage can at best be an ideological construct to justify higher wages for men, irrespective of the effects this might have on lowering the wages of women and withdrawing them from the workforce. For, even if wage labour were exclusively male, many workers would not be living in families, there would be different family sizes and different numbers of dependants, according to those able or expected to work.[6] Only if the working class pooled its income for consumption purposes could there be a consistent relationship between the value of wages for the individual worker and the value of labour power for the working class – but this would then strip away the individuality of the wage contract and, in the conventional wisdom, diminish work incentives.

There are then two aspects to the value of labour power: who works and how much, and the standard of living provided in return. In addition, the value of wages is distinguished from the value of labour power to signify individual or sectional differences in work and consumption around social norms. In short, in drawing the distinction between the value of wages and the value of labour power, with the one varying around the norms established by the other, these norms must themselves establish standards of who works and how much, as well as levels of remuneration to provide for consumption and, indirectly, the daily and generational reproduction of the labourer.

Irrespective, then, of the degree to which women work, there is a tension between the value of labour power as it operates through the labour-market to provide equivalent wages to each labourer for work done and the value of labour power as it establishes standards of consumption from the income of a variable number of household wage labourers. Moreover, this tension is reproduced within the households, and even within the individual worker. For individual household consumption levels are affected by the overall level of earnings which can be obtained through the household working longer (more workers offered by the household or overtime for the individual worker) or by working harder (on piece rates, for example).

These conundrums concerning the value of labour power might lead some to reject it as a useful concept in moving to a greater level of detail than the hours of work and wages of the working class as a whole. Certainly, this is as far as can be gone in abstractly analysing how capital provides for the reproduction of labour power and is perhaps the way to interpret Marx's enigmatic comment that, subject to the purchasing power of the value of labour power, the reproduction of the workforce can be safely left by capital to the proletariat's instinct for self-preservation. This is not to say that such self-preservation is unimportant or irrelevant because it is in some sense automatic, only that the analysis of capital does not directly encompass the relations of social reproduction, those lying outside the immediate circuits of capitalist production and exchange.

Here, there is an analogy with the Marxist analysis of wage labour. Whilst Marx did reveal the *qualitative* nature of the wage relationship in the exploitative class relations underlying the exchange of the commodity labour power between capital and labour, it is equally clear that this does not fix the *quantitative* relationship, either in terms of the level of wages or of the hours worked. Similarly, it is not possible to comprehend the structural connection between economic and social reproduction through scrutiny of the value of labour power, for many of its qualitative as well as of its quantitative dimensions remain unaddressed in an abstract analysis of capital, not least who shall work and for how long, and how reproduction should take place and with what standards of consumption and methods of their provision between the factory and the home.

This somewhat abstract discussion around the value of labour power and reproduction demonstrates that certain theoretical issues concerning (changing) social norms – such as whether women undertake paid work as part of a family labour power or as a separate labour power – cannot be answered by virtue of theory alone. What, for example, constitutes a norm as opposed to a variation around the norm in an analysis based on these Marxist concepts? Consequently, historical analysis is essential to address these problems.

Obviously, some of the analyses previously examined are designed to fill this void. The reserve army of labour, for example, proxies for the role that women play in social reproduction by assigning them to the margins of the workforce. The domestic labour debate takes a more direct approach in focusing attention directly on (one part of) the activity of social reproduction. And economic demography has constructed a calculus of choice and advantage around the allocation of labour between the sexes and between the public and private sphere. Within each of these approaches, however, a framework is adopted in which a sharp dichotomy is drawn between economic and social reproduction, although there is a fusion of the two within neoclassical theory (and neo-Ricardianism) in so far as labour, leisure and expenditure are traded off against each other in the two spheres of economic and family life.

Whilst this dichotomy is justified in structural terms as recognising the increasing separation of paid work from the home within the capitalist mode of production, it has considerable drawbacks in so far as the family, the presumed principal site of non-economic reproduction, becomes relatively fixed in conception. For there are not only enormous changes in the family's internal range and level of activities – in household production, in number of children, etc. – there are also shifting relations with economic and other aspects of social reproduction (as in state provision). This implies that the family, often conflated with the household, cannot be taken as a fixed foundation, a building block, for the study of changes in women's economic position – it does itself have to be explained and analytically constructed. This has been brought home forcibly at the empirical level with the archetypal family of parents and children being far from the universal norm – single parents have increased in importance, this quite apart from the household situation of single workers.[7]

If the family (and domestic labour, for example) is left as a neglected black box, it is far from clear how women's changing labour-market situation can be explained when analysis is encumbered with such a poor empirical and theoretical understanding of the changing domestic situation from which women have entered the labour-market in recent years. As McIntosh comments:

> The family and women's oppression also have a specific character in each different epoch.
>
> (McIntosh, 1979, p. 155)

It is necessary to identify those epochs and distinguish between them rather than leaving the family unexplored, and as often for patriarchy theory or sexist ideology, in the role of the residual explanatory factor.

> The family has come to serve as a final and last-ditch 'explanation' for the reproduction of labour power and relations of production, while at the same time its *operation* remains largely unanalysed, and apparently unanalysable.
>
> (Kuhn, 1978, p. 64)

If, then, discussion of the value and reproduction of labour power is the first component in exploring female labour-market participation, a second concerns the changing character of the family. Accordingly, in the following three sections, an attempt is made to periodise the family according to the stages of development of capitalism. Particular emphasis is placed upon the continuing opportunities for women to engage in earning income from and in the home, but most important proves to be the demographic transition in which family size is drastically reduced, thereby potentially releasing women from domestic to waged labour.

What transforms that potential into actuality? Here a third component is of importance, what will be termed the *access* to employment. Interestingly, this can be understood in the most abstract sense but also in the most concrete sense – and at all theoretical levels in between. Consequently, it allows the more abstract concepts to be reproduced at more detailed and complex levels of analysis. For Marx, for example, one way of distinguishing between one mode of production and another is through the methods by which labour gains access to the means of production. For capitalism, for example, it is only through the sale of wage labour – the capitalists' monopoly ownership of the means of production means that labour only gains access to (capitalist) production through sale of labour power, from which is generated both a source of profits and the means of working class consumption through wage revenue; for feudalism, the peasantry already has possession of the land. From conditions governing access to work, there follows, or is associated, a mode of generating and appropriating a surplus and the conditions of distribution and consumption.

At the most concrete level, and more but not exclusively associated with the simultaneity approach outlined above, access to the means of production is identified with those conditions of, or around, the labourer's access to jobs in terms of the cumulative effects of training, discrimination, etc. It can even be taken almost literally. How do people get to work? Given that women take primary responsibility for childcare (and domestic labour more generally) and the separation of work from home, then they are disadvantaged physically in their access to work, especially when work is situated further from home than within earshot of the now defunct factory hooter.

Clearly, women's, and men's, access to work is affected by the availability of transport. But here there is structured inequality in two ways. First, men and women have different transport *needs* given their division of responsibilities. Second, men and women have unequal *access* to transport itself. Despite this, Whipp and Grieco report that:

> The first official UK survey explicitly concerned with gender and transport did not take place until the mid–1980s.

In terms of transport needs, Hamilton and Jenkins (1989) find that men and women make about the same number of journeys. But more men (68 per cent) than women (31 per cent) are qualified to drive a car; more men (88 per cent of those with licences in the GLC area) than women (two-thirds of those with a licence) had primary access to a car; and shopping accounts for 25 per cent of women's journeys. Thus:

> While the male breadwinner, who has traditionally had first call on 'the car', has enjoyed the benefits of massive invest-ment in road construction, women have borne the brunt of diminished investment in public transport.
>
> (Hamilton and Jenkins, 1989, p. 33)

The advantages of greater access through travel are illustrated to some extent by the premium in earnings of 27 per cent for those women commuting distances between one and two miles to work as compared to those who travel less than one mile (Pickup, 1989, p. 214).[8] It is also crucial to recognise how the tendency to subordinate women's employment to that of her partner leads to the location of residences and the timing of mobility between them to suit his and not her career or employment prospects.[9]

Female access to wage employment can also be considered as a way of understanding a host of other factors ranging from dis-crimination by employers and employees: primacy or high priority to a domestic role; socialisation to stereotyped aspirations; and differential opportunities in education and training, etc. These in part reflect the duality of women's role in domestic and wage labour but equally reflect, although this is easily forgotten, the separation of most women (as well as men) from ownership or possession of the means of production. In this light, it can be argued that the working class in general, as a whole, shares a particular relationship to the capitalist ownership of the means of production, but that there is differential access to them through the labour-market, as between different, possibly overlapping, strata of the working class. Nor is this simply, then, a differentia-tion as between men and women, but also as between other strata in so far as it reflects skills, education, mobility, recruiting prac-tices, ethnic origins, etc.

There is, however, a major distinguishing feature in the dif-ferential access as between men and women, in so far as the latter take primary responsibility for domestic labour. Women, then, have primary access to means of production other than capital, since work is carried out in the home, whether for income or not, and they also have access to an alternative source of income and consumption to the extent that they are financially dependent upon their partners. In addition, women are responsible for a major part of the reproduction of labour power, what is for the family a potential source of income for the period over which children work and support their parents or the household economy.

For the current period of capitalism, a number of developments mark it off from earlier periods: commodification of household products and work; reduction in family size (with children constituting a cost rather than a source of income); and the assumption of greater responsibility by the state for many aspects of reproduction – such as education, health and welfare, and income support. All analyses which are not empirically blinkered point to these features, and seek to link them to an explanation of the increasing participation of women in the labour-market – whether it be as a consequence of shifting comparative advantage (as in the new household economics) or, as in patriarchy theory, as an escape from private to public patriarchy in response to the driving force of capitalist productivity and wage-cost reduction.

The approach adopted here is rather different. It is to recognise that analysis of the value of labour power based upon the work time of the family is no longer appropriate. At the time of Marx's writing, and for some time afterwards, women's production in the home, and of children, provided an alternative access to work with which capital competed. Consequently, conflict over the value of labour power did concern the extent to which women (and children) needed to work for wages for the household to attain a satisfactory standard of living. Thus, the major factor determining differential access of men and women to work has been the sexual division of labour as between domestic and paid labour. This even applied to many single women who were confined to domestic labour as servants.

Subsequently, the contribution that women could make through domestic labour has been subject to erosion, so that increasingly their access to means of production is through the labour-market – although not necessarily on equal terms with men. This quantitative shift has also been a qualitative shift in so far as the hours of female paid labour no longer form part of the collective contribution from the household in exchange for the value of labour power – a shift that is transparent in the case of the complete erosion of children's labour. Women enter the labour-market to earn a wage that is independent of their structured responsibility for housework, although how they enter and what they get paid remains influenced by this factor.

This is not to say, then, that the sexual division of labour in the home is finished as a continuing disadvantage to women in the labour-market. Rather, it is to argue that it constitutes one factor amongst many others and not the determining factor as previously. This might appear to be a dubious and, at best, a fine and academic distinction. From the point of view of the housewife, labour-markets are worse for them than for men, and it is of little consequence – in making the decision whether to work for wages or not, for example – whether this is perceived as being primarily or partially due to domestic responsibilities.

This is, however, to neglect the different modes of operation of the capitalist system and its labour-markets, according to capital's stages of development. Prior to the enactment of limitations on the length of the working day and other legislation on behalf of the working class, the effect of women going out to work was a tendency to depress the overall level of the value of wages and, thereby, to diminish the relative advantage of female wage-labour subject to households obtaining sufficient income for survival at socially defined norms. However, once legislation is effectively implemented on behalf of the working class, then the impact of women's employment becomes increasingly determined by the nature of state interventions – and less by the balance between what work is performed by the family as a whole and what rewards it commands collectively through wages.

This, again, is an unduly abstract discussion and one that might only detain the reader engaged in a dialogue with Marxist economic concepts. Perhaps the point involved can be put more simply: it is that as capitalism develops it is economically and socially structured in such a way that the relationship between women and the labour-market is no longer so decisively dependent upon women's role in the household which, instead, becomes one factor amongst others.[10] As a result, as other factors such as welfare measures, labour legislation, taxation, etc. become more important, so the way in which they have an impact on women's position in the labour-market may be both substantial and interactive with other factors. This is brought out by Lewis and Foord (1984), for example, who observe that the growth of women's employment and development planning (for new towns) are intimately linked with each other but not in the practice of planners themselves.[11] Consequently, the impact of this as well as of, for example, welfare measures will have (negative) implications for women's access to the labour-market, partly as a consequence of their own gender content, partly because of their co-existence with other measures. This is despite, or even because of, an ideology and practice of compartmentalising different areas of policy. As Creighton (1979) observes of the law in the context of the social security system, this has primarily been constructed for women on the basis of the dual roles of income support and motherhood. Thus, Creighton notes:

> The law singles out women for special treatment . . . because there are certain kinds of exploitation to which women are thought to be peculiarly susceptible (in labour-markets) . . . but in broad terms it can fairly be said the social security system has traditionally been based upon the premise that the family is the primary social unit, and that women's place is in the home.
>
> (Creighton, 1979, p. 18)

Another example is provided by childcare, with Bowlby (1990) specifically discussing this in terms of female access to employment. Childcare provision is as much a labour-market policy as a welfare measure – just as are taxation, transport and most other policies – and must be seen as having a particular impact on labour-markets and their gendering. The combination of these factors gives rise to women's labour-market position and, to the extent that it ever was, it can no longer be argued that the duality of wage and domestic labour alone is decisive in itself in determining the potential impact of other factors.

In the following sections, some rationale for this approach will be provided by a periodisation of the family in an attempt to explain the broad historical timing of women's greater labour-market participation in the most recent period. In Chapter 4 this is taken further, by specific reference to the British labour-market.

Thus, to sum up, in structural terms it has been traditional, outside the neoclassical household economics, to locate women's employment position as being heavily determined by the duality between domestic and waged labour. As women have increasingly entered the labour-market, this duality has been supplemented by other factors which might also be perceived as simultaneous sources of disadvantage – whether in training, recruitment, career prospects, or whatever. At the opposite extreme to the initial structural duality, this leads to neoclassical household economics in which all of these variables are seen as interacting harmoniously to give rise to an efficient sexual division of labour, reflecting comparative advantage and tastes (women are better at and prefer housework to men, respectively) – even though residual discrimination in pay still continues to be measured empirically.

The approach adopted here does not so much dispute the direction taken by these analytical tendencies towards taking account of a wider variety of structures and processes (especially in so far as domestic labour is set aside as the structurally prior source of women's labour-market disadvantage, a stance motivated by women's apparent exclusion from employment at an earlier stage). Rather, it seeks to interpret them differently by reference to *abstract* analyses of the value of labour power, the family and access to employment, whose interaction gives rise to historically contingent outcomes at more complex levels of detail.

PERIODISING THE FAMILY: ITS FORMAL SUBORDINATION

At first sight, the family seems both simple and transparent, all the more so for being familiar, as it were. Possibly for this reason, it has often been taken as a basic unit of analysis across the social sciences. Taken together, however, the various analyses reveal how complex is the family. It is the site of many different activities with social significance – production and consumption, reproduction and socialisation, quite apart from relations of power, oppression and solidarity. Necessarily, the family is not the only site of these activities and relations and the extent to which, and the manner in which, they are divided between family and society (once forcing this division) is historically and contemporaneously variable. It follows that the notion of the family as an analytical category must be treated with caution since it is liable to lead to some archetypal 'ideal type' being imposed where it is neither apt nor wanted – as if all were on the way to being, or were completing, the life-cycle of the two-child nuclear household or some other of a number of household models. More generally, it is necessary to treat the family as a complex and concrete consequence of underlying economic and social forces. In short, it is more appropriate to analyse the family system and to recognise that it is historically variable, much as the same is true of the firm as the site of capitalist production as it varies from the putting-out to the factory system. For Harris:

> 'The family' is still a sign which denotes on the one hand a distinct substantive area of social life, and on the other hand a complex of related issues.
>
> (Harris, 1983, p. vii)

How are they to be unpicked?

For Laslett (1971) and (1983), the nuclear family pre-dates the arrival of capitalism, and there is little evidence for a household made up of an extended family of kin relations that was transformed by the arrival of capitalism. This is, however, to construct the family on the narrow analytical terrain of kin and numbers. This is not to suggest that Laslett has nothing else of importance to consider, for he does see capitalism as breaking down patriarchy within the household as smaller numbers are located within it and as those that remain, and are subordinate to the head of household, become less so. Indeed, dependent servants are perceived as embryonic wage labourers, soon to be brought to maturity, historically speaking, by industrialisation. A similar history in many ways is presented by Lesthaeghe (1983) for whom the family system has moved through three successive phases under capitalism: from concern with the welfare of the household (displacing concern for the wider community) to concern for the welfare of its children, and ultimately to concern for the welfare of the individual. In this way the individualism and modernisation of capitalism appears to diminish the nuclear family to its nucleus, the individual.

But with these great historical themes, it must always seem, as today in the age of divorce and illegitimacy, that the family is on the verge of breaking down – if it has not already done so.[12] Thus, the family appears to combine a fragility and a permanence, both of which reflect the character of the era in which it is situated. Moreover, even superficial evidence suggests that the family has no autonomous, internal dynamic of its own with which it can confront external conditions (even if its own internal structure and composition were invariant, which they are not). As Coontz concludes:

> We should avoid the temptation to label the family as a dependent or independent variable, as a malleable object

acted upon by grand historical forces or an amazingly resi-
lient institution that organizes itself to deflect the impact of
social change, allowing its members to carve out their own
culture. The family cannot be separated from the total net-
work of social relations: when one changes the other changes,
and the seeds of change may derive either from the larger
structure or from the dynamics of family life within it.

(Coontz, 1988, p. 16)

This suggests, in addition, that the family as such should not be
examined prior to an understanding of it as a part of a historically
variable system tied to broader economic and social changes. This
is already explicit in those authors cursorily considered above, for
whom the family changes dramatically, if at times slowly, as between pre-industrial, industrial and modern capitalism – not only
in its composition but also in its functions and ethics. Consequently, it is imperative to seek a periodisation of the family (system)
linked to the periodisation of capitalism.[13]

Within Marxism, it has been standard to periodise capitalism.
Fairly uncontroversial has been the recognition of the two stages
of *laissez-faire* capitalism and monopoly capitalism, although the
basis for making the division and the defining characteristics of the
two stages have been at issue. Classical Marxism, for example,
defines the *laissez-faire* stage by reference to the predominance of
the mode of extracting surplus value through the production of
absolute surplus value, making labour work longer or more in-
tense hours as a source of greater profitability. This is closely
associated with the formal subordination of labour to capital, in
which the methods of production are not significantly transformed, but the appropriation of surplus value depends on the
extension of the working day as far as possible. Consequently,
competition between capitals is predominantly fought at the level
of markets, for which either free competition or protection may be
a preferred policy, although the implications for labour are downward pressure on wages and working conditions. At the level of
social policy, such as it is, the primary focus is upon enforcing work
through the principle of less eligibility.[14]

The stage of monopoly capitalism is based on the production of
relative surplus value, associated with the real subordination of
labour to capital, in which methods of production are transformed
through the introduction of machinery. Surplus value now comes

to depend on productivity increase which reduces the value of labour power. Competition between capitals is based on the ability to concentrate production within the factory system. Whilst this may also be associated with cartelisation, it is the least-cost, mass producers who are best able to survive and expand. The supremacy of monopoly over *laissez-faire* capitalism is marked socially by the limitation of the length of the working day and other measures to restrict the crudest forms of exploitation of labour. Consequently, the value of labour power is not only reduced through productivity increase in wage goods but also through the preservation of the labourer, whose working life is prolonged, often at a higher general level of skill, albeit at the expense to capital of higher consumption levels and a shorter working day.

A third stage, of state monopoly capitalism, is more controversial. Whilst, for any other than polemical purposes, its grounding in the fusion between the state apparatus and the agents of large-scale capital is to be rejected, a distinct stage can be identified with the extensive penetration of the agencies of the state into economic reproduction – through public ownership, taxation, and government expenditure across a range of economic and social policy areas. At this stage, whilst the working class continues to depend upon wage employment for social reproduction, its fortunes are increasingly tied to the economic and social policies of the state.

Even if universal agreement could be commanded for these principles of periodisation at the economic level, there exist other foci for dividing the development of capitalism into stages, some associated more directly with the family. Tilly and Scott (1978) look to a pre-industrial *family economy*, a *family wage economy* at the stage of early industrialisation and a *family consumer economy* for the modern period. They closely associate transformations of the family with the transformation of work.

The intimate and mundane experiences of men and women are not universally and at all times the same: rather these have changed over time. An unfortunate division of labour among scholars has prevented a full examination of the implications of these acts. Studies of demographic history often neglect the subject of the family. Yet the implications of each area for an understanding of the history of working women are important. The age at which a woman marries, the number of children she bears, the size of the household in which she lives, and the value of the children directly affect her working life. The amount of time required for household and childbearing activities affects the amount of time spent in productive work. A history of women's work must therefore also be a history of the family.

(Tilly and Scott, 1978, p. 7)

This leads to consideration of yet another periodisation, that bridged by the demographic transition, especially across the vast majority of western Europe. Although the timing and extent differ across countries, regions and different classes of the population, the 50 years or so around the turn of the twentieth century witnessed a major change in birth and death rates, with associated changes in the nature of the family. In England, population grew steadily over the 200 years to the middle of the eighteenth century, after which expansion was rapid for 100 years. Subsequently, both birth and death rates dropped from their high and often volatile levels, but the birth rate dropped even more than the death rate.[15]

The consequences for family size were dramatic. The average number of children per family in Great Britain dropped from 4.34 in 1890–9 to 2.24 in 1925. Whilst Anderson (1980) reports more than 50 per cent of children before the transition would have lived in families of six children or more, by the end of the Second World War, families with four or more children were rare – and to be found predominantly amongst the highly educated and, at the opposite extreme, in those who left school and married early (Mitchison, 1977). Thus, whilst the demographic transition took place over a short time in terms of the parameters of demographic history, in terms of economic and social history, it is long enough to be linked to a periodisation of three stages – before, after *and* during.

Oakley bases her periodisation on the work position of women as follows:

(1) from 1750 until the early 1840s, when the family was increasingly displaced by the factory as the place of production, but women followed their traditional work out of the home; (2) from the 1840s until 1914, when a decline in the employment of married women outside the home was associated with the rising popularity of a belief in women's natural domesticity; (3) from 1914 until the 1950s, when

118

there is a discernible, though uneven, tendency towards the growing employment of women, coupled with a retention of housewifery as the primary role expected of all women.[16]

(Oakley, 1974a, p. 34)

Seccombe (1983) periodises the family through four stages – peasant, proto-industrial, early proletarian and mature proletarian.[17] For the latter two, he argues that the joint family wage (for which all family members are collectively working) gives way to a wage norm paid to the husband alone, who supports a wife and family with patriarchy established in the home. He considers that this system has not proved sustainable, through economic crisis and cuts in state expenditure, so that the current period is one in which women have been forced to go out to work.

> The single-wage family system has collapsed . . . The proletariat compulsion to sell one's labour power at the best price has now pushed masses of women onto the labour-market, making 'working women' the norm for the working class as a whole, rather than the practice of a suspect minority.[18]
>
> (Seccombe, 1980a, p. 74)

For those emphasising the household as a site for consumption, the inter-war period is cited as a transitional period for the family. For Ewen (1976), for example, mass production required mass consumption, with the result that the market needed to penetrate the capitalist home with commodities and the housewife needed to be ideologically reconstructed as tied to the home as consumer and provider. This, however, placed the housewife in a dilemma, as she was needed at home but also at work to earn the income to buy the consumption goods.[19]

Although they differ in method and in detail, many of these periodisations have much in common: the transition to capitalism, industrialisation, and the drive to mass production and consumption are all taken as central. How do these and other phenomena – such as urbanisation, the demographic transition, female labour-market participation, etc. – mutually support or contradict one another? The contention here is that the Marxist periodisation, according to the three stages of *laissez-faire*, monopoly and state monopoly capitalism, is an essential component of an appropriate analysis.

Begin with the pre-capitalist family. Tilly and Scott offer the

119

following summary of their characterisation of the 'family economy':

> In the household mode of production typical of the pre-industrial economy, the unit of production was small and productivity was low. All household members worked at productive tasks, differentiated by age and sex . . . Within marriage, fertility was high. High mortality was, however, an involuntary check on net reproduction. Children were potential workers, but they were also potential heirs to limited resources. So households controlled the size of future generations by late marriage and enforced celibacy for some members. High fertility, high mortality, a small-scale household organization of production, and limited resources meant that women's time was spent primarily in productive activity. Unmarried women worked in their parents' households or in other households if there was no need for their labor at home. Married women were both producers and mothers. The household setting of work facilitated the combination of productive and domestic activities. Married women adjusted their time to meet the demands of production in the interest of the family economy.
>
> (Tilly and Scott, 1978, pp. 227–8)

It is, of course, important not to generalise an archetypal pre-capitalist family but a recurring emphasis, prior to the creation of wage labour, is the existence of a rural domestic economy in which the division of labour between the household and outside neither runs absolutely along the lines of a gender division of labour nor along the lines of sharply differentiated production for internal and external consumption. Nor is this to presume, without thereby embracing patriarchy theory, the notion of an absence of a sexual division of labour or greater equality between the sexes. As Branca puts it:

> One of the persistent myths pervading women's history is that at some point in the past there was that 'golden age' when women worked as equals to men, when women's influence was as important as that of men if indeed women did not dominate because of their vital production role.
>
> (Branca, 1978, p. 68)

According to Tilly and Scott, the rural domestic economy continued in France after 1750, but in England it was confined to cottages of domestic manufacturers – weavers, hosiers and nail and chain-metal workers. This should alert us to the fact that the rural domestic economy depended on exchange relations. Middleton (1979) recognises the three forms of feudal rent – in kind, in labour services and in money (for which he points to brewing, for example, as a source of income).[20] Labour services were predominantly confined to male workers, but the balance by which feudal dues were delivered did not comprise an unchanging traditional order – indeed, it must be expected that the money form of feudal dues would increase with the approaching capitalist order.

The significance of this is that the pre-capitalist family confronted by the emerging system of wage labour was one already experienced in a variety of methods for guaranteeing its survival in which women workers were fully, if not equally, involved. Consequently, far from simply dissolving the pre-capitalist family, the capitalist system and the household economy in part adapted to one another. This does not mean that the latter remained unchanged but nor was it necessarily split asunder by an unambiguous drive to create a wage proletariat out of all and sundry. It is instructive to see how the persistence of the pre-capitalist family form might be an essential part of the *laissez-faire* stage of capitalism rather than a relic of the previous feudal order. For, otherwise, but for inertia and cultural obstacles, comparative advantage would dictate the sweeping away of production within the home for all but the few activities over which capital could not establish superior productivity.[21]

First, and of necessity, male members of the household economy are drawn into wage labour, reflecting the advance of capitalist production and the pre-existing sexual division of labour – although women may also become wage labourers as a preferred source of income. To the extent that this is accompanied by driving the household out of possession of the land, there is a loss of alternative sources of household income through marketable, agricultural produce and a loss of alternative sources of domestically produced consumption goods. But these are not entirely curtailed. For the wage itself potentially provides for the purchase of means of production, for which domestic labour can then be used for household commodity production or household consumption, without there necessarily being a fine division in practice between the two. However, with the growing command of capital over the production of commodities, the ability of the household to survive through competition on the market will tend to make much sharper the division between those activities that are or are not moneymaking (without eliminating the latter). Also, capitalist production will tend to break down the household as the site of production, as wage earners travel to work – possibly even away from residence at home altogether.

Consider, then, a commodity such as cheese. According to Kleinegger:

> The first cheese factory in the United States was founded in 1831; by 1869, two-thirds of all cheese in the United States was manufactured in factories. By 1910, 99 percent of all cheese was made in factories.
>
> (Kleinegger, 1987, p. 163)

Where cheese did persist as a 'home' product in the nineteenth century, it was presumably linked to farms that found it worthwhile to manufacture it on their own account rather than sell their cream to a manufacturer. But cheese is not necessarily typical, although other activities such as butchering were also rapidly appropriated by the factory system. However, capitalist production also provided commodity inputs to the household as well as the commodity outputs to displace domestic production. And commodity inputs could include instruments of production, such as the spinning wheel and the stove as well as means of production such as finely ground flour and textiles with which, respectively, bread could be baked more easily and clothes cut and sewn at home. Whether in quality or quantity, whether for the market or consumption, capitalism both expanded and eroded the domain of domestic production.[22] As Kessler-Harris observes:

> Slowly, the process of manufacturing woollen, linen and cotton cloth became cheap enough so that more women preferred to buy than make fabric . . . By 1810 a third of the fabric in the United States was produced outside the home . . . After 1824, the proportion of homemade goods tumbled dramatically . . . By 1855 the state's [New York] households averaged only a quarter of a yard of fabric per

person. Household spinning and weaving had become dying arts.

(Kessler-Harris, 1982a, pp. 25–6)

But the loss of domestic material manufacture was, in part, compensated for by domestic sewing, especially with the rise of the sewing machine. More generally, as in brewing, the use of commodified ingredients could provide for domestic consumption and for sale. These observations are amply confirmed by Shammas' (1990) study of pre-industrial consumption. For the subsequent period, she finds that production potential was expanded by households taking on the production of items for preparation for consumption.

> It seems that many of the nineteenth-and twentieth-century alterations in household space and technology were connected to alterations in women's work and status. The sewing-machine and the cooking-stove and other kitchen innovations went along with women spending more and more time on such things as baking and sewing, the part of home production that one might term the finishing process.
> (Shammas, 1990, pp. 187–8)

If the waves of commodity production created their own undercurrents when breaking over family production, then much the same is true of household, if not family, formation as a means of providing a ready 'market' for domestic production and a reliable source of income. A popular theme across the literature dealing with different countries is the role played by women in supplementing family income through the taking in of boarders, what might be thought of as the urban counterpart to the possession of a plot of land, supplementing income if not generally adequate to survival on its own. Thus, as late as 1900, Brown (1987, p. 56) finds that as many as 25 per cent of US homes were taking in lodgers, and that flour baked at home was characteristic of over 90 per cent of households.[23] Davidoff points to taking in lodgers as part of a wider terrain of activities geared to the supplementing of family income through female labour:

> In summary, then, rather than investigating the supplying of lodging and boarding in isolation, it should be seen as part of a continuum of positions: wife or female relative helping to service apprentices, pupils, and others, childminding or

fostering children, taking in boarders or lodgers, keeping a small school, running private apartments, a lodging house or hotel.

(Davidoff, 1979, p. 89)

Taking together all these examples of the potential for work within the household, it emerges that there was more than enough to make housework long, arduous and varied.[24] The specific example of lodgings illustrates how the advance of capitalist wage labour both pulls the wage labourer out of the household production economy and provides a demand for the marketable services of the household economy. The process of urbanisation, greater facility in travel and the seasonal and variable demand for many sorts of labour power all made demands on more or less temporary and cheap forms of accommodation, with male lodgers outnumbering females by as much as three to one (Davidoff, 1979).

The situation with respect to women was rather different in so far as they flowed into domestic service. In this way, they were 'lodged' like their wage-earning male counterparts, but were able to contribute both to the 'domestic economy' of their immediate abode and to that of their origin as much as their earnings were remitted to their immediate family.

It is important to recognise both the extent of this activity and its scope. Branca (1978, p. 34) estimates that: 'up to a third of all women worked as servants at some point in their lives by the mid-nineteenth century in France and Britain'. MacBride reports that:

In 1866 domestics throughout France comprised 29 percent of the active female population, while in 1901 they constituted nearly 45 percent of all working women in Paris . . . in 1861 in London, one in every three women between the age of 15 and 24 was a servant.

(MacBride, 1976, p. 14)

Higgs (1986) warns that the *Upstairs Downstairs* image of servants is the equivalent to viewing the contemporary family through the pages of *Vogue*. A whole range of productive activities were undertaken by domestic servants, ranging from those equivalent to wage labour through to those now traditionally associated with domestic duties.[25] In this way, family income could be supplemented as well as saved by servants and a strain be taken off the accommodation and consumption budgets of the servant's own family. For Kent, writing for a century earlier:

> The petty bourgeoisie who were the principal agents of manufacture and commerce in eighteenth century London needed servants to free family members in the workshop or at the counter . . . It was their physical labour which mattered rather than the comfort they afforded to their employer.
>
> (Kent, 1989, p. 119)

And, as MacBride (1976, p. 30) observes, the availability of a large supply of cheap domestic servants provides potential disincentives to technological improvements in the home and, presumably, the purchase of commodities from outside it. More generally, Mac-Bride argues that the domestic servant revolution of the nineteenth century played a crucial role in proletarianisation, with migration from country to town on an unprecedented scale proving a stepping stone to more developed forms of wage labour in the cities. But, equally, it must be recognised that the stepping stone also proved to be a resting place – holding up both proletarianisation and commodification.[26]

Accordingly, domestic service was both a flexible and an uncertain source of family management. The daughter, usually dispatched from the family economy of the rural areas to domestic service in the cities, gained a degree of independence. At one extreme, some income may have been remitted home; at the other, all contact may have been lost. Alternatively, single women might remain as domestic 'servants' within their own home according to the costs and advantages of doing so (Tilly and Scott, 1978, p. 28). Higgs (1986) and (1987) reckons that between one third and one half of servants may have had some kinship relationship with their employers. Hill quotes from Cobbett in the 1820s as to why (rural) servants may have been increasingly discouraged by their employers from living in.

> Why do not farmers now *feed* and *lodge* their workpeople as they did formerly? Because they cannot keep them *upon so little* as they give them in wages. This is the real cause of the change.
>
> (Hill, 1989a, p. 79)

This suggests, at different times and for different individuals and households, a fine division and fluctuating balance between levels of wages, taking (on) employment as a domestic or not, and whether servants were to live in or not. And, to anticipate and to extrapolate, this balance would extend both to the end of the century and beyond and to urban employment.

It is against these various opportunities for alternative sources of income that the option of formal wage labour has to be considered. Consider Clark's (1919, p. 64) view for the seventeenth century, 'the more she was obliged to work for wages, the poorer was her family'. At greater length, Clark goes on to say:

> The value of a woman's productive capacity to her family was, however, greatly reduced when, through poverty, she was obliged to work for wages, because then, far from being able to feed and clothe her family, her wages were barely adequate to feed herself. This fact indicates the weakness of women's position in the labour-market, into which they were being forced in increasing numbers by the capitalistic organisation of industry. In consequence of this weakness, a large proportion of the produce of a woman's labour was diverted from her family to the profit of the capitalist or consumer.[27]
>
> (Clark, 1919, p. 145)

Just how much had changed by the nineteenth century? Were wages so much greater and the sweep of commodity production so much more advanced that the comparative advantage of abandoning domestic labour was paramount? Women's wages remained low, working conditions were hard and the potential for work within the home had also been expanded and would have to be sacrificed. Often this must only have been done in order to attain the minimum levels of income that were a pre-requisite for survival. As Black notes:

> Those who, because the family income is inadequate – whether from lowness of pay, irregularity of work or failure in some way, such as sickness, idleness, drink or desertion on the part of the husband – do earn . . . are the most overworked, the hardest pressed and probably the unhappiest of working women . . . concerned above all things (as are most of the mothers visited) about the future of her children and unable to secure, either by her husband's labour or her own, enough money for their healthy support. No 'driving' fore-

126

man, no greedy employer, can so spur the efforts of a worker
as her material affection spurs such a woman.[28]

(Black, 1983, p. 1–3)

The idea that women worked for wages out of economic necessity
is perhaps supported by the extent to which they were driven into
domestic service, which was far from popular, as evidenced by
desertion from it as both (male) income and alternative, better
paid, job opportunities expanded in the twentieth century, and by
the extent to which women were driven in lesser but significant
numbers into prostitution.[29]

In brief, the emergence of wage labour certainly created new
and different, often extreme, balances of pressures on the working
class family but it did not necessarily serve to transform it radically.
This is confirmed in examining the role of female wage labour. At
one level, the emergence of capitalist commodity production narrowed the range of commercially productive activities that could
be undertaken by the household economy. This had the effect of
forcing women into wage labour. Naturally, this occurred in
agriculture, especially in the absence of the small farmer through
enclosure in Britain. At the end of the eighteenth century, especially at harvest time, Pinchbeck notes the growth of female wage
labour:

> Wives, unable any longer to supplement their husband's
> wage by work at home, were forced to enter the ranks of wage
> earners and become like their husbands, day labourers in
> agriculture.

(Pinchbeck, 1969, p. 53)

But by the middle of the nineteenth century, such labour had
already disappeared. Without being overly economistic, the alternatives offered by the household economy and other forms of
wage labour must have been superior. But the extent of the latter
can only be exaggerated. Branca suggests that:

> In countries like England and Germany only about ten
> percent of all married women were reported as formally
> employed throughout most of the nineteenth century . . . In
> the cities, formal employment, which involved earning a
> wage and labour outside the home was not acceptable or
> feasible to working class culture. Men, and presumably
> women, found it inappropriate and degrading for married

women to take outside jobs. Thus, the working class family, well into the twentieth century maintained itself on the wage of the husband and older children alone.

(Branca, 1978, p. 32)

Thus, 'the history of working women in nineteenth century cities is the history of young single girls, spinsters and widows'.

It is doubtful that it was predominantly ideology that restrained the supply of married women's labour at this time and, as has been seen, the family maintained itself other than by the wage alone. Women's waged work could also take place within the context of the home, somebody else's where domestic service was concerned, or through the putting-out system. As John notes:

Waged work was not necessarily outside the home – as late as 1870 dressmakers outnumbered textile workers by nearly two to one, the majority of them working at home.

(John, 1986, p. 2)

And textiles, itself, provides a prime example of the persistence of waged work for married women, even immediately after childbirth. Osterud has this to say:

Instead of leaving the labour force during their childbearing years and returning when their children were older, as many women do now, wives in nineteenth century Leicester remained in the labour force when their children were young and stopped working for pay when their children were old enough to replace them as contributors to the family budget . . . when children left home, however, some wives had to return to the labour force.[30]

(Osterud, 1986, pp. 58–9)

For coalminers, the whole family could be employed in earning the 'family wage'. John observes that:

Traditionally payment had been via a family wage in the sense that the hewer was paid a wage which was supposed to cover the employment of his assistants. Until 1842 they had tended to be his wife and daughters.[31]

In summary, the period of capitalism up to the beginning of the demographic transition can be characterised as one of *formal subordination* of the family. In part, the term is chosen to reflect the

128

analogy with Marx's notion of the formal subordination of labour to capital. Just as the mode of production inherited from feudal society was not immediately transformed by capitalist relations, so the same applies to the family or household economy. Consequently, the *laissez-faire* stage of capitalism both restricted and extended the opportunities of the household economy to survive in its traditional form, as has been seen in citing different types of wage and non-wage labour that could be and were undertaken by women in and out of the home.

Thus, whilst these competing pressures on the family rarely ever remained in balance so that a typical family could emerge over an extended period of time, the demand for wage labour, on the one hand, and the commodification of domestic production, on the other, were never sufficiently strong to induce or to force married women into the labour-market. Pinchbeck explains why:

> Thus the necessity which first brought women's labour into the market to eke out the wage of the married man, not only prevented his wage from rising to an adequate standard, but resulted in a competition by means of which it was still further reduced. Moreover, had that competition been eliminated, the net family income would probably have been as high from the wages of the man alone as it was by the combined earnings, from which the extra wear on clothes and other costs incurred by his wife's absence from home had to be deducted.[32]

> (Pinchbeck, 1969, p. 102)

This suggests that the economic advantage of women going out to work was relatively limited, even as calculated by the individual household, because of the low wages involved. This is even more so if account is taken of the aggregate effect of the increased (female) labour supply on the levels of wages – as argued, for example, by Humphries (1977a) in explaining the persistence of the working class family. The argument being presented here is that the 'persistence' is explained by responses to economic pressures and opportunities in which collective action might have been quite limited.

Whilst wages and working class incomes were low, this limited the ability to purchase everyday necessities and made their domestic production more attractive. Equally, whilst capitalist methods of production remained relatively primitive and at low levels of productivity, domestic production for own or market consumption or through the putting-out system remained that much more viable. In this light, the parallel drawn between the formal subordination of the family to capitalism and of labour to capital goes beyond the terminological. For the two are intimately and causally connected. Whilst capitalism relies predominantly upon the production of absolute surplus value, its ability to provide both attractive (well-paid) wage labour and attractive (cheap) wage goods remains limited, so that the family (wage) economy and restricted female labour-market participation persist.

In view of the analysis given above, it is hardly surprising that a typical household economy should not emerge prior to the demographic transition. As Hudson and Lee argue:

> It is clear that some of the general assumptions concerning the impact of industrialisation on women's market and non-market employment, with the attendant implications for family organisational structures, are in need of modification and revision ... the development of industrial capitalism was not a linear process and the gap between the prevailing ideology and the reality of women's economic roles was often very wide indeed. Aside from the importance of life-cycle variations, the local and regional structure of production was crucial in influencing gender-specific economic roles. Thus analysis of the impact of industrial capitalism on women's employment and gender roles within the family must be conducted first on a disaggregated level.
>
> (Hudson and Lee, 1990, p. 33)

Consider children. They were predominantly looked upon as part of the household economy, as 'little workers' from the age of five or so. As Matthaei points out:

> Hence, in the family economy, children were treated as little workers, and workers (remaining in the household) were treated as children. Adulthood meant living in one's own household, as husband or wife, and working for oneself, as a farmer, craftsman, or putting-out worker.
>
> (Matthaei, 1982, p. 22)

This does not necessarily mean that children were bred for the sake of the income that they could earn. Tilly and Scott found that:

There is little evidence to indicate that these families bore more children so that they could eventually become family wage earners.

(Tilley and Scott, 1978, p. 141)

On the other hand, Levine (1985) associates changes in population growth over the period 1700 to 1914 with the variation in fertility, which is linked to the timing of marriage, itself a function of the fortunes of the 'family economy'. He states:

The gist of my argument is that adjustments in the age of and incidence of first marriage for women can be related to the family economy of the working classes, a massive and growing majority of the English population during this period. In fact, such adjustments appear to have been small-scale. But over a long time-frame . . . even small variations made a significant impact.

(Levine, 1985, p. 170)

What is far from clear is how a rational and longstanding calculation of desired family size might have been made. Economic conditions were extremely volatile, often by choice in terms of migration, and correspondingly uncertain. Equally, whilst methods of limiting pregnancy were known, it is uncertain how well-known, how well-practised and at what cost. Then, the high mortality rates, especially in the period through to the end of infancy but by no means ending there, and applying to parents as well as to children, made the process of family formation into something of a lottery. Yet this was part and parcel of a broader economic calculus. As Casey notes:

The bigger the household . . . the more self-sufficient it will tend to be in respect of labour and ability to supply its own food and clothes. However, cash is vital in several significant ways.

(Casey, 1989, p. 118)

Not surprisingly, then, prior to the demographic transition, there were no uniform movements of demographic variables across countries (and regions) and across time. Nor are there regularities correcting for the availability of income, employment, etc. Consequently, many theories are put forward to explain the details of these movements and each has its own degree of theoretical and

131

empirical validity, although it is difficult to discern cause and effect amongst variables that tend to move together – particularly in the absence of reliable data. Similar variables are used to explain the nature and timing of the demographic transition itself.[33]

Teitelbaum (1984), for example, explains the anomalies of the UK transition (late fertility decline and its relatively uniform decline) in terms of the late arrival of literacy (birth control knowlege), the decline of breast feeding (as 'natural' contraceptive), the easy availability of domestic servants, and internal and international (male) migration as an alternative to the restraint imposed by the burden of children. The process of urbanisation and the extent of retention of family farming is emphasised amongst others by Tilly and Scott (1978) who also observe that timing of marriage (and hence fertility) depends on economic and accidental circumstances, such as when wealth is passed on by a father's death. Branca (1978, p. 85) notes that nutrition has more than the obvious effects on the population growth rate through 'a decline in the age of female puberty from 18–20 years in 1750 to about 14–16 years in 1850'. For some, certainly those at the time, the system of welfare support is significant. Banks (1954), for example, emphasises the squeeze on the incomes of the middle classes, whose response of family limitation to maintain living standards was aped by the working class.[34] Crafts (1984a) and (1984b) examines the effects of the cost of contraception on a household attempting to act as a rational economic agent. Then there is the administration of health and the virulence of epidemics as set against the standard of living (see, for example, Woods and Woodward, 1984, and the work of Jay Winter, 1979). After all of this, there will always remain the customs and cultures of the people – which they may or may not observe.[35]

These and other factors often also have a direct influence on the participation of women in the labour-market, and an indirect influence through their effect on the family or household economy over and above the spatial and sectoral distribution and phase of growth of the economy. The crucial point is that these various influences interact without anyone able to exert overall and persistent influence. Nor is it possible for their combined weight to be overcome by (nor support sufficiently) the dull compulsion of economic forces, comprising the capitalist commodification of domestic production and the transformation of household into wage labourers. That is until, as a precondition, the stage of monopoly capitalism is established.[36] At this point, systematic increases in productivity and improvements in wages and conditions of work become increasingly influential.

THE REAL SUBORDINATION OF THE FAMILY TO CAPITALISM

In the previous section, the early development of capitalism is characterised as giving rise to the formal subordination of the family; this period is characterised as potentially extending wage labour to all members of the household but this is moderated by limited levels of capitalist productivity and by enhanced opportunities for making money or use values at or from the home. Accordingly, children become in part an economic asset as potential workers, providing wage income from an early age and for the old age of their parents.

By contrast, the real subordination of the family to capitalism, corresponding to the stage of monopoly capitalism, is associated with high levels of productivity increase, which increasingly undermine the ability of the home to sustain production, and it becomes the norm for children not to work but for (married) women to do so. Whilst this provides a neat logical division between the two periods, history has not proved so amenable, since women's labour-market participation remained low until long after the Second World War, long after the stage of monopoly capitalism had been established. The purpose of this section is to suggest that the periodisation of the family remains valid despite this huge historical anomaly. Essentially, the argument is that the very process of conflict necessary to establish monopoly capitalism is one that withdraws women from the labour-market at least until such time as the demographic transition is completed.

First, recall that the stage of monopoly capitalism is fundamentally associated not with the emergence but with the predominance of the factory system in industrial production. With the increasing introduction of machinery, the worker is displaced from various detailed tasks within the production process, although workers tend to be congregated together in ever larger numbers at the plant as the scale of production is increased. In this way, the heritage of pre-capitalist methods of production is abandoned, and Marx talks of the specifically capitalist method of production and the real subordination of labour to capital.

Such developments are clearly synonymous with increases in productivity. They result in the reduction in the value of labour power, and profitability is increased through the production of relative surplus value. Whilst this process can be traced in the case of individual industries – in which spinning and weaving, for example, are the classic instances – Marx argues that the stage of machinofacture requires social intervention for it to be fully established. The higher productivity of the factory system would, for example, release workers from employment who would then be open to weakened labour-market conditions, allowing and encouraging the persistence of backward conditions of production in the same or other sectors. Accordingly, Marx identified the stage of monopoly capitalism as depending upon legislative restriction against the crudest forms of exploitation. In this way, then, the value of labour power (production of relative surplus value) is not only reduced directly through the lower value of the wage bundle, it is also socially reduced through the more favourable labour-market conditions which tend to prolong the lives of the working class beyond the premature death associated with hard and long work and poor living standards.

In Marx's own analysis in *Capital*, particular emphasis is given to the struggle to limit the length of the working day. He concludes that such legislation was an inevitable consequence of the conflict between capital and labour but that its particular form and timing would be contingent upon the balance of class forces. None the less, one particular focus is inevitably the status of female and child labour. In so far as the production of absolute surplus value depends on the extension of the hours of wage labour to men, women and children, the struggle to limit the hours of labour offered in return for the value of labour power necessarily looked to, and often focused upon, the limitation of female and child labour.

In short, the process of *establishing* the stage of monopoly capitalism is one that tends to consolidate the withdrawal of women (and children) into the household (economy). This is despite the intensification of the pressures towards the capitalist commodification of both household production and household domestic labour power as productivity is increased through factory production. These pressures are associated with the real subordination of the family to capitalism. As Jensen observes:

The 1920s and 1930s were important decades in the transition of women from household production to wage labor. To maintain the standard of living that women's work in the home had previously allowed, they now began to work outside the home at wage labor. Work at home was no longer productive because the services and commodities that women had produced had become commercialized – capitalist structures could perform them more cheaply than could women.

(Jensen, 1980, p. 21)

Similarly, Power argues:

They could no longer contribute directly to family support through this work, probably for the first time in history . . . women lost their ability to contribute to the support of themselves and their families through their work in the home.

(Power, 1983, p. 80)

At a very general level it has been suggested why the real subordination of the family should have lagged behind that of wage labour: reduction in the wage labour of women and children as the factory system was generalised. This can be looked at in slightly more detail across a range of factors. First, consider children. Around the turn of the century, there is a distinct change in the rearing of children which is not only quantitative but also qualititative. The limitation of children from waged work and the introduction of compulsory education increased the financial burden of having children. Also, the rising standard of living was ultimately associated with falling mortality rates for children and infants. Consequently, to the extent that commercial considerations entered into the choice over family size, etc., decision-making was dictated by a smaller and more certain number of children. This may well have released mothers more easily into wage labour except that the removal of children from wage labour gave rise, at the turn of the century, to the twin ideas and practices of childhood and motherhood for which the mother was required to remain at home.[37] Indeed, the very notion of childhood first comes to full fruition. In his classic work, Aries (1962) traces the emergence of childhood back to a point after the Middle Ages.

135

In medieval society the idea of childhood did not exist; this is not to suggest that children were neglected, forsaken or despised . . . as soon as the child could live without the constant solicitude of his mother, his nanny or his cradle-rocker, he [sic] belonged to adult society.

(Aries, 1952, p. 128)

And, as Vann suggests:

After the period of gross physical dependency . . . he or she was treated as a miniature adult . . . No games or stories were reserved for children; Louis XIII of France, who grew up in the early seventeenth century, played golf and tennis as a child, while the adults around him did not feel silly playing with hoops.

(Vann, 1977, p. 205)

But these are examples drawn from the upper or middle classes. For the working class, the arrival of childhood had to wait upon such youngsters giving up work. At the ideological level, this transformation in the role of children has been most sharply brought to the fore by Zelizer (1985). She observes how children were reconstructed from being economic assets to being priceless due to their sentimental value. She does so through examining the changing evaluation of children across three separate areas – as a consequence of accidental death, and by reference to insurance and adoption. Her starting point though is that of the child worker in the nineteenth century; for families under economic stress, children could contribute as much as a third of household income, thus 'in the late nineteenth century a child, not a wife, was likely to become the family's secondary wage earner' (Zelizer, 1985, p. 59).

In the case of accidental death (as, for example, negligence by a railroad company), damages were assessed by reference to the earning power of the child. Today, it would be more by monetary assessment of the sentimental loss to the parents. Zelizer records two case histories:

In 1896, the parents of a two-year-old child sued the Southern Railroad Company of Georgia for the wrongful death of their son. Despite claims that the boy performed valuable services for his parents – $2 worth per month, 'going upon errands to neighbors . . . watching and amusing . . . younger child,' – no recovery was allowed, except for minimum burial expenses. The court concluded that the child was of 'such tender years as to be unable to have any earning capacity, and hence the defendant could not be held liable in damages.' In striking contrast, in January 1979, when three-year-old William Kennerly died from a lethal dose of fluoride at a city dental clinic, the New York State Supreme Court jury awarded $750,000 to the boy's parents.

(Zelizer, 1985, pp. 138–9)

For insurance, working-class policies were taken out to pay for children's burials, these taking up as many as 40 per cent of policies for major companies by 1928. They were then transformed from a burial to an educational fund as infants' lives became more secure and their futures had to be secured.

Finally, Zelizer considers adoption, with the transition from the unwanted child, falling as a burden upon the local state or charities, to its commanding a healthy price for adoption:

As the market for child labor disappeared, a market price developed for children's new sentimental value. In 1975, a second Congressional hearing on black-market practices estimated that more than 5,000 babies were sold in the United States, some for as much as $25,000.

(Zelizer, 1985, p. 201)

Zelizer's emphasis on the emergence and changing ideology of the value of children is remarkable for pinpointing the rapidity and the nature of the transformations involved. There is a close relationship with the material position of children and the family: the significance of education, the decline in family size, and the end of child labour. Minge also notes:

In the middle of the nineteenth century the development of the need for educating wage-laborers created a previously unknown institution of 'childhood', which soon extended children's dependency into adolescence. The cost to the family soon became considerably greater than the forgone labor of children who no longer worked for the family.

(Minge, 1986, p. 24)

Also, child labour was not always eliminated immediately. Van Horn (1988, p. 19) sees in the early twentieth century that:

'children still represented an economic asset and source of labor for many people'. This was particularly so in rural areas or areas of poverty and was not curtailed by legislation until well into the twentieth century. As Van Horn remarks:

> The laws prohibiting employment of children under age 16, passed in almost all the states by the 1920s, gave the final blow to what remained of children's economic value in the family.
>
> (Van Horn, 1988, p. 37)

Zelizer (1985) suggests that for the southern states, child labour legislation was seen as a northern conspiracy to render them uncompetitive. As a result, there was no national legislation possible in the United States until 1938. Meanwhile, one million children between 10 and 15 years of age still remained at work in the 1920s, especially in the southern cotton mills (Zelizer, 1988, pp. 64–6).

In short, the erosion of children as an economic asset (and their becoming a liability to the family in terms of costs) was by no means immediate but it has been a prerequisite for reduction in family size. Second, this in turn has been a general pre-condition for releasing married women into paid work. As Richards observes:

> The mid-nineteenth century probably experienced the highest average size of family in British history. The tyranny of repeated pregnancy *and* continuous childrearing was at a peak, and this may have helped to reduce the female participation rates.
>
> (Richards, 1974, p. 349)

The ideology and practice of confining married women to the home was in part a reaction against the double burden of bearing both children and the conditions of wage labour. Thus, Winter (1982) observes that in the middle of the nineteenth century, maternal mortality was not, relatively speaking, a major component of the pattern of female mortality. This was mainly due to the severity of other causes of death. Winter also reckons that the increase in life-chances among Europeans from the mid-nineteenth century onwards probably more than matched any gains made over the previous thousand years. But the decline in the death rate was far from uniform across the population. As Winter notes:

The onset of aggregate decline in death rates in the 1870s can be ascribed almost entirely to improvements in the life-chances of people aged 2–35. Twenty years later, older adults (aged 35–65) began to register significantly lower death rates. Finally, only after the turn of the twentieth century did infant mortality rates and death rates for the elderly begin to drop.[38]

(Winter, 1982, pp. 103–4)

Elsewhere, Winter (1979) finds that the maternal mortality rate had remained stubbornly high at about 4 per 1,000 births until the mid–1930s. In other words, the physical dangers for mothers of having children remained as high as they had always been, despite the uneven rhythm of fall in death rates across the rest of the population. This is an indication of the incentive for mothers not to engage in waged work even with modest increases in the standard of living. It was also an incentive to have fewer children, for, as Lewis observes:

Wives aged under 45 suffered a higher mortality rate than unmarried women prior to World War I . . . the difference is not solely explicable in terms of maternal mortality . . . The causes of the low health status of working class wives were related to frequent pregnancies, poor nutrition, hard household labour in often depressing conditions, and lack of leisure.

(Lewis, 1984, pp. 23–4)

And Chinn also notes:

In 1900 the life expectancy of a woman aged twenty was forty-six years. She could expect to spend a third of that time pregnant or nursing infants, with the consequent effect on her ill-health and premature ageing.

(Chinn, 1988, p. 134)

Women's taking on paid work would have proved an additional burden to be avoided except when income from such a source proved imperative.[39]

Third, increasing productivity brought with it increasing levels of real wages and established with it the ideology of the family wage. However, the increasing standard of living was only achieved painfully slowly. Recall that the Rowntree survey at the end of the nineteenth century uncovered that forty per cent of the York population found itself in primary poverty at some time during its lifetime. Grown children's wages still remained important contributions to the family household. This suggests that the continued reliance on household production would have been, in part, a consequence of limited purchasing power.

Fourth, the need for a wage from a working wife may have been diminished by the newly introduced welfare benefits which made their appearance with the stage of monopoly capitalism. Tilly and Scott recorded that:

> In the 1920s and 1930s, the advent of social welfare measures – unemployment insurance, health and accident compensation, family allocations – alleviated some of the need in working families, some of the dependence on children's earnings.
>
> (Tilly and Scott, 1978, p. 186)

Apart from this, the increasing regularity of employment may have raised the potential of the male wage to provide adequate family income.[40]

Fifth, at least in its earliest stages, monopoly capitalism may, as previously discussed for formal subordination, have increased the opportunities for making income from home. This is most clear in the case of taking in lodgers, as the building industry, especially in Britain, has shown itself incapable of providing cheap, mass production of housing (see Ball, 1983). Equally, the increase of working class income and consumption was also supportive of petty (retail) trading, often of mass produced goods, and other economic activity that could be based from home.[41]

To summarise, through a number of factors, the conditions that established the stage of monopoly capitalism, such as limitation of the working day and welfare measures, also tended to counteract the forces associated with it which would tend to break down the formal subordination of the family to capitalism. Rising standards of living without drawing married women into wage labour also became possible through the more certain limitation of family size. In Matthaei's View:

> There were counter-currents operating: while homemakers could fill family needs through the purchase of commodities, and the purchase of such commodities allowed them to

concentrate on the special personal aspects of homemaking, their investments in homemaking as a vocation pressured them to hold onto their 'work', even to reintroduce home production into the family . . . the transformation of woman's work from production to consumption . . . filling the particular needs of the family though the purchase of commodities with the earnings of the head of household.[42]

(Matthaei, 1982, pp. 164–5)

Writing in 1933, Pinchbeck assessed the situation as follows:

Her own labour was often exploited and in many instances women's earnings only served to keep their husbands' wages at the level of individual subsistence. In this sense the industrial revolution marked a real advance, since it led to the assumption that men's wages should be paid on a family basis, and prepared the way for the more modern conception that in the rearing of children and in home-making, the married woman makes an adequate economic contribution.

(Pinchbeck, 1969, pp. 312–13)

But the position of women in the labour-market was already beginning to change in response to the real subordination of the family to capitalism, as real wages rose in line with the mass availability of consumption goods. First of all, female participation in wage labour was beginning to rise. Whilst it had always been high amongst young, single women and stood at well over 70 per cent for these in the UK in 1931, the following decades were to witness a dramatic increase in the labour-market participation of married women. Between 1931 and 1951, the participation rates of married women more than doubled to the level of 21.7 per cent, whilst for younger married women it was bordering on 40 per cent.[43]

The waged work that women were doing was also changing. Slowly but surely, domestic service was disappearing. Even in 1930, over a fifth of the female workforce was still engaged as private domestic servants (almost twice the number of textile workers) compared to a quarter 20 years earlier. But 20 years later, less than 6 per cent of women worked as such servants. During the 1920s, although still so important, domestic work was taken unwillingly, servants increasingly lived out, and the job served as a route from countryside to town and as an expedient in the absence of other waged work.

The jobs that grew were in clerical work, various retailing activities, and other forms of service employment, each of which was as important in employment as textiles and as clothing in 1931. Some of these jobs were the extension of domestic labour to the market place. Others drew upon the elementary education that all children now received, requiring the ability to read, write, add and subtract.[44] To a lesser extent in absolute numbers, women were drawn into the professions that they were to come to dominate numerically – nursing and teaching. But women were also to become wage workers for the new mass-production consumption industries – especially, for example, in electrical engineering, female employees rising from 69,000 in 1931 to 204,000 in 1951.[45]

No doubt the deep recession of the 1930s may have dulled some of these trends. But women's wage labour had certainly begun to respond significantly to the pressures to obtain income other than through the circumscribed route of domestic production. Associated changes around fertility and labour-market participation were by no means historically novel. As Hewitt reports of Victorian workers:

> These women deliberately controlled their own fertility partly to avoid the physical rigours of bearing children in quick succession, but partly also that the standard of living made possible by the wife's contribution to the family income might not be imperilled by a large family, whose demands might force the mother to give up her employment.
>
> (Hewitt, 1958, p. 95)

But such behavioural patterns could only be systematised within the period of monopoly capitalism after the pressures to withdraw family labour and the demographic transition had worked themselves out historically. In the post-war boom, the real subordination of the family to capitalism was to be fully realised but, once again, economic and social conditions were to be transformed.

THE SOCIAL SUBORDINATION OF THE FAMILY

Writing at the beginning of the 1950s, Titmuss summed up the major changes associated with the demographic transition as follows:

> It would be probably true to say that at the beginning of the century about half of all working wives over the age of forty had borne between seven and fifteen children . . . it would seem that the typical working class mother of the 1890's, married in her teens or early twenties and experiencing ten pregnancies, spent about fifteen years in a state of pregnancy and in nursing a child for the first year of its life . . . the expectation of life of a woman aged twenty was forty-six years. Approximately one-third of this life expectancy was to be devoted to the physiological and emotional experience of childbearing and maternal care in infancy. Today the expectation of life of a woman aged twenty is fifty-five years. Of this longer expectation only about 7 percent of the years to be lived will be concerned with childbearing and maternal care in infancy.
>
> (Titmuss, 1963, pp. 90–1)

Titmuss (p. 98) draws the conclusion that these changes favoured the entry of married women into the labour-market but, as has been argued, the very process of establishing the real subordination of labour and the family to capital had the effect of withdrawing women from the labour-market. Hence, the inter-war period, whilst witnessing considerable changes in the position of women at home and at work, still left the extent of female waged labour at relatively low levels, particularly for married women (with children).

Following the Second World War, the economic pressures on, and ability of, women to work were substantially increased. Society entered the era of mass consumption in which an ever-increasing number of consumer durables entered into the norms of the standard of living. To some degree these eased the burden of housework, releasing women to work outside. On the other hand, women's wage income became essential to meet consumption norms that were ever unattainable. For Tilly and Scott (1978), this has led to the *family consumer economy*. Matthaei takes a somewhat different view:

> Universalisation of needs and differentiation in family purchasing power were enmeshed in a competitive hierarchy of

consumption and situated within a dynamic process of economic growth and a rising overall standard of living . . . Wealth was no longer an absolute phenomenon, a particular standard of living; wealth became having the most commodities, having commodities that others did not own. Poverty was no longer an absolute phenomenon either; it meant having less than the majority of Americans, rather than the absence of some fixed necessities.

(Matthaei, 1982, pp. 242–3)

The OECD has this to say:

The increasing participation rates of married women with husbands present also suggests that, for most families, single income is no longer regarded as sufficient and that the threshold at which total family income reduces the motivation of both spouses to undertake paid employment is high . . . the economic trade-off point has shifted in favour of outside work.

Interestingly, the release of women into the labour-market in pursuit of consumption norms is reflected by their changing participation as affected by their husband's income, although there is no reason to expect hard and fast empirical relations to emerge. Initially, the higher paid the husband, the less the need for a wife to work. Subsequently, in recent years, given the generally close association between socioeconomic status of husband and wife, the greater the incentive for the wife to work because of greater earning power from higher qualifications. Thus, Van Horn notes:

In 1940 the inverse correlation between husband's income and women's work persisted.

(Van Horn, 1988, p. 67)

Subsequently, she observes:

By 1963 a small positive correlation between the income of a husband and his wife's employment appeared, as work rates for women between the ages of fourteen and thirty-four who had no children under eighteen were *higher* the greater their husband's income.

(Van Horn, 1988, p. 133)

At lower levels of income, however, once a notion of poverty becomes relative, rather than relying upon an absolute standard of subsistence, then the importance of women's work in avoiding poverty becomes clear. The pressures of consumerism do not simply rest on the attainment of luxury. In the UK, four times as many families would be living in poverty – below income support entitlement level – if wives did not work.

Thus, by the 1980s the participation of married women in waged labour exceeded 50 per cent in many of the advanced capitalist economies, and each of these had experienced high growth rates in the numbers of working women (see Mincer, 1985, and OEEC, 1985). For most countries, females made up at least a third of the labour force and, for many, it exceeded 40 per cent.

But this drive of women into waged work has been countered by other pressures, those associated with the formation of the nuclear family, where present, as the unit of consumption. It takes domestic labour time to use and enjoy the benefits of consumer durables. For Wilson (1978, p. 61), following the creation of the ideals of childhood and motherhood around the turn of the century, there came 'women's important role after the [1939–45] war as consumer, or spender of the man's wage'. These activities require time out of wage-labour.

How have these tensions between the needs of the family and the needs of the labour-market been resolved? Within an orthodox neoclassical view, it is a matter of individual optimisation around the time available, taking account of potential family earnings, desire for, and costs of, children, productivity within the household and the incentive to work created by the level of wages. In charting the increase in women's participation rates in the labour-market over the post-war period, the conclusion is reached that the incentive for women to work due to higher levels of wages has heavily outweighed the disincentive effect of the higher wages of their husbands in providing sufficient household income.[46] As observed previously, this is little more than a tautology for, if the history of female labour participation had been different, so it would have been 'explained' by a different balance of incentive and disincentive effects. In addition, this neoclassical view faces serious problems once closer attention is paid to more detailed developments in the labour-market. Gregory et al. point out that female employment has increased relative to male employment even though wage relativities have also narrowed:

145

> Female employment relative to male has continued to rise despite the 30% relative wage increase in response to the introduction of equal pay for women . . . we are always led back to a view of the economy that stresses that relative wages are institutionally determined and that the most important point in explaining relative employment growth is job segregation and the changing demands for different types of jobs.
>
> (Gregory *et al.*, 1985, p. S294)

Joshi finds that the orthodox explanation is thrown into doubt by its failure to distinguish between female participation in labour-markets as full-or part-time workers:

> Another source of doubt as to whether wage-pull is the sole determinant of long-run changes in participation propensities is that regression analysis of 1980 cross-section data suggests that it is full-time participation which is the component particularly sensitive to wage effects, yet it was participation in part-time jobs which actually rose.
>
> (Joshi, 1985, p. 75)

Here emerges a key development in the form in which married women have entered the labour-market – as part-time workers. As the OEEC (1985) reports, as many as 40 per cent of female workers are part-time in Sweden, Denmark, Norway and the UK, and such countries tend to have 90 per cent of part-time jobs taken by females. Where males do engage in part-time work, they tend to be older, whereas part-time females tend to be at an age which is primary for male workers.

This is because they are mothers with small children. Over the post-war period, there has been a trend towards earlier marriage (and greater rates of marrying).[47] Women continue to work until their first child is born, Rockeis-Strugl notes for Austria the trend:

> toward earlier marriage with the young wife remaining in the workforce in order to help buy and equip a new home.
>
> (Rockeis-Strugl, 1983, p. 156)

Subsequently, a smaller completed family size has accompanied shorter gaps between births so that the childbearing years have been compressed. And there has often been a return to part-time work. In Canada, for example, Lupri and Mills recorded that:

> 78% work less than 30 hours per week. More married women

would like to work full-time, but family obligations, childcare responsibilities, and a severe shortage of adequate childcare facilities are barriers to full-time employment.[48]

(Lupri and Mills, 1983, p. 65)

Over time, the most important determinant of married women's participation has become focused upon the age of the youngest child, especially when the latter is pre-school. For Britain, Joshi notes that:

Though the presence of children in the home lowers the probability of employment this is a relatively transient phenomenon, reducing as children pass through their school age years and, by 1980, virtually negligible by the time the youngest child reaches secondary school age. Once one allows for the presence and age structure of the youngest child, the presence of additional siblings makes little difference to the chances of their having a job outside the home, whatever their age.

(Joshi, 1985, p. 71)

This has been particularly important for middle class women with children under eleven for whom increases in participation rates have been the greatest, matching the previously higher levels of working class women (Joshi, 1985, p. 77).[49] Marriage as such has become a much less significant obstacle to women's participation in paid work.

One resolution, then, of the economic pressures associated with the real subordination of the family has been the U-shaped pattern of employment participation of married women over their lifetimes, with the trough of participation during childbearing years being sandwiched by periods of full- and part-time employment. Some have projected these changes into more dramatic resolutions, in particular for women ultimately to enter the labour-market on equal terms as men and for men to share equally in domestic labour.[50] Others consider that men have abandoned their (financial) responsibilities for children, as the latter have become an economic liability rather than an asset for old age.[51]

The current divorce rates for teenage brides in Britain is one-third (Craven et al., 1982), and this figure would apply to the whole population within 20 years if current trends continue (Murphy, 1985). However, this reflects no leap into the world of freedom

147

and equality but is often the response to economic stresses. Murphy reports that marital breakdown is more likely the earlier the marriage, the shorter the interval to children (especially for pre-marital conception), and according to affluence of housing tenure (private rented and then, in ascending order, council housing as opposed to owner-occupation).[52] In the 1980s the number of children in the UK in one-parent families reached one and a half million, and this constituted a major source of poverty.

This suggests that the real subordination of the family does not yield a well-defined nuclear family with a readily recognisable pattern of life-cycle behaviour for women. Pratt and Hanson (1991) powerfully argue how household and family strategies, including employment decisions, are both influenced by various spatial and temporal constraints. Nor do these strategies necessarily lead to women moving to a position of parity with men in and out of the home. On the other hand, those who project an image of increasing equality do so on the basis of economic *and* social change. Thus, for Matthaei (1982), emphasis is given to the process of 'social homemaking', which she associates with public provision of teaching and nursing, for example. She argues that great stimulus is given to this through women's employment in these areas as an extension of their domestic homemaking, particularly after universal suffrage when women's interests can be expressed and acted upon politically. In other words, the functions of the family and of domestic labour are increasingly provided through the state.

Whatever the historical validity of this account, it clearly points to the increasing role of the state in economic and social reproduction, as has previously been associated with the stage of state monopoly capitalism. The results and conditions of the real subordination of the family to capitalism are soon integrated with this stage to give rise to the social subordination of the family to capitalism. As Wilson describes it:

> The period since the Second World War is marked off from what went before by an intensification of state interest in family life and in the child. The earlier periods had given expression through social policy to an interest above all in the maintenance of the adult worker . . . The ideology of the Welfare State has changed. In its beginnings, greater emphasis was placed on the immediate reproduction of the

worker. Malthusian ideas meant that the dangers of over-population were stressed, rather than care for chldren already born. Increasingly, and especially since 1945, the main emphasis has been on the reproduction of labour power in terms of children, the next generation.

(Wilson, 1977, pp. 35–9)

Significantly, then, OEEC argues that:

Inequality in the education system, in employment and in the tax and social security systems, along with the domestic division of labour have combined to perpetuate occupational segregation and women's greater vulnerability to poverty and dependence.

(OEEC, 1985, p. 11)

Other factors, particularly those associated more widely with welfare provision (childcare), could be added also but what stands out is that these influences are a product of contemporary capitalism, with the exception of domestic labour, and would not and could not be brought forth as explanatory variables for the female role in the labour-market in earlier times, except in very special cases.

As already remarked, some have responded more favourably and optimistically to the social subordination of the family, seeing it as potentially releasing women from the various forms of domestic oppression. Others, most notably Zaretsky (1985), have adopted an opposite point of view. For him, the role of the state has been to prop up the family which would have otherwise have been shattered by the pressures of capitalism:

Rather than the state undermining the modern family, it is difficult to imagine how any form of the family could have survived the enormously destructive uprooting that accompanied industrialisation without some intervention by the state. The issue is not whether the welfare state eroded the family, but rather in what form it preserved it . . . the family has been preserved as an economically private unit and that most of the normative aspects of state policy are based on that.

(Zaretsky, 1985, p. 195)

Yet another way in which these developments have been understood is through the public/private dichotomy – with state

149

intervention being seen as shifting the boundary between the two, either as interference or as support, or as a social surrogate for patriarchy.[53]

Not surprisingly, these different attitudes reflect particular theoretical simplifications of a complex and contradictory interaction around the state, capital and the family.[54] The result is that these interpretations tend to be one-sided, reading off concrete developments in the family from the possibilities, rather than the necessities, that have been created by the stage of state monopoly capitalism. What does result, however, is an increasing dispersion of household formation, as reflected in, and responding to, fewer children, their timing (and of marriage or not), divorce, increasing female labour-market opportunities, welfare provision, etc.

As is well known, many state policies affect employment: those that do so directly through economic management and industrial policy at the macro-level; those that operate at other levels, such as training, the welfare benefit and tax system and employment legislation; then there is childcare and maternity provision and equal opportunities which are overtly geared towards women. The effects of these policies cannot always be anticipated in advance, they may not even have been taken into account.[55] For, as Mincer observes:

> Public policy that affects labour supply, fertility behaviour, and more generally the family institution does not necessarily emanate from a concern with these matters and is not necessarily designed to change them.
>
> (Mincer, 1985, p. S28)

Consequently, the effect of state intervention on the role of women in labour-markets is by no means pre-determined but depends on the evolution of a set of policies which have an imperative which may be derived from quite separate considerations. This is more so, with more uncertain effects, the less prominent and explicit is women's employment treated as a matter of policy and conflict.

To summarise, in the period of state monopoly capitalism, the delayed drive towards the real subordination of the family to capitalism is achieved, but in a context heavily influenced by the increasing social subordination of the family. The net result is increased participation of women in the labour force, especially married women (possibly on a part-time basis after the youngest child has reached school age). Women's position in the labour-market, however, like men's but differently, will be profoundly affected by the economic and social policies of the state.

4

WOMEN AND THE BRITISH LABOUR-MARKET

THE THREE 'LOWS' AND WOMEN'S EMPLOYMENT

The current period of capitalism has previously been characterised as one of state monopoly capitalism. What implications does this have in particular for the British labour-market and for women within it, given the social subordination of the family? Elsewhere, Fine and Harris (1985) have argued that the British economy is itself characterised, within the advanced capitalist countries, by the 'three lows'. It is a low wage, low investment and low productivity economy. These are all intimately connected to each other. Low productivity is a consequence of low investment, and wages must remain low in order for products to be cost-competitive.

It is important to acknowledge these aspects of the British economy but also to recognise that they do not, as such, constitute an explanation for relative industrial decline. This is linked to the absence of a coherent and long-term agency committed to the reorganisation of British industry. It is not that industrial policy, for example, has been negligible, but that it has lacked coordination both within and between sectors. This in turn is explained by the global orientation of the transnationals that dominate British industry, the international and short-term financial strategies of the City (rather than commitment to long-term industrial investment), and the weakness of the labour movement in pressing for and establishing long-term economic policy-making.[1]

The resulting weaknesses in the British economy have been particularly exposed by the intensity of competition for markets that have followed on from the growth slow-down of the early 1970s. This has accelerated the trends associated with deindustrialisation – the (absolute) decline in manufacturing employment and the increasing role of the service sector as a major source of employment.[2] This, then, is the context in which women, as in other countries, have been entering the labour-market in Britain.

From the *Women and Employment Survey*, Martin and Roberts (1984) provide a detailed picture of the conditions of female wage labour – as discussed below if not otherwise indicated by alternative references. From the mid–1960s to the end of the 1970s growth in employment has been associated almost exclusively with the entry of part-time married women into the workforce, with this providing over one and a half million jobs. Of the total workforce, 18 per cent had become part-time, 94 per cent of them women.[3]

Most analyses of part-time work focus upon the joint impact of supply and demand factors.[4] For demand, employers are seen as seeking lower wage costs and flexibility in numerical, financial and functional control, with the first two of these in particular being provided by part-time workers.[5] These factors, however, have to be set against the extra recruitment costs associated with higher numbers and, potentially, turnover of employees. In addition, as the sectoral composition of output shifts towards services, these may be more (female) labour-intensive and more amenable in certain areas to casual and part-time work. All of these considerations have to be set against alternative possibilities of achieving flexibility through overtime or short working of full-time employees. On the supply-side, it is generally argued that women may prefer part-time employment given childcare and other domestic responsibilities.

To a large extent the supply and demand framework based on cost-effectiveness and flexibility can chart the conditions in which part-time working is liable to be more prevalent. But it does not paint a full picture. Dey (1989), for example, observes that hours worked are not bimodal, failing to fall neatly into distinct numbers of hours worked corresponding to part-time or full-time work:

> Not far short of one in ten part-timers work close to 30 hours, while approaching one in three works over 21 hours a week.
>
> (Dey, 1989, p. 469)

He also emphasises that flexibility in hours has been most readily pursued through use of part-time labour rather than through variation in full-time hours. Thus, he observes:

> The distinction between full-time and part-time work has been eroded by the growing range and variety of work patterns . . . [which] can be attributed almost entirely to the growth of part-time work and not to any significant changes in full-time hours. The growing diversity in work patterns reflects the development of part-time alongside full-time work rather than a revolution in the latter.
>
> (Dey, 1989, p. 471)

This suggests that the demand for part-time labour is dominated by considerations of cost, and that flexibility is more in response to employer needs. In short, it is low pay that employers are pursuing, and this can even be at the expense of other advantages. As Dey notes:

> Firms adopting this approach cut labour costs at the expense of 'functional flexibility', accepting low productivity as an inevitable concomitant of low paid labour in low skill jobs . . . the potential skills and resources of the part-time labour force are being wasted through the exploitation of low-status, low paid employment.
>
> (Dey, 1989, p. 473)

Dale and Bamford also point to the heterogeneity of the flexible workforce but confirm that the latter may provide a 'peripheral' workforce with the following characteristics:

> There is a real danger that, in those industries which are increasing their use of 'peripheral' forms of labour, employer flexibility is only gained at a cost to the employee. This cost may be the absence of any training or career prospects, the lack of any job security or the ineligibility to claim redundancy pay or receive maternity leave.[6]
>
> (Dale and Bamford, 1988a, p. 32)

Dale and Bamford also find that those few men who do work part-time are liable to be the young or old, and are on the margins of entering or leaving the labour-market, respectively. For women, it is more associated with marriage and children, although Dey argues that these factors should not be exaggerated, given the numbers, especially of older women without children, who tend to work full-time. Further, Dale and Bamford report that part-time work has increased most in those sectors where it was already well-established – as in distribution, hotels and catering. Both of these contributions discover that part-time workers are not necessarily less attached to the labour force or to particular jobs and, thereby, liable to impose recruitment costs on an employer. This is examined in great detail by Dale (1986) who observes, however, that part-time workers, especially when compared to full-time male workers, are less liable to move to a new job within a firm and are more likely to move not only to a different firm but to a different occupation or sector of work. This suggests that part-time workers are denied career paths and are neither able to exploit nor to accrue on-the-job training – again, consistent with low-wage cost as the primary motive for their use by employers.

In the case of qualified workers, Bonney (1988) finds that such married women are more likely to work full-time (49.3 per cent) than the unqualified (23.5 per cent) but that each is equally liable to work part-time (17.2 per cent and 16.8 per cent, respectively). Consequently, she argues that:

> Qualified women constitute the vanguard of women's full participation in the labour-market. They are increasingly forging labour-market careers approximating the male norm of continuous full-time paid employment.
>
> (Bonney, 1988, p. 100)

But the counterpart to this is the creation of heavy dependence on part-time, careerless employment for many women, especially for those without qualifications and unable to compensate for this through work experience.[7]

For British women, the most important determinant of whether they work or not is the presence of a child under five, after which age or for the presence of other older children, there is a much reduced disincentive effect. Marriage as such does not affect whether women work or not but is a strong influence on whether they work full-time or part-time – suggesting that domestic duties in marriage, even in the absence of children, inhibit labour-market participation.[8] The significance of the constraints imposed by childcare is demonstrated by women working at short journeys from home and taking regular employment on a five-day week, with reduced hours rather than days of work, in order to fit in with the hours of children's attendance at school (or taking evening work).

As already observed, women are especially concentrated in a

few service sector jobs (health, education and welfare, selling, catering and cleaning, etc.) and repetitive manufacturing assembly, and are more concentratedly so when doing part-time work. In manual service work, 70 per cent of female employees are part-time. There is a 15 per cent differential between hourly earnings for full-time and part-time workers, but a large part of this is explained by the difference in rates for full-time non-manual and part-time manual workers. Indeed, by the hour, part-time non-manual earnings are more or less the same as manual full-time earnings. Thus, female manual part-time workers are particularly badly paid (and this also applies to sales staff within the non-manual).

Many of these features of part-time work in Britain are to be found in other countries. But it would be a mistake to believe that all trends are common and equal across all economies. Indeed, the extent of part-time labour is marked in Britain, as is the strength of the association of part-time working with the presence of children and of low participation rates with young children – even if the growth of part-time female labour in services is uniform across different countries. But as Dale and Glover (1990) report, there is no necessary connection between high levels of female labour-market participation and high levels of part-time working. France and the UK, for example, seem to be at the opposite of two extremes. As Dex and Walters (1990) report, whilst both countries share a female labour-market participation rate of just under 50 per cent, twice the proportion of women work part-time in the UK as compared to France. French women tend to work more continuously or not at all, non-workers being less qualified and having larger families.[9]

Differences also emerge from the study of part-time work in Britain and West Germany by Schoer (1987). For 1983, part-time employment is depended upon more in the UK, 19.4 per cent of employment as opposed to 13.5 per cent in West Germany, even though it is over 90 per cent female in both countries. This is strongly linked to the demands of childcare, but in the UK a greater proportion of part-time workers are drawn from the very young and the very old, suggesting that weaker sections of the workforce in general support the market for part-time labour. The dependence of the UK economy on part-time labour is illustrated by as many as 9 per cent of all part-time workers holding two or more jobs. Nor is this a consequence of the preference of profes-

sionals for varied work, for both countries have a similar proportion of part-timers in high status jobs, but the majority are
concentrated in the service sectors and low status.

Further, whilst the UK has a higher share of service industries,
and hence an implied bias towards a higher share of part-time
workers, it also has a higher share in each separate service industry
than West Germany. Again, the UK is seen to be more dependent
on a low-wage female workforce, and this is supported by employment tax policy. The National Insurance threshold, earnings
above which attract contributions, is higher in the UK, excluding
30 per cent of part-timers as compared to 11 per cent in West
Germany. So, for employment tax when compared with West
Germany, women workers in the UK are discouraged from working other than part-time.[10]

From most studies of differences in the operation of female
labour-markets as between countries, much emphasis is put upon
the role played by childcare arrangements and taxation (and
welfare payments). Here attention will only be paid to the first,
although the two are not independent of each other. How (married) women are taxed influences when and whether they are
going to have children. And the treatment of childcare provision
– by the fiscal system as a fringe benefit or not if provided by
employers, or as a tax deductible cost if paid for by an employee –
is of importance.

In a comparative study across the EEC, Moss (1988) brings out
the special character of the UK in childcare provision, and it is
worth dwelling on his findings. First, Britain is unique in the
extent to which female labour-market participation is influenced
by the presence of pre-school children.

> Employment rates among women with children aged 5–9 are
> generally similar to those for women with children under 5.
> Only one country shows a change of more than 5 points. In
> the UK the employment rate increases by more than half,
> from 29% to 45%.
>
> (Moss, 1988, p. 5)

Moss goes on to say:

> The UK has two peak ages for [female] employment – 20–24
> and 45–49. This reflects the UK's unique pattern of employ-
> ment, with women leaving the labour force when they have

157

their first child, then returning in large numbers after their children start at primary school, most to part-time work.

(Moss, 1988, p. 22)

Second, the UK stands out (other than the Netherlands which, in addition, has extremely low female participation rates) in the extent of part-time working by mothers, with most working less than 30 hours per week (and between 15 per cent and 30 per cent working less than 10 hours per week). This is especially so for those with children under five and (in the Netherlands too), fathers tend to work compensatingly longer hours. Thus, as Moss finds:

The UK has 40% of all part-time workers in the European Community. Most are poorly paid, with 4 out of 5 earning less than the Council of Europe's 'decency threshold' for wages of £4.25 an hour. Many are not covered by basic employment rights, such as maternity leave.

(Moss, 1988, p. 18)

Third, as compared with France, for example, British women are much more likely to leave work upon having a child without returning soon after.

A large-scale survey in France in 1981 of women with at least one child under 16 found that just over a third of the mothers had remained in employment except for periods of maternity leave. In the UK, by contrast, more than 80 per cent of women leave the labour-market for a period after the birth of their first child, and only 3 per cent remain in the labour-market throughout their childbearing years.[11]

(Moss, 1988, p. 21)

Not surprisingly, then, in the study for the EEC of childcare in Britain, Cohen (1988) finds that it has the weakest policy across Europe. Further, in the UK, the benefits of private provision do not accrue either. As Dex and Shaw (1986) report in comparing the US with the UK, the arrangements for childcare are quite different. In the US, it has become usual to make use of paid childcare and, with the associated tax relief, this has proved more successful than the limited extent of state provison in the UK. Here, the main form of childcare provision is, in the absence of tax relief on costs incurred, through the assistance of a relative, normally the husband. Consequently, women will often be in

158

part-time jobs either during the school day or in the evenings when their husbands come home from a normal working day. Yet another factor favouring women's participation in the US is the greater access to (second) car ownership which widens the travel to work area as compared to the UK where (local) public transport has to be relied upon.

How do these various aspects correspond to the workings of the British economy? First, a large proportion of female employment, including part-time work, has been through the state in central and local government. Women have been used to provide a cheap labour force, and this has not been at the expense of manufacturing employment nor symptomatic of labour shortages there.[12] For, whilst female (part-time) service employment has been rising, full-time male manufacturing employment has been declining (see Dex, 1987b). Services have not been taking jobs away from manufacturing. But the decline of manufacturing has provided a source of cheap female labour for services. A typical employment profile for a woman has been to move from full-time manual work through childbirth and back into part-time service employment (Dex, 1987b). And, as Dale notes, part-time work has been used as a means of shifting towards services:

> Women part-timers are more likely than any other group to move into clerical work from different occupational groups.[13]
>
> (Dale, 1986, p. 19)

Further, in both manufacturing and services, women have been used to compensate for low productivity because of their low wage costs. Dex observes that:

> When women have been working in manufacturing industries at cheaper wage rates, they have been supporting, in Britain, an ailing manufacturing sector, allowing it to limp along and be slightly more on a par with the cheap labour production of developing countries in textiles and clothing. Given that productivity gains have been restricted in service industries, then women are also the obvious choice of workers to try and keep down costs in these industries.
>
> (Dex, 1987b, p. 127)

But the special significance of women's work for the British economy is brought out by comparisons with other countries, something that Dex and Shaw (1986) have done for the United States.[14] They find that the US is more advanced than the UK in drawing women into the labour-market, and this is especially true for the continuation of work around childbearing and not just for an early return afterwards. Only women above 40 are more likely to work in the UK than in the US although they are more liable to be part-time when they do so, and this probably reflects greater income needs. A greater attachment of women to the labour-market in the US might also reflect that fewer have children and divorce is more common, enabling and necessitating an independent source of income.

Perhaps some of these differences might be explained away by the higher per capita income in the US, but the most startling difference between it and the UK is brought out by looking at employment histories over childbirth. Although women in the UK are to be found more in semi-skilled factory and unskilled jobs, the occupational structure for women is similar between the two countries. However, over all, in moving in and out of work because of childbirth, US women experienced upward mobility in the sense of finding a better job. In contrast, the net effect for women in the UK was for downward mobility, especially for those not returning to full-time work immediately. As Brannen observes:

> The majority of women who remain in full-time employment with their pre-birth employers enjoy a relatively advantaged situation in the primary sectors of the labour-market, the most significant benefit being an increased chance of upward mobility. In addition they are more likely to have access to job security, occupational pension schemes, and paid holidays . . . In contrast women who find new part-time work after childbirth move into secondary sectors of the labour-market and are vulnerable to downward mobility. Many make no further use of their former skills, seniority and experiences. They also lose out on pay, job security and employment rights, both statutory and employer related. Those who have a second child are rarely eligible for maternity leave, maternity pay or reinstatement.
>
> (Brannen, 1989, p. 196)

Mann and Elias observe, from a survey, the presence of:

Evidence to suggest that there is a resultant underutilisation of the skills and experience of these returners.[15]

Rothwell (1980) sees this as a consequence of limited employment policy for women – in contrast, presumably, to inner-city youth which has had a higher policy profile:

> By default, if not by deliberate action, the employment problems of mature women re-entrants tend to be relegated to the back of the queue . . . women are obviously seen as having alternative occupations open to them, and they represent no threat to law and order if unemployed.
>
> (Rothwell, 1980, p. 161)

The US/UK comparison supports the idea that women's wage labour plays a crucial role in supporting the low-wage economy in the UK. Women are so poorly supported in their attempts to work through public provision of childcare, and wages are so low that private provision of childcare with tax relief has proved more successful in the US – where Blau and Robins (1988) find that female labour supply is affected by the availability and cost of childcare. In addition, the low-wage economy in the UK has made use of women as a cheap labour force, as reflected in downward mobility over childbirth, even at the expense of under-utilising the skills and experience that women do have from their previous employment and training.

These comparisons are important in considering the likely future prospects and role of women in the British labour-market – unless there are profound changes in economic and social conditions and decision-making. For, whilst part-time working, especially where pre-school children are involved, is an important and continuing feature, particularly of the UK labour-market, there are increasing trends across many countries towards women working full-time with shorter breaks for bearing children. Thus, part-time work might be seen as a transitional phase towards full-time work in the female labour-market, as economic and social adjustments are made in response to this initial form in which increasing female labour-market participation has occurred.

Thus, Humphries and Rubery (1991) point to changes in women's employment in the UK by reference to three processes – integration, differentiation and polarisation. Integration is the increased participation and greater spread of women across

161

sectors and occupations; differentiation is the gap between male and female pay and conditions; and polarisation signifies the differentiation within the female labour force. Especially marked is the gap between those in some professions who achieve a degree of parity with men and those who are marginalised within the labour-market (and who remain segregated from men and face the poorest pay and working conditions).

That polarisation within female employment is the outcome of integration and differentiation is a reflection of the limited extent to which women have been supported in the labour-market in the UK. Thus, just as the relatively large share of part-time work has corresponded to Britain's position as a low-wage economy so, as that part-time component becomes increasingly full-time, it is to be suspected that such jobs will continue to be low-paid and limited in skill and conditions.

To some extent, then, those who point to the extreme position of women in the labour-market in the UK seek to remedy it through adopting more progressive policies around women's access to, and benefits from, paid work – through childcare, transport, taxation and welfare policies, education and training, etc. No doubt this would have some significant impact. But such an approach fails to address analytically why the policies that have been adopted in Britain should have been so: implicit is the assumption of incompetence or sexism rather than these serving more to reinforce the employment role of women in the context of the 'three lows' character of the British economy.

However, a further analytical step has been taken by those who trace the origins or ethos of British policy. A popular starting point is to quote from Beveridge, as in Crompton and Sanderson:

> The attitude to the housewife to gainful employment outside the home is not and should not be in the same as that of the single woman. She has other duties . . . to do in ensuring the adequate continuance of the British Race and of British Ideals in the World.[16]
>
> (Crompton and Sanderson, 1990, p. 50)

Here is made explicit the intended role for women as mothers as opposed to wage labourers, but it has also been intended that welfare policy and employment should be treated as separate as far as women are concerned. Consequently, in the UK, the implications of welfare policy for women's employment have been neglected along with corresponding measures to support women in the labour-market, as most notably brought out by childcare as considered above.

It is not satisfactory, however, to rest an explanation for this on the ideology and even the institutions laid down in the wake of the Beveridge Report – for these are subject to change much as has occurred for the imperialist ideology in which Beveridge stated his view. In addition, though, the UK has lacked long-term, coherent labour-market policy in general, and in correspondence with its lack of long-term industrial strategy and agencies. So, by comparison with elsewhere and what might have been, labour-market policy for *women* has been weak because it has been so across *all* workers and because its relation to welfare policy has been set aside, both in design and implementation. This is all the more paradoxical given the extent to which the expansion of state welfare has depended primarily upon female workers.[17]

In short, the argument here, although it has not been documented in detail, is that the particular weaknesses of the British economy have led it to draw upon an impoverished female labour-market and to reproduce it – most notably in correspondence with the character of industrial, welfare and employment policy. These have lacked general coherence within and between themselves and, in particular, in their lack of concern for the labour-market position of women.

This perspective can be brought out through comparison with other countries. In Ruggie's (1984) study of Sweden and the UK, the differential impact of legislation and policy on women's labour-market position is taken much deeper. He argues that Sweden has developed a corporatist economy with an approach to labour-markets that is universal in recognising the needs of both men and women as workers. For the UK, it is suggested that economic policy is more market-oriented, although this is better seen as a lack of coordination of policy rather than its absence. Thus, as Ruggie observes:

> In Britain economic policies and anti-discrimination employment measures each function in their own separate spheres, neither influenced by the other, and the result for women is less than the sum of the parts.
>
> (Ruggie, 1984, p. 99)

163

Given, in any case, the weakness of employment measures in the UK, such as in training, Ruggie goes on to note:

> Labor market polices in Britain reveal that the role of the state is secondary to market forces in allocating resources . . . In contrast, the Swedish labor market policies indicate that the state is taking a strong role in directing the best use of all labor resources in conjunction with a well-developed industrial policy.
>
> (Ruggie, 1984, p. 181)

Brown and Wilcher (1984) further reveal the contrast by pointing to the links made in Swedish policy between female employment and regional development and in allocations to new jobs and in training. In an accompanying comment to this paper, Ginsburg adds the commitment to employment policy (even when unemployment is low), public works, equality legislation, trade-union low-wage policy, and parental leave.

The supposed free- market attitude to labour-market and economic policies in the UK is supplemented by social policy which takes the 'traditional' role of women (as wives and mothers) as its point of departure. As Brown and Wilcher note:

> In general, the British are more traditional in their conception of the role of women . . . Swedish policies indicate a prevailing conception of women as potential or actual workers.
>
> (Brown and Wilcher, 1984, p. 294–5)

Thus, whilst part-time work and occupational segregation are comparable in the two countries, female workers in Sweden have a wage differential with men of around 10 per cent, whereas it is around 30 per cent for the UK. There appears to be a close link between the lack of coherent industrial and social policy in the UK and the deeper dependence on women as a cheap labour force. Moreover, this has been particularly important in the public sector itself, and not just in policy in general, since the public sector employs so many women and has been a major source of employment increase for them in health, education and welfare. The state as employer must have had a profound and direct effect on the conditions in which women have been employed. In Sweden, as Adams and Winston (1980) report, this is approached positively, working mothers being consistently supported by welfare programmes.[18] This corresponds to a broader framework of always linking welfare to employment:

> Social spending has been closely related to manpower [sic] policies . . . expanding social services and full employment policies have been mutually reinforcing in Sweden's postwar economy.
>
> (Adams and Winston, 1980, p. 188)

Similarly, Gordon (1988) emphasises in West Germany how a high priority has been placed on the opportunity to work rather than to live on transfer payments. Gordon argues that, by increasing female labour-market participation:

> The government [of West Germany] has responded by stressing the need to improve training opportunities for women and by specific measures that will, among other things, permit a mother (or father) to remain out of the labor force as long as five years following the birth of each child without losing eligibility for training allowances or for placement in a work creation programme.
>
> (Gordon, 1988, p. 259)

And the contrast is drawn with the UK and the US:

> Some countries such as Sweden and West Germany have had continuous and consistent emphasis on labor market policies, whereas others, like Britain and the United States, have had 'stop-and-go' policies . . . There is a persistent need for training and retraining programmes, not only for the unemployed and persons entering the labor force, but also for the employed. Stop-and-go policies must result in deficiencies of training personnel and facilities.
>
> (Gordon, 1988, p. 343)

This analysis, then, carries a number of implications. First, the theoretical suggestions of the previous chapter are confirmed. Women's positions in the (British) labour-market are decreasingly determined structurally and quantitatively by their primary responsibility for domestic labour. This must be considered in conjunction with other, equally important, factors which directly and indirectly influence the conditions under which women enter, and continue within, the labour-market.

Second, measures to enhance women's labour-market position,

such as childcare provision, are of considerable potential, but they are liable to be subject to erosion and to be of limited impact in the absence of measures to restructure the relations around employment and welfare more generally. For, otherwise, the UK economy will continue to depend upon a large strata of low-paid workers of which women will form the major part.

Finally, it follows that policy should be geared not only to promoting the position of women in the labour-market. This should also be part and parcel of more general policies to regenerate the levels and quality of employment, welfare and economic performance for the benefit of the workforce as a whole.

CONCLUDING REMARKS

One of the difficulties in engaging in analysis of women's employment, whether theoretical or empirical, is to avoid restating the obvious. To court that very danger, how many studies have found that women take disproportionate responsibility for domestic labour, that they work in the worst jobs, are paid the lowest wages for jobs that make equal demands upon them as better paid men, and that they are systematically discriminated against in appointments, training and promotion. And how much has women's work been devalued in social esteem? In a, possibly unconscious, parody of Marx's letter to Kugelmann, Scott observes:

> From the point of view of capital, try to imagine what it would mean if women laid down their tools.[19]

> (Scott, 1984, p. 58)

As remarked, we all know this now, although not all share the passion expressed by Olive Schreiner:

> The fact that for equal work equally well performed by a man and by a woman, it is ordained that the woman on the ground of her sex alone shall receive a less recompense, is the nearest approach to a wilful and unqualified 'wrong' in the whole relation of woman to society today. That males of enlightenment and equity can for an hour tolerate the existence of this inequality has seemed to me always incomprehensible; and it is only explainable when one regards it as a result of the blinding effects of custom and habit. Personally, I have felt so

166

profoundly on this subject, that this, with one other point connected with woman's sexual relation to man, are the only matters connected with woman's position, in thinking of which I have always felt it necessary almost fiercely to crush down indignation and to restrain it, if I would maintain an impartiality of outlook.

(Schreiner, 1911, pp. 24–5)

However, not all remains the same. For she also observes:

On the entire field of woman's ancient and traditional labours, we find that *fully three-fourths of it have shrunk away for ever, and that the remaining fourth still tends to shrink.*

(Schreiner, 1911, p. 66)

But, whilst occupational segregation remains a continuing feature of women's employment, we are now almost certainly witnessing a historically delayed, if nevertheless permanent, increase – both in female labour-market participation and breadth of occupations. This is itself associated with dramatic changes in women's (and men's) lives more generally. It is not simply that the family is in 'crisis' once more – with high and rising levels of divorce, illegitimacy and single parenthood – but that the certainty of changes is, as it were, the only thing that has remained constant. It must be recalled that, little more than a century ago, few married women undertook wage labour and each on average took responsibility for five children or so. Even a little more than 50 years ago, the single most important employment for women was domestic service.

With rapid change such as this, the gap between restating the obvious and being proved hopelessly empirically wrong is extremely narrow. This, then, is not a fertile area in which to sow predictions, unless they be surrounded by a thicket of caveats. The analysis in this book has, however, attempted to highlight tendencies, structures and processes that determine the progress of women's employment and root these in historically contingent outcomes. As it happens, the breaking down of the barriers to women's participation in employment is proceeding apace and, it can be anticipated, that the conditions under which they enter and continue in paid work will also improve, not least as their own influence is increasingly exerted through trade unionism and the political arena. But, as has been demonstrated for the increasing levels of female labour-market participation, the economic and social processes involved are neither automatic, direct nor pre-determined – whether in pace, level or detail. Hopefully, the analysis offered here, whatever its continuing validity, will serve as a contribution in how to understand and examine the complexity of the changing position of women in and out of the labour-market, and that others can employ it either by drawing upon it or through critical reassessment.

APPENDIX

REVIEWING THE DOMESTIC LABOUR DEBATE

Domestic labour and value theory

Central to the debate over domestic labour, other than in the new (neoclassical) household economics, has been its relation to Marxist value theory. Contributions have fallen at, or between, two extreme positions. For one, domestic labour produces value, much like wage labour and as measured by labour time. Or, to be more accurate, domestic labour can be treated as if it does produce value like wage labour. From this perspective, domestic labour can be analysed accordingly to reveal the extent of the specific exploitation of female labour – once corresponding levels of consumption are taken into account. The more women work relative to what they consume, the more they are exploited.

The other extreme position denies the immediate relevance, or direct application, of such value theory to domestic labour. Consequently, it opens, but does not necessarily fully engage in, a richer specification of the relationships between domestic and wage labour. As the second extreme position has emerged as a critical response to the first and has become the conventional wisdom,[1] it is as well to begin with the theory of domestic labour as equivalent to value-producing labour.

The clearest statement of this position is perhaps to be found in Harrison (1973), although it is undoubtedly to be found in the earlier analytical work supporting wages for housework. In arguing for such wages, domestic labour is likened to waged work without the payment of the wage (or subject to discretionary levels of marital support) and is necessarily exploitative of women by

169

men. Consequently, in relation to each other, each of the sexes then constitutes a class. Harrison does also consider women to be a separate class, which is exploited, but this follows from his taking the analysis further by treatment of housework as a separate mode of production in its own right.[2] He explicitly denies that housework is able to produce value as such, since it is not subject to competitive mechanisms to establish norms or standards of labour time corresponding to (capitalistic) socially necessary labour time, a competitive standard set through the market. However, he then proceeds to add together value as determined in the capitalist sector with labour time performed in the domestic sphere so that, despite his denial of the latter's capacity to produce value, domestic and wage labour are treated as equivalents for the purposes of adding them together.[3]

This raises the issue of when is it legitimate to add together two qualitatively different quantities – to set aside their differences for quantification purposes. An example is provided by apples and pears, for which the more general category of fruit will suffice and which encompasses both. Consider a further example. In travelling from A to C via B, different modes of transport may be used in going from A to B than in going from B to C. Clearly, this is irrelevant to comparison of the distances AB and BC. But there may be considerable qualitative differences involved – not least in the time taken, the comfort, the cost, etc., quite apart from a potentially infinite number of other differences such as fuel used, pollution to the environment, public versus private provision, and so on. On one of the journeys, long breaks may be made for purposes other than the travel itself, and walking might serve both for leisure and to achieve some distance. This may actually make difficult even the identification of journey time. On the other journey, speed may be of the essence. Clearly, for Harrison the differences as between domestic and wage labour are not sufficient that these labours are rendered incommensurable with each other (and, often neglected, that domestic labours are equivalent with each other as well as with the different value producing labours). Indeed, Harrison does observe that there are substantial differences between the labour performed by housewives and by wage-workers – that the former is not subject to direct coercion over the labour process, that there is limited specialisation and division of labour and production is not for exchange. There is then a strong argument that the commensuration of domestic with wage labour will conceal much more than it reveals, quite apart from the difficulties of identifying and standardising domestic labour even theoretically.

None the less, Harrison adds together domestic and wage labour. For each individual, exploitation can then be gauged by consumption relative to work done. By this mechanism, Harrison is able to argue that the surplus labour performed by the housewife is essentially divided between the male husband/worker and the capitalist. Thus, the more domestic labour the wife performs, *ceteris paribus* (and with fixed consumption levels in particular), the more surplus labour is transferred to the capitalist and is appropriated as profit. This follows because, with domestic provision by the housewife, the husband can attain a high level of consumption even with a lower wage. This is of benefit to the capitalist (e.g. when paying low wages, since bread is baked more at home than bought from a shop). On the other hand, if the consumption of the husband/worker is increasingly supplemented by domestic provision, then ultimately he will consume more than he produces and the capitalist's sole source of profit will be the surplus labour of the housewife, transferred through the lower wage (but high consumption level) of the male worker. It becomes possible for profits to depend exclusively on the non-wage labour of the housewife, appropriated by the capitalist through paying the husband a lower wage which is compensated for by high levels of housework.

A similar analytical position is adopted by Gardiner (1975) and (1976) in her earliest work on domestic labour, although the possibility of male workers enjoying positive levels of exploitation through domestic exploitation does not arise. Rather, the equivalence between the different types of domestic and wage labour is brought into effect through varying the ways in which consumption levels are maintained. More domestic labour is needed to compensate for a lower wage, as in a recession for example – so that profits can be indirectly supplemented by reducing wages. As Gardiner puts it:

> The labour time spent by the housewife in caring for husband and children will normally vary inversely with the wage, as she will be forced to substitute her own labour for commodities which the labour is insufficient to buy.
>
> (Gardiner, 1976, p. 113)

Like Harrison, then, Gardiner does not perceive domestic labour as value creating but surplus value transferring:

> Domestic labour does not create value, on the definition of value which Marx adopted, but does nonetheless contribute to surplus value by keeping down necessary labour, or the value of labour power, to a level that is lower than the actual subsistence level of the working class.
>
> (Gardiner, 1975, p. 58)

This approach, especially for Harrison, reflects a broader methodology towards value and labour time. It is one in which *all* labours can be measured against each other, even if they are not and do not all necessarily count equally, and in which exploitation then follows by comparison with corresponding levels of consumption. There is no doubt that this is possible as an academic or conceptual exercise but the question remains as to whether it is justifiable theoretically. For Gough and Harrison (1975), there is a justification. This is, that, like wage workers, other workers:

> can contribute to relative increases in surplus value in a way that is *materially* identical (producing in less labour time use values which enter directly or indirectly into the means of subsistence of workers in the capitalist sector).
>
> (Gough and Harrison, 1975, p. 2)

This argument has been appropriated from the debate over productive and unproductive labour. Gough and Harrison (1975) note, for example, that both commercial workers and those engaged in the welfare state (especially in education) contribute equally to profit, to the extent that they both perform surplus labour, and that this is what makes them 'materially identical' with one another.[4]

As such, this argument that all surplus labours are materially identical does not address the issue of whether the material differences in the (surplus) labours may render them incommensurate. Within Marx's own theory, different types of (concrete) labour geared towards exchange are commensurate as abstract labour even though those labours perform different tasks for capital according to what is produced and how. On the other hand, commercial labour is exploited as wage labour and is employed by capital but it does not produce a commodity (but the circulation of commodities and money). State employees are exploited as wage labour but are not employed by capital and do not produce commodities in general. Finally, domestic labour is exploited but not as wage labour, nor does it produce commodities.

These are all substantial reasons for recognising that these different types of labour are not materially identical, or not sufficiently so for the purposes of commensuration between them. Indeed, there is a glaring contradiction in the work of Harrison which appears to have gone unnoticed. For, whilst maintaining that housework and wage labour are materially identical for the purposes of uncovering the origins of surplus labour, he has equally argued that the two are governed by totally different relations of production; so much so, that housework is conceived as constituting a separate mode of production itself. It is strange to argue both for material identity and difference in mode of production in equating labours with each other!

Effectively, as is often explicitly recognised, the analysis of Harrison (and Gough) employs a general category of labour commensurable across all social structures, so that all labours are 'materially identical' in this sense. This inevitably implies a lack of historical specificity, but also an inability to deal with historical change to supplement what is otherwise a simple specification of static structures of exploitation – in which all labours contributing more than they consume are treated as equivalent.

Pressing this further, it can be shown that this approach to domestic labour does not depend upon value theory at all (and hence the equivalence between housework and wage labour becomes unnecessary). This conclusion will come as no surprise to those familiar with the debate over the transformation problem and the Sraffian critique of Marxist value theory.[5] Those unfamiliar with these issues may wish to skip to the next paragraph. Indeed, the treatment of (unproductive) state workers as equivalent to those who produce surplus value for private capital does not depend upon Marxian value theory either.[6] Rather, there is only a need to differentiate between the different types of labour and how much each receives for consumption. This can be laid out very clearly in algebraic terms:

$$pA (1 + r) + w_1 l_1 + w_2 l_2 = p$$

Here, p is a price level, A the input requirements for capitalist production, r the rate of profit, w_1 and w_2 the consumption levels of men and women, and l_1, l_2 the unit labour inputs for capitalist production and domestic production, respectively. This is, of course, the normal Sraffian equation for prices – only with the extra term, $w_2 l_2$, added to represent the consumption taken by women as if they were paid w_2 for each unit of domestic labour l_2. The displacement of value equations by price equations in this approach is appropriate because, for example, capital intensity in wage labour as opposed to domestic labour is liable to be different (the former generally presumed to be higher), so that the transfer of domestic labour to profits will take place at prices and wage levels that diverge from values. In any case, the very division between what is produced in the home and for the home will be dependent upon the market mechanism which will lead to results that diverge from calculation at values. Choice between domestic and commercial laundry will depend upon availability of credit to buy machines, etc., and not just on relative labour times, for example.

For the reader unversed in value theory, the previous paragraph may be mystifying but the results it entails are simple enough. It shows that there is merely a three-way trade-off – given capitalist and domestic technology – between the rate of profit and the levels of consumption of men and women. To boost the rate of profit, however, whilst men's work and consumption position remain the same, it would be necessary to reduce womens' consumption or increase their hours of work (so that women's unit 'wage' is reduced). Further, in this way, exploitation can be measured by levels of consumption relative to hours of work.

There is, of course, a striking parallel between this model and dependency theory except that the exploitation of one nation by another is now replaced by the exploitation of women by men. In the formulation of Emmanuel (1972) – and Amin (1974), but especially (1978) – and employing value theory, relative prices are struck to the disadvantage of the Third World through the paying of lower wages there. However, this model should also be reformulated as above and will necessarily lead to a three-way split between profit, male wage and female 'wage' – where the latter are now the wage levels in the exploiting core and the exploited periphery, respectively. As before, it is possible that wages in the core could rise to such a level as compared to those within the periphery that, whilst profit remains positive, core workers as well as capitalists are exploitative of the workers in the periphery. Not surprisingly, then, Harrison (1973, p. 35) sees an analogy between his analysis and that of the relationship of capital with the Third World and feudalism. He also considers the example where male workers consume more value than they produce as analogous to the theory of the labour aristocracy (which feeds on the bounty of colonial exploitation). Similarly, Gardiner (1975) points to the lack of labour-market mobility for women (tied by the marriage contract rather than by national boundaries) and emphasises the lack of equal exchange within marriage.[7]

It is worth noting the work of Samir Amin, who treats all labours around the world as equivalent and quantitatively identical, so that exploitation is measured by differing levels of consumption. When such world-systems theory is combined explicitly with the household, all labours differ only in the way in which they yield up surplus value to global capitalism, so that the household becomes an institution within a historically evolved structure of institutions. For Wallerstein this serves as:

a system of polarizing distribution in which the majority of the world population serve as a labor force producing surplus-value, which is somehow distributed among the remaining minority of the world population.

(Wallerstein, 1984, p. 17)

In these terms, it can be seen that the theory of domestic labour lying at the extreme of treating all labours as essentially equivalent can at best merely *measure* the extent of the extra-exploitation of women (according to work done as opposed to consumption received). There is little chance of *explaining* why such exploitation exists and persists or how its form and extent are liable to change.

This is made explicit by Harrison when he seeks to use such measures to provide the basis for a history of women's exploitation through the relative labour time and consumption of men and women. Here, though, he does add some further analytical considerations of considerable importance. He recognises that (the growth of) productivity in the capitalist sector may be higher than in the household sector. Consequently, there may be some tendency to shift production from the household to the commercial sector, even to the extent of housework being eliminated altogether, although he continues to allow for lower productivity in the household so that comparative advantage between waged and non-waged work does not, by analogy to neoclassical economics, operate fully. This suggests that Harrison's approach has some analytical affinities to the neoclassical household economics of Becker. In effect, the latter allows the household to act as if it were fully incorporated into (his understanding of) the capitalist economy. Harrison essentially recognises the structural separation between the two. Consequently, he differs from Becker by employing a labour theory of value to measure exploitation, although reliance for this upon costs of production as measured by labour time of production is unnecessary (and Sraffians would argue it to be undesirable). There are also frictions in the allocation of such labour time between the capitalist and household modes of production.[8] Nonetheless, comparative advantage adjusts allocation of labour as capitalism increasingly exceeds household productivity. As Himmelweit and Mohun observe:

> This leaves any conception of the dominance of the capitalist mode purely static and fails to provide any way of relating changes in domestic labour to the laws of capitalist development.
>
> (Himmelweit and Mohun, 1977, p. 21)

Gardiner's approach, in moving from the analytical measurement of exploitation, is slightly different, although she too tends to set the comparative advantage of household labour against that of wage labour. Her method of doing so is essentially functionalist, in seeking explanations that rely upon changes as they are or are not to the advantage of capitalist profitability (or stability by reference to the ideological functions of the family). Thus, socialisation of housework (through the state or commodity provision) is seen to follow the greater is the demand for female wage labour (Gardiner, 1976, p. 114), although it is recognised that childcare may not be cost-effective for capital (Gardiner, 1975, p. 54), and that other economic forces may be at work, such as the search for markets for consumer goods during boom periods (Gardiner, 1975, p. 55).[9] For both Gardiner (1975, p. 57) and Gough and Harrison (1975, p. 5), women tend to move in or out of the labour-market (and correspondingly do less or more domestic work and buy more or less commodities) as the accumulation of capital goes through its cyclical rhythms.

As a consequence of the wish to historicise what is essentially a structural measure of the exploitation of domestic labour, Gardiner and Harrison create an implicit tension in their analyses. For, whilst they seek to deny that domestic labour produces value (although it is readily rendered commensurate with wage labour), and however much hedged by frictions, the law of value does operate to allocate labour between the domestic and the capitalist sphere according to comparative advantage, the needs of capital or the criterion of profitability. This is explicitly recognised by those who argue that domestic labour does produce value, the leading representative of whom has been Wally Seccombe (1974 and 1975).[10] He argues that domestic labour contributes to the value of the commodity labour power. The male worker's wage is then divided into two parts, one of which sustains him and the other of which sustains the wife (and generational replacements for both, respectively). That part allocated to the wife represents the value that she has produced:

> She creates value, embodied in the labour power sold to capital, equal to the value she consumes in her own upkeep.
> (Seccombe, 1975, p. 89)

This is, however, extremely problematical. As Gardiner (1975, p. 50) points out, this means that if the husband hands over less of his pay packet, then the housewife is deemed to have produced less value even if she works exactly as before. By the same token, if the housewife changes the amount of labour that she performs within the household, then it follows that this also has no effect on the value created unless, as is by no means necessary, she is more amply rewarded. Of course, it might be argued that such *ceteris paribus* comparisons are illegitimate – in the absence of an explanation of what determines the standard level of domestic labour time performed or the standard level of remuneration to housewives. But the existence of such standards has yet to be established, and their existence must be doubted given the emphasis placed on the privatised nature of domestic labour and its remuneration.[11] There are not norms established as such for these – as on the contrary, can be argued for the hours of wage labour and its levels of remuneration. Yet this is what is required for Seccombe's argument, as he makes explicit:

> The housewife's labour is compelled directly by the demands placed on her by her husband and children . . . Assume that the average wage, the price of wage goods and the normal living conditions of the proletariat in a given capitalist nation are known at any given point in time. Since these three

177

factors completely surround housewives' labour, its intensity is also determined and knowable. Average domestic labour time will therefore be that labour time necessary to convert the average wage into the average proletarian household, at the average price of wage goods.

(Seccombe, 1975, pp. 88–9)

Ultimately, armed with these averages and in order to sustain what appears to be an impossible argument, Seccombe relies upon two different lines of defence. The first, and least compelling, is to appeal to Marx's proposition that underlying relations (wife's production of value) are concealed in the form that they assume (husband receives the wage). But this general proposition cannot be used to justify what not only appears to be false (that the housewife produces value) but what is actually false, since domestic labour is not coerced to be at a socially necessary minimum. Second, and not unconnected to the first, Seccombe (1980b, pp. 231–40) appeals to the very special nature of the commodity labour power to explain why domestic labour produces value despite its considerable divergence from wage labour (and petty commodity production). The list ultimately runs to six peculiarities. Whilst, once again, simple empirical observation is to some extent being presented as abstract theoretical insight, it is precisely features such as these that lead Seccombe's critics to argue legitimately, not that domestic labour produces value in a special way, but that it does not produce value at all.

Despite this, not surprisingly because of Seccombe's view that domestic (indeed all) labour is subject indirectly to the law of value (1975, p. 88), he, like Gardiner and Harrison, is drawn towards what is essentially a frictioned comparative advantage analysis of the allocation of the wife's labour time. Because he expects that the capitalist productivity for consumption goods (Department II) will outstrip what can be provided in the home, ultimately women will gain by entering, and will be forced to enter, the labour-market:

Domestic labour is nowhere near the productivity of simple labour time in Department II . . . *it has been falling farther behind the rising productivity of industrial labour in general and of Department II labour specifically* . . . On taking a second job, the bulk of her productivity gain will be extracted as surplus value. Nevertheless, she will receive a fraction which is more than sufficient to make up for labour time lost at home. It is the incentive of this fraction which compels her onto the labour-market. Provided the structural limit of the exchangeability of Department II goods for household labour has not been reached, and provided childcare can be found, then the widening productivity gap will push more and more women onto the labour-market.[12]

(Seccombe, 1975, p. 93)

In subsequent work (Seccombe, 1980b), further account is also taken of the tendency towards the growth of state provision of domestic services, although this is tempered at his time of writing by the drive to economic austerity.

The duality of domestic and waged work

The response to Seccombe, and further development of the theory of domestic labour, ran along a number of different tracks. One was to accept that domestic labour contributes to the (re)production of the labourer through the production of use values in the home but to deny that this entailed the production of value itself or the commodity labour power as such. A second was to continue to recognise the structural separation between capital and the household but to emphasise much more strongly the dual labouring role of women both as domestic and as wage workers. The third placed more emphasis on historical change and the forces underlying it. It is worthwhile dealing with each of these in turn and in more detail.

In arguing against the notion that domestic labour produces value, the case can be made at a number of different levels. The most abstract concerns the value form. Following on debates over value theory itself, value production is specified as requiring that the product take the commodity form and that production be for the market. Once it is accepted that domestic labour is not confined to servicing the (male) worker (and hence open to interpretation as part of a production process that ultimately leads to the commodity labour power), then it cannot produce value since it is not labour exclusively directed towards the market. Moreover, the different types of labour brought into equivalence with each other through the production and exchange of commodities render such concrete labours both social and abstract.

This does not occur for domestic labour which remains private and individually specific. Thus, for Adamson *et al.*:

> Seccombe has clearly confused concrete labour and abstract labour. It is the fact that commodities are the product of abstract (social) labour, products of the same homogeneous substance that allows them to be measured, compared and exchanged.[13]
>
> (Adamson, *et al.*, 1976, p. 11)

Thus, as was realised by Himmelweit and Mohun (1977, p. 28), there is much in common between Harrison and Seccombe, despite their differences over whether domestic labour produces value or not:

> Seccombe's assertion, that domestic labour produces value but no surplus, and Harrison's, that a surplus is produced but no value, both rest on the same faulty foundation: the attempt to quantify domestic labour and wage-labour in the same units.
>
> (Himmelweit and Mohun, 1977, p. 28)

Smith (1978) also criticises Seccombe for not having recognised the presence of the abstract character of labour for the commodity form and the absence of this for domestic labour. But, in addition, he points to the absence of equilibrating mobility between households (by analogy with a labour market) so that domestic labour time is not allocated by a social mechanism such as the law of value. The mirror image of this is the absence of competition in the product market which would establish norms for the time taken by domestic labour to produce use values (by analogy with the socially necessary minimum labour time associated with the values of competitively produced commodities). In a rather different vein, Gardiner *et al.* (1975) make the same point by emphasising how domestic labour differs from wage work. There is no rigid distinction between work and leisure and between production and consumption, and there is no immanent pressure to increase productivity or reduce costs, and there is no immediate external control over the production process.[14]

In placing domestic labour beyond the direct ambit of value production (and theory), a different aspect of female labour was able to assume prominence: the division between, and combination of, domestic and wage work. Whilst Harrison had suggested that domestic labour could, in principle, be totally displaced by capitalist provision of commodities, this was denied in examining conditions governing the sexual division of labour. Some level of domestic labour needs to be retained.[15] None the less, as capital expands extensively into more sectors, so increasing female wage labour serves as the necessary counterpart to the commercial production of domestic goods. Adamson *et al.* sum it up thus:

> The inadequacy of this [domestic labour] debate so far . . . rests on its inability to show the absolute limits to the socialisation of domestic work under capitalist production.
> (Adamson *et al.*, 1976, p. 9)

What these *absolute* limits are is never specified. And it seems more likely that what is meant is that there are structural limits, in the sense that there must always remain a, possibly substantial, residue of domestic labour to be performed by women irrespective of the extent to which individual tasks or products are commercialised. Whilst there may be greater difficulties in commercialising some household tasks rather than others, with childcare being the most frequently quoted example, it seems impossible to anticipate in advance which tasks will remain within the domestic and which within the commercial sphere.

Particular emphasis on the dual labour role of women was also made by Coulson *et al.* (1975) and Gardiner *et al.* (1975). As a consequence, the structural division between capital and the home, and their being straddled by the law of value, comparative advantage or whatever, becomes replaced by a division between female domestic and wage work.[16] This dual role, rather than domestic labour as such in isolation, is taken as the key to women's oppression. Whilst, in the absence of commensurability across the two spheres of work, it is impossible to assert that women are more exploited than men in the strict technical sense, this is clear when both husband and wife are working and the latter also does all the housework. As Gardiner *et al.* see it:

> What this discussion has rejected is an analysis which calculates a transfer of labour from domestic labour into profits. What it has not rejected is the idea that husbands may benefit from the work of their wives . . . a family where husband and wife are both working, and for the sake of the argument are

181

gaining identical wages, but where the wife is still performing all the housework and child care.

(Gardiner *et al.*, 1975, p. 7)

Being tied to domestic labour also seriously disadvantages women in the labour-market so that they are not, in practice, liable to earn the same level of wages as men. For Coulson *et al.* (1975), the pressures to combine and combat the conditions surrounding the two roles is potentially a source of unity and radicalisation, given the appropriate revolutionary strategy and organisation.

In short, in rejecting value theory or some equivalent version of it, the duality between domestic and wage labour is displaced by what Himmelweit and Mohun describe as:

a different duality of women's position under capitalism: they are both domestic labourers and wage-labourers, roles which are contradictory and provide the specific dynamic of their situation.

(Himmelweit and Mohun, 1977, p. 23)

This, in turn, leads to the third development in the debate, a corresponding re-examination of the commercialisation of domestic work – for this becomes central in the mediation between domestic and wage labour. It is also potentially theoretically innovative given the rejection of commensuration between the two spheres, since this does not allow a structure nor a dynamic based upon a simple calculus of exploitation alone. It is no longer analytically permitted to be a matter of quantities of work and levels of remuneration but is one of the (qualitative) relations between domestic and waged work.

Two aspects are involved here. The first is the recognition that capital has a tendency to bring many of the use values produced in the home into the orbit of commodity production, thereby tending to release women for wage work. The second is the recognition that these tendencies had been and were being realised historically. For example:

The percentage of women (fifteen years and over) involved in wage labour has risen . . . Necessarily complementary to this expansion of the labour force has been the 'socialisation' of aspects of domestic labour – a partial appropriation by the state of many of the traditional duties of the housewife . . .

182

such as feeding, cleaning, education, health-care and some aspects of child care.

(Himmelweit and Mohun, 1977, p. 23)

In short, an apparently more sophisticated position – reflecting a double duality between capital and the home and between female domestic and wage labour – had, none the less, reached remarkably similar conclusions to earlier analyses. Value theory was correctly set aside as inappropriate to non-commodity, privatised production within the home, but tendencies to commodification of housework and for displaced housewives to enter into wage work were accepted. Whilst previously these economic pressures had been appropriately tempered by frictions associated with the ideological role of the housewife in socialisation or whatever, now they were to be encompassed within, and accounted for by, a broader appeal to history. Just the passage of a few years was sufficient, for example, for that history to experience a change in emphasis. The economic crisis of the mid–1970s was initially expected to lead to shortages of male jobs and lower wages, with women being forced back into the home (as a reserve army of domestic labour) as a compensating factor. Subsequently, the continued trend for women to enter the labour-market meant that this overrode any such cyclical movements which might, in principle, have led to the growing labour-market participation of women being reversed.

The demise of the debate

It is from this point on that the dissatisfaction with the domestic labour debate arises. An exercise in value theory had been concluded. But, otherwise, little more had emerged other than to correct the theoretical propositions with which the debate had begun in response to empirical observations concerning the importance of domestic labour in oppressing women at home and abroad. In addition, it was increasingly realised how narrow a terrain had been occupied in the course of the debate and this was true both theoretically and empirically.

Empirically, there were a number of problems. First, on housework itself: this had never been examined in any great detail, either by divisions of tasks undertaken or by historical change.[17] Some criticisms of the debate at the theoretical level emphasised that within the home the very distinction between production and consumption, and between leisure and work, were far from clear.[18] Housework was not simply housework but contained a whole variety of detailed and general categories of work. Further, to have gone into greater empirical detail at the outset may have led theoreticians to have been somewhat more cautious in translating particular tendencies into realised outcomes. Foremost, the historical evidence suggests that commercialisation of domestically produced use values had not released women from the burden of housework. As Vanek observes:

> One would suppose, in view of all the household appliances that have been introduced over the past 50 years, that American women must spend considerably less time in housework now than their mothers and grandmothers did in the 1920's. I have investigated the matter and found that the generalization is not altogether true. Nonemployed women, meaning women who are not in the the labor force, in fact devote as much time to housework as their forebears did. The expectation of spending less time in housework applies only to employed women.
>
> (Vanek, 1980, p. 82)

This suggests that women who take on wage work do perform less housework but this is not necessarily because of the simple substitution of the commodities that they can purchase for the time lost to domestic labour. Otherwise, it is difficult to explain why housework has not decreased for the non-employed housewife (irrespective of income level) with the availability of a wider range of commodities, and why the employed housewife undertakes even more hours of work in total. Vanek makes the observation that:

> Indeed, for married women in full-time jobs the work day is probably longer than it was for their grandmothers.
>
> (Vanek, 1980, p. 90)

The reasons for this are quite easy to identify. The availability of commercial products together with advances in the standard of living have tended to extend and even to intensify domestic labour. As Fox puts it:

> Because household work is, simultaneously, family con-

sumption, there are two opposing forces perpetually at work in the household: one to decrease work time and the other to increase it. Depending on the nature of an inflation in the product expected of the domestic labourer – namely family subsistence – it may or may not make sense for the domestic labourer to intensify her efforts in the home.

(Fox, 1980b, p. 190)

As histories of the (technology of) housework reveal, the 'industrialisation' of the home both allows more and different use values to be produced there, even if economy of time can be found in sustaining a fixed level of 'domestic output'.[19] So there are competing tendencies operating on the time made available from the commercialisation and increasing productivity of housework. In the case of consumer durables, for example, these provide a market for the capitals concerned but only at the expense of tying the housewife to the home (*and* subverting the example of commercialisation through laundrettes or laundry services). Capital's production of the sewing machine and of mass-produced textiles shifts some production to the home, not away from it, even if there is also the growth of ready-to-use clothes and curtains. As Probert observes:

The introduction of manufactured cotton cloth meant that women did more sewing than previously, and a great deal more laundering. The more washable clothes became, the more they had to be washed, so it was only in the nineteenth century that doing the laundry became a major chore – and one loathed by most women . . . The women in the household had to wash the clothes, tablecloths and sheets in a cauldron of boiling water, before rinsing, wringing, bleaching, starching or mangling them as required. A mountain of ironing resulted.[20]

(Probert, 1989, p. 78)

Nor are these considerations relevant only to the duality between wage and domestic labour – value and non-value production. For it is also possible for capitalist production to enhance, as well as to erode, the ability to produce *commercially* within the home. It is not necessary to accept Delphy's (1984) argument that, because some French peasant women produce commodities for the market, all domestic labour must be treated as (surplus) value producing. But it has been established that, around the turn of the century, women were able to make considerable contributions to household *income* through their domestic activities, such as taking in and serving boarders.[21] This is of importance in explaining the history of female labour-market participation as well as the changing nature of domestic labour itself. Significantly, the importance of income-earning activity through domestic labour has been particularly emphasised in considering Third World households.[22] This, however, not only exposes the limited scope of domestic labour being considered by the debate, but also placed the ideal type of household, characteristic of the debate, into question.[23]

Thus, there is no necessary relationship between the commercialisation of housework and the freeing of domestic time. By the same token, presumed correlations between the level of (male) wages or employment, over the business cycle for example, and women being forced into or out of the labour-market simply cannot be sustained. At one and the same time, higher wages allow women to remain within the home because of the adequacy of income level *and* permit the purchase of what may, or may not be, labour-saving devices for use within the home (with consequential effects on the freeing of female labour for wage employment). It follows that the history of women's dual labour role is not one of a simple trend in which capital overcomes the obstacles constructed by domestic labour (whose origins usually remain unexplored in terms of why women were not already in waged employment). It is more the outcome of contradictory tendencies, which both displace domestic labour and extend and intensify it. The relative strengths and the forms of resolution of these tendencies is contingent upon other factors, as will emerge in subsequent discussion.

Nor, however, is this resolution liable to be uniform either in nature or in extent across the various activities that encompass domestic labour. The debate has legitimately been criticised for lumping the different types of domestic labour together indiscriminately, an empirical counterpart to the previously noted theoretical objections to treating all domestic labour as homogeneous.[24] Although there is token listing of the work that actually makes up domestic labour – cooking, cleaning, childcare, etc. – these have not, within the domestic labour debate, been differentiated analytically nor historically researched. It is as if they are subject to identical, if not equal, pressures and determinants. But the factors determining domestic labour and the way in which they determine it are highly variable, and surely not reducible to a generally lethargic invasion of the home by capital, or reducible to contingent response to the general conditions of the labour-market.

One way in which the distinction between different aspects of domestic labour has been recognised is through analysis of reproduction. Since the value of labour power is associated with the cost of reproducing the labourer and this occurs outside the immediate control of capital, reproduction and domestic labour have been closely linked with each other. None the less, it was soon recognised that reproduction itself involved a number of processes, for the social formation, or society as a whole, as well as for the family on a daily and a generational level. Admittedly, even if remaining at an abstract level, this was to accept that childcare, education, etc. are rather different as products of domestic labour than cooking and serving the Sunday lunch. Indeed, it also becomes inescapable that the state is heavily implicated at all levels of reproduction and, in all but the most reductionist and functionalist explanations, this implies that an even more complex and discriminating analysis is required of the determinants of women's position as dual workers.

But of most importance is the failure of the domestic labour debate to have made anything other than token reference to childcare (other than a nodding acceptance of the costliness of commercialising it). Given, over the past century, the dramatic falls in family size (and an even greater fall in the number of pregnancies) and the changing patterns in age of (female) marriage and sequencing of childbearing years, then sources of change in the amount of domestic labour to be performed, and its impact on women's working lives, become more readily transparent.

The value of labour power

By mustering together arguments such as these, Molyneux reasonably concludes that:

> Within this multiplicity of determinations, the contribution of *housework* to establishing the value of labour power plays a relatively minor role. Indeed, it cannot be assumed *a priori* that housework plays any significant role in this determination at all. For the relation domestic labour/value

of labour power is also subject to historical/ cultural variations.

(Molyneux, 1979, p. 10)

This exposes a problem within the domestic labour debate around the notion of the value of labour power. As is well known, this has two aspects. On the one hand, it is the competitively socially necessary labour time required to produce the bundle of wage goods, the value of which may be reduced by increasing productivity (producing relative surplus value in Marx's terms). On the other hand, the bundle, or standard of living, is itself historically and socially determined. In the domestic labour debate, there has never been any examination of what determines the bundle through time and through society, although at times it has been assumed directly to vary inversely with domestic production without mediation by other factors. It has generally been assumed to be a bundle fixed at a particular level (or possibly pre-determined to rise with economic and social progress). In this way, it has been possible, of course, for those such as Gardiner and Harrison to argue that domestic labour can substitute for commodities in making this bundle available when wages fall. Much the same is true, with caveats, of the more subtle analyses that distance themselves from such immediate accounting of labour time across different forms of production.

But this begs a number of questions. First, it must be doubted that the historical and social level of consumption can be so simply conceived. Surely it involves implications for levels of consumption across different strata of the working class, but according to where and how they live and number of family members, etc. In other words, it must be linked to quite a complex *system* or mode of consumption. It cannot, therefore, be presumed that changes in the mode of provision of consumption, as between home and market, can be simply effected without any relationship at all to the historically or socially determined level of consumption itself.[25]

Second, from Marx's analysis of capital, a reduction in the value of labour power, through the increasing productivity in the elements that comprise the wage goods, is based upon a fixed standard of living of the working class as far as the commodities consumed are concerned. Consequently, it cannot be assumed that the effect of productivity increases is simply to leave the overall standard of living unchanged by relying even more upon market provision. For then, inconsistently, an analysis based on a fixed wage bundle of commodities is being used to draw implications for how that bundle changes – by greater reliance upon those commodities whose productivity increases in place of those produced within the home.

There is another way of viewing these problems. In arguing that increasing productivity of consumer goods leads to an erosion of domestic labour, the mechanisms through which this occurs, rather than the logical or arithmetic possibility, are never distinguished from those which would permanently establish a new value of labour power (either in the total value of the given commodities consumed or in the quantity and mix of what is consumed). This is so even though the time over which erosion of domestic labour is liable to be effective is potentially of long duration, and certainly greater even than a business cycle. Thus, the large-scale commercialisation of shopping in superstores, the availability of convenience foods, the creation of a welfare system, etc. are more to be associated with establishing a new value of labour power than they are to be linked to the daily, weekly or even annual substitution of one form of women's work for, or on top of, another.

In addition, Marx's view, for example, of the nineteenth-century labour-market is that the working women (and children) represented an increase in the hours of labour contributed by the family (production of absolute surplus value) in return for the value of labour power (variously collected through individual wages taken together). Thus, family labour became the norm for many working-class families. Consequently, it is again questionable whether women can be viewed as moving in or out of wage labour on the assumption of maintaining a given value of labour power. Variations in and around the value of labour power are being conflated.[26]

In short, even in its most sophisticated form, the domestic labour debate never addressed the issue of determining historically and socially the value of labour power. Consequently, it was able to focus upon and highlight tendencies in the duality of women's labour but only by the dual and mutually supporting errors of reducing the analysis to narrowly defined economic factors alone and of conflating (certain) short-term movements in the conditions governing the value of labour power with longer-term changes in its social and historical determinants.

Once again the results are very similar to those that had been relied upon at an earlier stage in the debate. Then, it had been argued that domestic labour could have the effect of lowering the value of wages below the value of labour power.[27] Here, there were resonances, not always explicitly acknowledged, with the notion of cheap labour power, as associated with Wolpe's (1972) theory of apartheid labour being reproduced in rural areas costlessy for the benefit of capital – although this did depend upon a readily distinguishable mode of production other than the capitalist and, associated with the latter, a permanently higher (white) level of the value of labour power. However, for the domestic labour debate, if the value of wages were to fall permanently below the value of labour power or the latter to be permanently cheaper, then it becomes an immediate puzzle why these lower levels do not define the *actual* rather than the deficient level of the value of labour power.

This points to a separate but related issue. It has all too frequently been assumed that movement of female labour in and out of the home, or simply intensifying labour in the home, is a response to the pressure passed on by capitalists over the course of the business cycle. Capitalists remain secure in the knowledge that the labourer will be reproduced. In other words, it is assumed that domestic labour effectively forms part of wage labour as far as overall tasks to be done are concerned – feeding, clothing, etc. The parallels here with Malthusianism stand out, for there the reproduction of the workforce occurs like a pseudo-market. He, however, allowed an alternative possibility – that working-class families would not be able to reproduce themselves: that children, for example, would die (although family size could be restricted). If, however, capitalists are able to force down wages and force up domestic labour when times are bad, why should they not do so when times are good. They will, after all, always force down wages to the lowest level allowed by the labour-market, regardless of the impact on reproduction (rather than its being guaranteed). Marx, of course, argued that legislation to protect the labourer and the family represented a social recognition of the potential to reduce the value of labour power by prolonging working life and spreading reproduction costs over more labour time. This entailed the state to intervene to blunt the animal spirits of capitalists in the labour-market. Such arguments illustrate again how too readily the domestic labour debate has only looked at economic forces partially and by collapsing them into immediate empirical results, unmediated by other economic pressures and social interventions.

NOTES

INTRODUCTION

1 See also Vogel (1981, p. 204) and Ferguson and Folbre (1981) for whom:

> Long run changes in the size, composition, and stability of the family, as well as the character of social relations there, inevitably affect the production of labour power. Yet most of the literature concerning domestic labour and value theory ignore these factors. The major issue in these debates is whether the use values which wives provide affect the value of their husband's labour power, and thus, the production of surplus value as a whole. 'Reproduction of the laborer' is pictured as the physical reproduction of the adult male. The nature of the labor that wives and mothers perform is seldom explored. Furthermore, the labor time which mothers devote to their children – future workers – is never discussed.
>   (Ferguson and Folbre, 1981, pp. 316–17)

2 See Dalla Costa and James (1972), and Malos (1982) for a review of the debate over wages for housework.

3 See Delphy (1984), and Barrett and McIntosh (1979) and Molyneux (1979) for a critique.

4 For other reviews of the debate, see Smith (1978), Kaluzynska (1980), Himmelweit and Mohun (1977), Fee (1976), Holstrom (1981), Molyneux (1979), Williams (1988), Glazer-Molbin (1976), Curtis (1980) and Fox (1980b). It is not intended here to provide a comprehensive review. Indeed, it proved impossible to obtain easily all the relevant literature due to gaps in holdings in the university libraries in the London area. A minor but interesting obstacle was the far greater extent than normal to which articles on the subject had been torn from journals. Readers are left to draw their own conclusions. The best bibliographies are to be found in Fox (1980) and Williams (1988).

5 See Wolpe (ed.) (1980), for example.

6 On the issue of reproduction, see Edholm et al. (1977), Seccombe

(1980a), Duchen (1989), Himmelweit (1974 and 1984a), Barrett (1980), Fox (1980a), Mackintosh (1977), Redclift and Mingione (1985), Mingione (1985), Blumenfeld and Mann (1980), Close and Collins (1983), Seccombe (1980a), Creighton (1985), Harris (1983), Kaluzynska (1980), Bryceson and Vuorela (1984), Humphries and Rubery (1984), Bowlby (1990), Landes (1977/8) and Evers (1984).

7 See Mitchell (1975) and for an assessment explicitly recognising its Althusserian origins, Barrett (1980). See also McDonough and Harrison (1978). In retrospect, it might be crudely argued that Althusserianism imposed the structures of psychoanalysis on to Marxian concepts. Consequently, in turning to sexism, it readily provides a psychoanalytical framework for explaining female oppression by inverting the previous intellectual route.

8 See also Redclift (1985).

9 See also Close (1989).

10 For further discussion of the problems of the distinction between public and private, see Showstack Sassoon (1987) and Siltanen and Stanworth (1984).

CHAPTER 1 ON PATRIARCHY

1 See Hart (1989), Crompton and Mann (1986) and Crompton (1989a), for example.

2 See Rowbotham (1973).

3 See Feldberg and Glenn (1984) and Kendrick (1981). Of course, models of the male labour-market alone continue to persist as if women were not there, as in Ermisch (1988), Shah (1990) and Congdon (1988).

4 See Scott (1983) for whom women were written into history rather than history rewritten. See also Scott (1986), Rose (1986), Buhle (1989) and Kessler-Harris (1989).

5 See Crompton et al. (1990).

6 See Stacey (1981) and Oakley (1989).

7 For a review of the earlier literature, see Beechey (1987). See also Mark-Lawson and Witz (1988).

8 In the debate between Rowbotham (1981) and Alexander and Taylor (1981), it is perhaps significant that the latter do not defend patriarchy against the charge of being ahistorical even though they see a notion of patriarchy as essential to move history beyond the confines of atheoretical narrative.

9 For a careful elaboration of the relation between discovery, exposition and causation in Marx's method of abstraction, see Lee (1990).

10 Seccombe also seems to base his understanding on the unrealistic assumption that the male becomes an owner-occupier as a necessary form of tenure.

11 Connell (1987, p. 92) also points to the way that a descriptive identification of some aspect of women's inequality is associated with, 'the

much more numerous cases where anything that shows a detectable pattern at all is called a "structure"'.

12 See also the *Grundrisse* for relevant discussion of Marx's method.

13 See also Middleton (1988) who distinguishes between explanation and independence in the use of the concept of patriarchy but concludes that the latter cannot be sustained as a category of analysis without relying upon:

> the changing *forms* of patriarchy . . . the patriarchal *essence* must presumably remain the constant – immune as it were from historical influence. The concept fails to acquire the explanatory power it is intended to have since things have to happen *to* patriarchy to precipitate the observed changes. It is not a motor of history itself.
>
> (Middleton, 1988, p. 70)

14 The following lines from Walby make clear how the duality between patriarchy and the capitalist mode of production has been fudged:

> Patriarchy, then, is composed not only of a patriarchal mode of production, but also sets of patriarchal relations in the workplace, the state, sexuality and other practices in civil society.
>
> (Walby, 1986, p. 247)

15 See also Walby (1988a, p. 23), (1986, p. 89) and (1985, p. 162), and Lown (1990).

16 See also Walby (1990a), where the periodisation between private and public patriarchy is associated with two crucial moments, the extension of the franchise and the potential to enter work:

> In the first moment women won political citizenship, which gave them not only the vote, but education, and hence access to the professions, property ownership, and the right to leave marriage. In the second moment women gained effective access to paid employment and the effective ability to leave marriages.
>
> (Walby, 1990, p. 96)

Consequently, Walby places emphasis on the importance of the first wave of feminism around the turn of the century.

17 See also Crompton and Sanderson (1990, p. 17).

18 Similarly, Eisenstein (1979) seeks a synthesis between capitalist patriarchy and socialist feminism; Sen (1980) a synthesis between class relations and the subordination of women; Beechey (1988) seeks an account that combines analysis of the family and the workplace. Brenner and Ramas (1984) criticise Barrett (1980) for creating a dualism between women's material oppression and the ideological construction of gender. In her response, Barrett (1984), criticises Brenner and Ramas for their alternative of a degree of biological determinism, but confirms her own position as one of synthesising the material with the ideological, with some emphasis on the role played by the latter in determining women's oppression in employment.

CHAPTER 2 WOMEN AND THE LABOUR-MARKET

1 See, for example, Crompton and Sanderson (1990) and Crompton (1988).
2 See also Fine (1990) for a shorter version.
3 In general, however, SLM theory has been interested in those female segments comprising the low paid.
4 See also Sokoloff (1980, p. 64) who criticises dual labour-market theory for being too simplistic. He further states that:

> Although dual labor market theory acts as a critique of the idea of equality existing between men and women in jobs and wages, the discussion remains basically descriptive. It does not explain how labor markets came to be structured in the first place to segregate women from men.
>
> (Sokoloff, 1980, p. 64)

5 For a critique of such tautologous reasoning, see Beechey (1987, p. 33 *et seq.*), for example.
6 See Martin and Roberts (1984).
7 Dex (1987b) also identifies an overlapping industrial segmentation for women's employment with five segments (see p. 126). Dex (1988a) argues that women's employment should be divided down into even finer segments to take account of differences between full-time and part-time workers. Through cluster analysis, Burchell and Rubery (1989) find five labour-market segments, three of which contain women.
8 For gender-neutrality of capital, see also Phillips and Taylor (1980) who argue that:

> In principle, capitalism is the first mode of production which treats all members of society as equals . . . Capital is interested only in labour-power – of whatever sex, race or rank in society – and selects its labour-power on the purely quantitative basis of how much it can contribute to profits. How then do ghettoes of 'women's work' arise?
>
> (Phillips and Taylor, 1980, p. 80)

9 She also finds that employment places and conditions depend on a variety of factors. See also Hartmann (1987b).
10 See also Walby (1988a, p. 23).
11 See also Walby (1986). Contrast with Delphy (1984), for whom:

> The position of women in the labour-market and the discrimination that they suffer are the result (and not the cause as certain authors would have us believe) of the marriage contract.
>
> (Delphy, 1984, p. 96)

And also contrast with the ultimate conclusion of the domestic labour debate, for which domestic and market labour are a dual, articulated burden.
12 There is a parallel history that searches further back in the past for

the origins of patriarchy itself (and not just for its division of labour). Whilst apparently originating with Engels' associating it with control over private property, many justifiably see this as a worthless exercise: see Connell (1987) and Mitchell (1975, p. 365). See also Lerner (1986) and Coontz and Henderson (1986).

13 For the implications of capitalism for the family in this light, see Seccombe (1986) and Zaretsky (1976) and, for a critique, Folbre (1980) and McDonough and Harrison (1978).

14 See also Middleton (1988) for a general historical critique of Hartmann's theory of historical exclusion and, on the sexual division of labour:

> The most striking empirical point to emerge must surely be the sheer longevity of some highly familiar features of gender stratification. Segregation and inequality in the organisation of wage labour have persisted with remarkable tenacity through profound changes in the wider social order of class and gender relations.
>
> (Middleton, 1988 p. 67)

15 Middleton (1985) strings together writers such as Clark (1919), Pinchbeck (1969), Tilly and Scott (1978), Oakley (1974a) and Zaretsky (1976) to suggest that if all were correct, then women must have experienced an uninterrupted long-term decline over many centuries in employment opportunities and even general welfare.

16 See also Clark (1919), Hill (1989a), and Earle (1989) who concludes:

> Women were expected to work for their living, in addition to their multifarious domestic duties, and indeed the low productivity and low earnings of the society made their earnings imperative if families were to survive in any comfort. In this respect, the London of Queen Anne may have been a different place from the London of Queen Victoria but, in most other respects, the working lives of women in the London of 1700 were remarkably similar to those exposed by Mayhew and the mid-Victorian censuses a century and a half later.
>
> (Earle, 1989, p. 346)

17 See also Charles (1985), Berg (1988), Hewitt (1958) and Earle (1989).

18 See also MacBride (1976).

19 See Phillips and Taylor (1980), Rose (1988), Lewis (1984) and Lown (1983) and (1990), for example.

20 For the collapse of the male union as women are introduced with mechanisation in the case of cigar manufacture, see Kessler-Harris (1982a) and Prus (1990). Haddad (1987) also observes that new technology in cigar making can lead to the displacement of women by yet other women even more poorly placed in the labour-market.

21 See Lazonick (1986), and also Valverde (1987/8) for whom male control of spinning required its reconstruction as a male trade from its previous identification with housebound female work. See also Freifeld (1986).

22 See also Coontz (1988), Brenner and Ramas (1984) and Zeitlin (1989).
23 See Jordan (1989), for example.
24 For discussion of unions pursuing equal pay for women, see, for example, Rose (1988), Cohn (1985) and Coontz (1988).
25 See Turbin (1984) and Coontz (1988).
26 See Kessler-Harris (1982a), Lehrer (1985) and Harrison (1990) who notes:

> in textiles, for example, the mills simply worked the hours laid down for women.
>
> (Harrison, 1990, p. 89)

27 In a critique of Brenner and Ramas, Lewis (1985) attempts to sustain the otherwise limited impact of exclusionism by seeing it as a cumulative part of an ensemble of other factors.
28 See Kessler-Harris (1982a, p. 112) and Walsh (1989), the latter compiling a general bibliographical essay on working women in the United States.
29 Zeitlin (1989) observes that most theories of female labour-market exclusion do not rely upon material factors alone but complement them with ideological considerations.
30 See Jordan (1989) for strong support for this view.
31 For Lown:

> The Married Women's Property Bill . . . served, however, to highlight a realm of subordination which, though differently experienced, was common to women of divergent social and economic positions. It encouraged a political alliance which altered the traditional demeanour of philanthropic activity. There were continuing tensions in these cross-class contacts since middle-class feminists were affected by a world view bestowing on them a sense of superior social status in the Victorian hierarchy.
>
> (Lown, 1990, pp. 190–1)

See also Perkin (1989) and Hill (1989a and b).
32 Although Higgs (1986) estimates that as many as one-third of domestic servants may have had some kin relationship to the household members for whom they worked. See also Higgs (1987).
33 Silverstone (1976) pointedly observes that in 1851 42 per cent of women in Britain between the ages of 20 and 40 were spinsters. There were nearly two and a half million spinsters over the age of 15 in 1866, nearly half a million in London alone.
34 For a critique of the division between gender and job models in sociology see, for example, Beechey (1987, pp. 15–16), Feldberg and Glenn (1984), Dex (1985) and Jenson (1988).
35 See also Wajcman (1981). Similar considerations apply to work orientation. Because the work of Goldthorpe *et al.* emphasised the external family orientation of men, some consideration had to be given to the effect of women on men's orientation. Dex (1985) argues that:

very little, if any consideration had been given since Goldthorpe *et al.* to the potential or actual role that women might
play on men's orientation formation.

(Dex, 1985, p. 36)

This has obviously changed with analysis of sex-stereotyping in work.

36 See Mallier and Rosser (1987), for example.
37 See also the critique of Beechey (1987) by Anthias (1980). The latter
   is in turn criticised by Power (1983) for neglecting the trend to
   displace domestic by capitalist production and for lumping all domestic production into a set of undifferentiated tasks. Empirically, the
   notion that women constitute a reserve army has been challenged by
   Milkman (1972), Bruegel (1979) and, implicitly, by Joshi (1984) by
   looking at the effects of recession on women's employment (to see if
   they are first out, as it were). See also Owen and Joshi (1987).
38 See Cockburn (1986) and Knights and Willmott (eds) (1986).
39 For critical assessments of Braverman, see Wood (ed.) (1982).
40 On the social construction of gendered skills, see Phillips and Taylor
   (1980).
41 See also Appelbaum (1987), and Baran and Teegarden (1987) for
   whom computerisation of insurance can lead to added functions and
   responsibilities for women operating machines – because of their
   dealing, for example, with claims.
42 See also Beechey (1987, p. 163) who points to the importance of the
   extension of domestic labour into paid work. Pinchbeck (1969, p. 148)
   explains women's loss of cotton spinning to men, with the introduction of the mule after 1788, in terms of the required strength of men.
   Yet women can acquire that strength when it is necessary. As Pinchbeck describes, women were:

   drawn into agriculture during the Napoleonic Wars [for which
   one in six males were absent] including heavy work from which
   they were displaced subsequently.

   (Pinchbeck, 1969, pp. 62–3)

   Exactly the same considerations apply to the use of women's work
   during the two world wars. On women's employment in the wars, see
   Summerfield (1984), Braybon (1989) and Braybon and Summerfield
   (1987).
43 See Arnold and Faulkner (1985), and Griffiths (1985) for whom the
   industrial revolution through exclusion of women from work and
   from property ownership, was effective in gendering technology.
44 See also Osterud (1989) for this in the context of Leicestershire
   hosiery and Lancashire cotton, if not for London tailoring. See also
   Osterud (1986).
45 Most important is the idea that women are unsuitable for combat.
46 This leads Enloe (1980) to see women as a potential reserve army of
   army labour.
47 Racism has also been important. As Williams notes:

> Black nurses were allowed to work only on all-black wards in hospitals with a sufficient number of blacks to warrant having a separate ward. Black female nurses were also used to tend German prisoners of war during the war, but *not* white American soldiers.
>
> (Williams, 1989, p. 38)

48 It is uncertain to what extent this depends upon the erosion of the glamour of being a stewardess as the clichéd dream of every little girl, as opposed to the extent to which the mystique of travel has been eroded, together with sexist attitudes and the creation of broader job opportunities for women.

49 See Hacker (1989) and (1990).

50 See especially Cockburn (1983) and (1985), and also Game and Pringle (1984).

51 See Griffin (1984).

52 See also Bridges (1980).

53 Joseph (1983) reports on uncertain results for the UK, but the evidence points to a lower level of men's wages when they work in sectors where women are heavily concentrated.

54 Cohn (1985) suggests that, apart from the usual complaints about toilets, sexual hanky panky, etc.:

> Managers in the Great Western Railway and the Post Office certainly perceived women as being sickly, physically frail, and incapable of performing tasks requiring intellectual sophistication or training.
>
> (Cohn, 1985, p. 37)

For a review of theories of women's employment with some emphasis on the neglect of management strategy and behaviour, see Collinson *et al.* (1990).

55 See also Davies (1982), Anderson (1988), Dohrn (1988), and Holcombe (1973) who notes:

> One device which the government adopted to keep down wages was the 'downgrading' of clerical work, that is, the introduction of new grades of workers to perform at lower pay some of the duties of higher grades.
>
> (Holcombe, 1973, p. 173)

56 Berk and Berk (1983) argue that the emergence of the neoclassical household economics is in part a response to the vacuum created by the over-abstract treatment of the family by sociology.

57 The obsession with exclusive reliance on the assumptions of neoclassical economics is indicated by Becker's 'rotten kid theorem' which is a defence of the analysis' dependence upon absence of conflict within the household. It argues that with a head of household who is altruistic and a child who is selfish the household will still exhibit optimal behaviour. See McCrate (1987).

58 Fuchs has the strongest of beliefs in the commitment to children as the explanation of women's economic inequality:

> It is not employers who cause the wages of married women relative to those of unmarried women to fall 20 percent as the women age from 25 to 40. It is not employers who cause the wages of mothers in their thirties to lag (relative to childless women). It is not employers . . . Discrimination against women undoubtedly persists, not only in the labor market but in most economic and social institutions. But the biggest source of women's economic disadvantage – namely, their greater desire for and concern about children – is more fundamental, though it is impossible to say how much results from 'nature' and how much from 'nurture'.
>
> (Fuchs, 1988, p. 140)

59 See also Ermisch *et al.* (1990), Ermisch and Wright (1988), Wright and Ermisch (1990) and Moss (1988/89).
60 See also the debate with Polachek: England (1985) and Polachek (1985a and b), and Beller (1982).
61 As quoted in O'Neill (1985, p. 71).
62 For Miller:

> Future anti-discrimination legislation should be directed more at promoting equal pay within occupations than at promoting a more equal distribution of the sexes across the various occupations.
>
> (Miller, 1987, p. 894)

But he concludes:

> The depreciation effect associated with non-participation accounts for the major part of both the gender wage gap and the disparate occupational distributions of male and females. To the extent that this reflects a true productivity differential, further erosion of sex differentials in the labour-market may be difficult without a simultaneous revamping of traditional family roles.
>
> (Miller, 1987, p. 894)

See also Reilly (1991), Kidd (1990) and Dolton and Kidd (1990) and the debate between Borooah and Lee (1988) and Zabalza and Tzannatos (1988). Elliott and Murphy (1987) find that comparisons between men and women's pay have to be calculated carefully to take account of hours and age but also that movements for each are different as between the public and the private sector.
63 Jacobs (1989a) reports a survey of empirical estimates by Elaine Sorenson which finds for them that the wage gap due to occupational segregation ranges between 9 per cent and 38 per cent of the residual (averaging 25 per cent) but concludes that even small changes in occupational segregation may lead to major changes overall.
64 It is important to recognise that fringe benefits also make a major

difference in men's and women's working conditions. Perman and Stevens, for example, find that:

> The magnitude of the gender gap in health insurance coverage was mainly produced by the distribution of men and women across different industries. Industrial segregation influenced the gap in two ways. First, a large proportion of US women workers were employed in industries with a large gap *between* men and women workers. Second, women were overrepresented in industries where all types of workers were less likely to receive health insurance.
>
> (Perman and Stevens, 1989, p. 401)

See also Even and MacPherson (1990).

65 Shelton and Firestone (1989) find that household labour time spent by women appears to reduce their wage rate after correcting for other factors. Coverman (1983) finds this for men and for women, especially for high paid women. For graduates, Dolton and Makepeace find that:

> Female participation is conditioned by marital status and the presence of a child, and that earnings, given participation, are not affected by the presence of a child ... men's earnings are not influenced by the presence of a child ... residual earnings differentials indicate that being married affects male earnings favourably by up to 5.8% and female earnings unfavourably by up to 4%.
>
> (Dolton and Makepeace, 1987, pp. 919–20)

Coverman also finds that an egalitarian sex-role ideology on the part of men does not mean that they do more housework – more the opposite:

> Neither attitude change nor socioeconomic status will alter the domestic division of labor. Rather ... younger men who have children, employed spouses and jobs that do not require long hours of work are most likely to be involved in housework and child care activities.
>
> (Coverman, 1985, p. 94)

66 See also Beggs and Chapman (1988).

67 See also Joshi and Owen (1988) and Joshi and Overton (1988). Gomulka and Stern (1990) examine married women's labour-market participation by a time-series of cross-sections. Their estimates from a human capital model find that over time the coefficients on their variables explain more change than the changes in the variables themselves (which implies that little has been explained:

> A large part of the rise in participation over the 1970s would not have been forecast on the basis of the precise knowledge of how the characteristics of the population were changing

together with standard participation models using data for the early years.

(Gomulka and Stern, 1990, p. 193)

68 See also Maconachie's (1989) study for South Africa:

> A central constraint on white married women's employment was found to be the responsibility for the care of their children, particularly younger children . . . wives were most likely to be employed on a full-time basis if they had either no or limited child-care obligations, or if their husband's incomes were relatively low and they had access to domestic help. They were least likely to be employed when they were mothers of young children and their husbands earned a high income.
>
> (Maconachie. 1989, p. 143)

CHAPTER 3 GENDER AND ACCESS TO THE MEANS OF PRODUCTION

1 On internal labour-markets, see Ford *et al.* (1984) and, on 'gatekeeping', see Borman and Frankel (1987). See also Curran (1988) and Crompton and Jones (1984).
2 See Robinson and McIlwee (1989) for the case of engineering.
3 Jacobs (1989b), somewhat perversely, sees his approach as compatible with neoclassical economics (p. 184) but incompatible with labour-market segmentation theory:

> Both the internal labor market thesis and the segregation as segmentation thesis hinge on the infrequency of mobility between male-dominated and female-dominated occupations.
>
> (Jacobs, 1989b, p. 165)

4 For consideration of the current state of homeworking in Britain, see Hakim (1987).
5 See Land (1980) and Barrett and McIntosh (1980).
6 Land (1980) quotes Eleanor Rathbone's argument against the family wage:

> Provision would be made for over 16 million phantom children in the families containing less than three children, while those in excess of that number, over one and a quarter million in all in families containing more than three children, would still remain unprovided for.
>
> (Land, 1980, p. 62)

The preference is for a system of family allowances, on the struggle for which, see MacNicol (1980).

7 The breakdown of the nuclear family seems to have gone furthest in Sweden, see Popenoe (1987).
8 See also Fagnani (1990) and Pickup (1984) and (1988), but Madden

and Chiu (1990) find that distance travelled to work does not affect wages.

9 See also Leopold (1989, p. 1) who finds that: 'wage poverty among women is linked to lack of mobility in housing'.

10 This suggests, paradoxically, that the domestic labour debate's emphasis on the duality of domestic and waged work emerges just as this is becoming of decreasing causal significance for women's labour-market position.

11 Hence there is a literature also now emerging around geography and gender, not just in response to the presence of the women's movement in this academic discipline but also because of the increasing importance of female employment. See Little *et al.* (1988), Halford (1989) and Bowlby *et al.* (1986), for example.

12 For Thompson:

> Many early Victorians supposed that they were witnessing a 'crisis of the family' that threatened, unless successfully tackled and resolved, to undermine the entire fabric of society and to sweep the nation into turbulent, uncharted, and perilous times of chaos and anarchy.
>
> (Thompson, 1988, p. 85)

13 It is also imperative to recognise differences in the family system as between different classes and strata in society.

14 For a fuller discussion of the periodisation of capitalism, see Fine and Harris (1979).

15 See Wrigley (1969) and Wrigley and Schofield (1981).

16 For a similar periodisation, see MacBride (1977) and Lopata *et al.* (1986).

17 See also Seccombe (1980a, 1980b and 1986).

18 Methodologically, Seccombe's is closest to the analysis offered here, but there are two major differences. He tends to translate empirical developments into the categories of Marxist theory without explaining the history involved, and he relies too much on an archetypal family.

19 See also Wandersee (1981). This approach also has its counterpart in regulation theory. For a critique of the theoretical and empirical basis for the existence of a Fordist consumer revolution in the inter-war period, see Mavroudeas (1990) and Brenner and Glick (1991).

20 For a periodisation of feudalism according to the forms taken by rent, see Volume III of Marx's *Capital*. For a discussion of this see, for example, Fine and Harris (1979).

21 For Hill:

> The process of transformation and almost complete undermining of the family economy has extended over a long period of time, starting in the sixteenth century and, in areas of Ireland and Wales, still not completed today. All one can say with confidence is that the undermining had gone further in 1750

than 1700, and further still in 1800. In some areas transformation was rapid, in others extremely slow.

(Hill, 1989a, p. 47)

22 Thompson observes:

Mechanisation of one sector or process in an industry, and its
move into the factory, could well generate increased demand
for handwork and outwork in other sectors.

(Thompson, 1988, p. 31)

23 See also Folbre (1980), Matthaei (1982), Power (1983), Jensen (1980)
and Branca (1978, p 32) who estimates that as many as a third of the
women in the urban working class took in lodgers to supplement the
family income. See also Kessler-Harris (1982b), van Horn (1988) and
Walsh (1989). For Roberts, in England:

The most usual kind of lodger was in fact a relative who might
or might not, depending on age, health and job, have paid for
lodgings.

(Roberts, 1988, p. 17)

The pressure for lodgings through urbanisation is indicated by the
growth of population in large towns outside London, their numbers
growing from one to nine million between 1831 and 1901. London
itself increased its share of the British population from 11.5 per cent
to 17.8 per cent, Thompson (1988, p. 29).

24 See Harrison (1989) and Kessler-Harris (1982b).
25 Branca reckons that:

the upper servants combined, male and female, were vastly
outnumbered by the lowly general servants, who comprised
two-thirds of all servants in France, three quarters in England.

(Branca, 1978, p. 36)

26 For a discussion of this in the context of the eighteenth century, see
Fine and Leopold (1990).
27 See also Hill (1989a, p. 119).
28 See also Hewitt (1958).
29 See Kessler-Harris (1982a, p. 58) and (1982b, pp. 69–70). Thompson
(1988, p. 257) reports estimates of the number of prostitutes in
London in 1850 as lying between 8,000 (as recorded with the police)
and 80,000 (by Mayhew's survey). For 1806, Hill (1989a, p. 171)
suggests a figure of 10,000.
30 None the less, 'most female factory workers were young and single:
in 1841 in England fifty percent were under twenty years of age'
(Branca, 1978, p. 41).
31 For female surface workers in the nineteenth century coal industry,
see John (1984).
32 See also Minge (1986).
33 For a review of theories of the western family under the four catego-

ries of psychohistory, demography, sentiments, and household economics, see Anderson (1980).

34 The idea that the working class picked up limitation of family size from the example of the middle classes seems to be the opposite of the truth. The idea that women should not take waged work formed a pillar of the ideology of working-class respectability. Middle-class women could hardly go out to work, despite their superior qualifications and earning power, when it was not respectable for those beneath them to do so. Hence, work for middle-class women took the form of activity in charity organisations. Once working-class women were entering waged labour, welfare work became a paid profession and the highly educated have caught up in recent years in labour-market participation rates. For the role of middle-class women in providing the unpaid functionaries of the welfare state around the turn of the century, see Summers (1979).

35 One customary way of controlling fertility has been through late marriage. It has also been customary to marry where control has failed. Thus, the modern rise in the illegitimacy rate. As Anderson notes:

> A period of stabilising small-family size suggests not so much a rise in frequency of unmarried sexual intercourse, for the level of bridal pregnancy was already high, but the abandonment of the shotgun wedding.
>
> (Anderson, 1980, p. 75)

36 For a general review of demographic change in Europe, see Coale and Watkins (1986). For the US, in the context of female employment, see Goldin (1990). For an argument based on the continuing significance of economic rationality, but in which wealth flows from children to parents are reversed, see Caldwell (1982), for whom:

> The transition from familial to capitalist production is a process rather than a sudden change. What is formed first and is sustained for long periods of time is a two-tiered system in which the two forms of economies co-exist.
>
> (Caldwell, 1982, p. 173)

For a further variety of arguments, see also Haines (1989), Woods (1989), Greenhalgh (1990), Hill (1989a), Crafts (1989), England and Farkas (1986) and Folbre (1983).

37 For this in the context of the development of the welfare state, see Wilson (1977, pp. 15–17). For Minge:

> Since the beginning of the concern with education, children have subtly but rapidly developed into a labor-intensive, capital-intensive product of the family in industrial society.
>
> (Minge, 1986, p. 24)

38 See also Schofield (1986) who reckons that maternal death rates from childbirth itself were no lower in the 1930s than in the middle of the previous century – and forty to fifty times greater than today. Even

so, the rate was low in the sense of impressing itself as a general experience – no greater than the chances today of a child dying before the age of seven.

39 See also Chinn (1988) for a discussion of the importance of women's work and family income for the height and weight of infants. McDougall (1977, p. 274) reports 68.8 per cent lost children for a sample of working mothers in Bradford in 1870, and 55.5 per cent for a sample of those working in the smaller London trades, even in the early twentieth century. However, there is little evidence to suggest that mothers working as such was a cause of higher infant mortality.

40 See, for example, Barnsby (1971) and Roberts (1977) for the effects of unemployment on the standard of living during the nineteenth century.

41 On homeworking, in particular, see Pennington and Westover (1989).

42 See Power (1983, p. 79) who, slightly differently, also draws the distinction between home production and home consumption, doing so both conceptually and historically by reference to home production and home maintenance.

43 For details, see Joseph (1983), for example. There was no census for 1941 which, unfortunately, makes indistinguishable the separate contribution of each of the two decades to the changes involved.

44 Tilly and Scott (1978) report on posts and telecommunications in France, for which:

> In 1892 only 205 men had applied for 1,151 positions. In contrast, after 1892 the Postal Administration reported as many as 5,000 female applicants for some 200 positions. The situation in England was similar. There the post office doubled its workforce between 1891 and 1914 and by the latter date became the largest single employer . . . in the country of female white collar workers.
>
> (Tilly and Scott, 1978, p. 158)

45 See Glucksmann (1986). She notes that:

> So, although the proportion of women working was relatively low overall, women accounted for around 27 percent to 29 percent of the total workforce and for far more in those industries and occupations where women were concentrated. Even looking in very general terms, women accounted for 43 percent of all semi-skilled manual workers and 37.5 percent of all factory operatives between 1924 and 1935.
>
> (Glucksmann, 1986, pp. 21–2)

46 See Mincer (1985) who summarises the evidence as suggesting an elasticity of unity for the substitution effect (work for household time) of women's wages and an income elasticity on husband's wages of minus 0.4.

47 This has not been monotonic given the baby boom of the 1950s and

1960s in most advanced countries. For some discussion of this, see Teitelbaum and Winter (1985), Mallier and Rosser (1987), England and Farkas (1986), Goldin (1990) and Van Horn (1988).

48 This is a crude summary of a number of different interacting trends. Liberalised life-styles, for example, have led couples to live together out of marriage. Marriage came later in the UK in the 1970s. Older married women are tending more to full-time work, etc. And, as female employment opportunities have opened up, the trend to earlier marriage and childbearing can be reversed to some extent in deference to most advantageous timing of career breaks to have children.

49 In orthodox terms, even this greater increase of middle-class married women tends to underestimate the substitution effect over the income effect, since such women tend to marry men in higher paid and more secure jobs which ought to act as a greater discouragement to work. This relatively greater participation of the middle class, with presumed higher educational attainment, will also tend to bias upward any simple measure of the female–male wage ratio.

50 See Matthaei (1982, p. 322) and Nazzari (1980), for example.

51 See Brown (1981) who argues that men no longer value their children and that the advantage of women's domestic labour has been devalued by the rise of convenience products.

52 Interestingly, Gittins (1982, p. 48) notes another effect of housing, with the accommodation size of council house provision limiting family size.

53 See especially Showstack Sassoon (ed.) (1987).

54 See Bittman and Bryson (1989, p. 42) who point to a 'trinity of state policy, a capitalist labour-market as well as particular forms of the family'.

55 Even where these effects are taken into account, they can pose irreconcilable objectives. Consider family taxation for example. If the wife receives no allowance, this constitutes a tax on marriage, which is ideologically frowned upon, or a disincentive for her to work to the extent that the husband receives a married man's allowance. If the wife does receive a single person's allowance, this is a high subsidy to the family with two working adults and a tax on motherhood as a full-time occupation. Family allowances encourage children and discourage work, etc. All of this is the conflict over less eligibility and family allowances reproduced atthe stage of state monopoly capitalism.

CHAPTER 4 WOMEN AND THE BRITISH LABOUR-MARKET

1 These propositions are discussed in detail with case studies in Fine and Harris (1985).

2 For a recent account of de-industrialisation, see Rowthorn and Wells (1987).

3 For a detailed study of UK part-time employment, see Wallace (1985). For experience from different countries, see Jenson *et al.* (eds) (1988).
4 As Wallace observes, however:

> As employment of any kind other than for a regular full-time working week was ignored by statisticians until at least 1951, it is hardly surprising that part-time employment has been neglected in labour-market literature . . . There has to date been no attempt to place the growth of part-time employment in an historical context, except as a function of female labour supply, nor has there been an adequate recognition of its significance in recent theoretical studies of labour-market behaviour.
>
> (Wallace, 1985, pp. 412–13)

5 See Atkinson (1984) on flexibility and Pollert (1988) for a critique.
6 See Robinson (1988), Dale and Bamford (1988b), Bakker (1988) and Harrison and Bluestone (1990, p. 356).
7 See Phipps (1990) for the idea that women are being polarised in the labour-market between careered and careerless employment.
8 Joshi (1987) estimates the effects of such factors on women's labour-market participation and the overall cost in terms of wages forgone over a lifetime.
9 See also Crompton *et al.* (1990) and Beechey (1989) for comparison of UK and French female employment.
10 The papers in Epstein *et al.* (1986) also point to a number of cultural and ideological factors which induce greater labour-market commitment amongst female workers in West Germany. Epstein's own paper (in Epstein *et al.* (eds), 1986) has harder evidence in terms of educational achievement, with 77 per cent of men and 62 per cent of women in West Germany holding an occupational qualification. For 16–18-year-olds, 19 per cent of males and 13 per cent of females were attending occupational courses.
11 Brannen (1987, p. 164) suggests that, in the UK, women continuing to work through childbearing is seen as a 'deviant course of action'. Moss (1988) points to the extremely poor level of childcare provision in the UK as compared to the rest of the EEC. For Sweden, by comparison, see Sandquist (1987).
12 See Beechey and Perkins (1987) for the idea that part-time work is a source of cheap labour rather than a response to labour shortages. Montgomery (1988) also finds that part-time workers are more liable to be found in small-scale establishments in private industry, these are usually associated with lower wages and conditions. See also Leopold (1989).
13 See also Bird and West (1987, p. 182) and Wallace (1985) who notes that:

> The utilisation of female part-time labour has therefore provided the mechanism for redistributing labour resources along the lines to be expected in an advanced industrial economy.

14 See also Dex and Shaw (1988) and Dex and Walters (1989) for a three-way comparison between the US, UK and France where many of the conclusions reported here are confirmed.

15 Elias (1988) links downward mobility in employment to return to part-time work after break for childbirth. He also finds under-usage of qualifications in female workers in the age group of 25–29 years, the peak period for family formation. On women's presumed loss of work experience over childbirth, see Dey (1989), Bird and West (1987, p. 190) and Select Committee (1982). Gallie (1988) argues that in the 1980s there has been an increasing gap between skills in the UK, with women being particularly further disadvantaged. Horrell *et al.* (1988 and 1989) find that it is the undervaluation of women's skills in work rather than their lack of them which is the major source of pay inequality.

16 See also Wilson (1977) and Cohen (1988) who also quotes from Beveridge:

> The great majority of women must be regarded as occupied in work which is vital though unpaid, without which their husbands could not do their paid work and without which the nation could not continue.
>
> (Cohen, 1988, p. 4)

17 For some discussion of the state as employer, see Wills *et al.* (1987) and Brackman *et al.* (1988).

18 This is other than for single mothers who receive higher benefits without working.

19 See Marx's letter to Kugelmann of 11 July 1868. Marx writes:

> Every child knows that a country which ceased to work, I will not say for a year, but for a few weeks, would die . . .

APPENDIX REVIEWING THE DOMESTIC LABOUR DEBATE

1 Those that argue that domestic labour does not produce value include Scott (1984), Himmelweit and Mohun (1977), Coulson *et al.* (1975), Carter (1975), Adamson *et al.* (1976), Briskin (1980), Benston (1969), Fee (1976), Smith (1978), Holstrom (1981) and Molyneux (1979). Those that consider it produces value and, for some, surplus value include Smith (1984), Evers (1984), Gerstein (1973), Blumenfeld and Mann (1980), Delphy (1984), Dalla Costa and James (1972) and Seccombe (1974, 1975 and 1980b).

2 Harrison accordingly relies upon a restricted, as opposed to an extended, notion of the mode of production as defined by Wolpe (1980) – for which the relations of production alone are specified without any further specification of the mode of production at the economic or other levels.

3 It is also possible that the two types of labour be commensurate but not equal in the sense that one counts more than the other.

4 For a review of this debate and a critical stance to the one adopted by Gough and Harrison, see Fine and Harris (1979).

5 See Fine and Harris (1979), Elson (1979) and Steadman *et al.* (1981).

6 This is made explicit in Rowthorn's (1974) equivalent model for educating workers with embodied teaching labour – to which Gough and Harrison refer approvingly.

7 See Himmelweit and Mohun (1977) who refer to:

> the attempt to draw an analogy of the role of capital in relation to domestic labour to its role with respect to pre-industrial modes of production in an imperialist world.
> (Himmelweit and Mohun, 1977, p. 21)

and to:

> a model of unequal exchange, first, between capitalist and worker, over the purchase of labour-power and second, between husband and wife, over the exchange of her labour-time for part of the commodities bought with his wage.
> (Himmelweit and Mohun, 1977, p. 24)

Note that Nazzari (1980) treats the crisis of marriage as progressive by analogy with the dissolution of feudalism and a parallel proletarianisation of housewives.

8 To anticipate, such is the criticism of Seccombe by Fox (1980a). Becker (1981) is the classic statement of household economics from the neoclassical stable. For some assessments of it, see Berk and Berk (1983), Brown (1982), McCrate (1987), Walby (1988b), Feiner and Roberts (1990), Gwartney-Gibbs (1988), Korneman and Neumark (1989), England and Farkas (1986) and Cass and Whiteford (1989). In a critique of Becker and Barro (1986), David (1986, p. 78) points to significant problems in their approach to altruism within the family.

9 Gardiner also tempers these processes according to the differing interests of competing sectors of capital.

10 There has been a minor controversy over the spelling of Seccombe with, the first c frequently missing or replaced by an a.

11 This is not to deny the possible existence of norms of consumption within the household, and even of accepted levels of income for wives to handle (out of their husband's pay packet) – see Pahl (1984); only that such norms are not produced by standardised quantities of domestic labour and hence also unit rewards for wives.

12 See also Seccombe (1980b, p. 261):

> The impact of the law of value upon domestic labour is very much weaker than its impact upon capitalist labour processes. It runs up against an imposing principle of labour organization, based upon the direct use of domestic labour to proletarians themselves. Its *domination* of this antagonistic logic is a relative one, therefore. In the very way in which the

housewife organizes her labour time and manages the household, both principles can be seen to operate. But, ultimately, the law of value dominates. This is because the *sine qua non* of proletarian subsistence remains the capacity to sell labour power on a competitive basis to employers who find it useful for their purposes in capitalist production. Domestic labour in the private household *must* bow to this exchange value imperative.

13 See also Carter (1975), Coulson *et al.* (1975), Himmelweit and Mohun (1977), Morton (1972), Seccombe (1980a), Curtis (1980) and Rowntree and Rowntree (1970).

14 See also Himmelweit (1983), Oakley (1974a), Jamrozik (1989), Close (1989) and Quick (1972).

15 See especially, Himmelweit and Mohun (1977).

16 The dual labour role of women was hardly discovered by the domestic debate, its tensions having already having been explored by Parsonian sociology (for a critique of which, see Beechey (1978)). See also Young and Willmott (1973) and Myrdal and Klein (1956).

17 It is significant that the literature on housework itself, from a historical and empirical point of view, has been neglected by the domestic labour debate – even though the two were simultaneously inspired for the same reasons at the same time. See Oakley (1974a and b) and Lopata (1971).

18 Significantly, Glazer (1984) puts forward a theory of four different types of labour structurally burdening women, adding to domestic and wage labour that which is imposed by private capital in shifting costs of purchasing to the shopper, and that which is imposed by the state in shifting care to the home. Close (1989) separates out care, and Finch (1983) the labour of supporting a husband in his (professional) work. See also Himmelweit (1984a) and Holstrom (1981).

19 See Cowan (1983a and b), Ironmonger (1989), Rothschild (1983) and Arnold and Burr (1985). The latter emphasises how important it is to recognise the commodifications of housework that were *not* taken up.

20 She also recognises that there may be shifts of the burden of domestic labour from males to females through commodification. This is related to the gendering of domestic labour, on which see Close and Collins (1983), Rothschild (1983), Close (1989), Coltrane (1989) and, in the context of socialisation through child labour in the home, White and Brinkerhoff (1981a and b) and Goodnow (1988).

21 For the importance of the household as a source of income, especially in the literature on the United States at the turn of the century, see Folbre (1980), Hareven (1982) and (1991), Jensen (1980), Ehrenreich and English (1978), van Horn (1988), Brenner and Ramas (1984), Kessler-Harris and Sacks (1987) and Fox (1990).

22 See Young (1978), Mackintosh (1979), Babb (1984), Mies (1986), Folbre (1986), Smith *et al.* (eds) (1984) and Deere (1976), for example.

23 Thus, it is necessary to draw a distinction between family, household and kin. See Creighton (1985), Coontz (1988), Harris (1983) and

Yanagisako (1979). See also Hareven (1991) and the special issue of *Social Research* (on the home) in which Hareven's article is included.

24 See Williams (1988), Duchen (1989), Jamrozik (1989), Goodnow (1989), Curtis (1980), Ironmonger (1989), Ironmonger and Sonius (1989) and Close and Collins (1983, p. 34) for whom the domestic labour debate has not succeeded in exploring 'empirical connections between the capitalist mode of production and gender relations which operate by way of the practice of domestic labour'.

25 See Fine and Leopold (1992) for a wide-ranging discussion of modes or systems of consumption.

26 These issues were taken up in Chapter 4.

27 For those who argue that domestic labour can cheapen the value of labour power, see Friedman (1984), Fox (1980b), Holstrom (1981), Smith (1984) and Beechey (1987).

REFERENCES

Abrams, P. *et al.* (eds) (1981) *Practice and Progress: British Sociology, 1950–1980*, London: George Allen & Unwin.

Adams, C. and Winston, K. (1980) *Mothers at Work: Public Policies in the United States, Sweden and China*, New York: Longman.

Adamson, O. *et al.* (1976) 'Women's oppression under capitalism', *Revolutionary Communist*, no 5, Nov, pp. 1–48.

Alexander, S. and Taylor, B. (1981) 'In defence of "patriarchy"', in Samuel (ed.) (1981).

Allatt, P. *et al.* (eds) (1987) *Women and the Life Cycle: Transitions and Turning Points*, Basingstoke: Macmillan.

Amin, S. (1974) *Accumulation on a World Scale: A Critique of the Theory of Underdevelopment*, New York: Monthly Review Press.

—— (1978) *The Law of Value and Historical Materialism*, New York: Monthly Review Press.

Amsden, A. (ed.) (1980) *The Economics of Women and Work*, Harmondsworth: Penguin.

Anderson, G. (1988) 'The white-blouse revolution', in Anderson (ed.) (1988).

—— (ed.) (1988) *The White-Blouse Revolution: Female Office Workers since 1870*, Manchester: Manchester University Press.

Anderson, M. (1980) *Approaches to the History of the Western Family*, London: Macmillan.

Anthias, F. (1980) 'Women and the reserve army of labour: a critique of Veronica Beechey', *Capital and Class*, no 10, Spring, pp. 50–63.

Appelbaum, E. (1987) 'Technology and the redesign of work in the insurance industry', in Wright *et al.* (eds) (1987).

Aries, P. (1962) *Centuries of Childhood: A Social History of Family Life*, New York: Alfred A. Knopf.

Arnold, E. and Burr, L. (1985) 'Housework and the appliance of science', in Faulkner and Arnold (eds) (1985).

Arnold, E. and Faulkner, W. (1985) 'Smothered by invention: the masculinity of technology', in Faulkner and Arnold (eds) (1985).

Atkinson, J. (1984) *Flexibility, Uncertainty and Manpower Management*, IMS Report no 89, Brighton: Institute of Manpower Studies.

213

Babb, F. (1984) 'Women in the marketplace: petty commerce in Peru', *Review of Radical Political Economics*, vol 16, no 1, Spring, pp. 45–59.

Bakker, I. (1988) 'Women's employment in comparative perspective', in Jensen *et al.* (eds) (1988).

Ball, M. (1983) *Housing Policy and Economic Power: The Political Economy of Owner Occupation*, London: Methuen.

Banks, J. (1954) *Prosperity and Parenthood*, London: Routledge & Kegan Paul.

Baran, B. and Teegarden, S. (1987) 'Women's labor in the office of the future: a case study of the insurance industry', in Beneria and Stimpson (eds) (1987).

Barker, D. and Allen, S. (eds) (1976) *Dependence and Exploitation in Work and Marriage*, London: Longman.

Barker, T. and Drake, M. (eds) (1980) *Population and Society in Britain 1850–1980*, London: Batsford Academic.

Barnsby, G. (1971) 'The standard of living in the Black Country during the nineteenth century', *Economic History Review*, vol XXIV, no 2, pp. 220–39.

Baron, A. (1987) 'Contested terrain revisited: technology and gender definitions of work in the printing industry, 1850–1920', in Wright *et al.* (eds) (1987).

Barrett, M. (1980) *Women's Oppression Today: Problems in Marxist Feminist Analysis*, London: Verso.

—— (1984) 'Rethinking women's oppression: a reply to Brenner and Ramas', *New Left Review*, no 146, Jul/Aug, pp. 123–8.

—— and McIntosh, M.(1979) 'Christine Delphy: towards a materialist feminism', *Feminist Review*, no 1, pp. 95–106.

—— (1980) 'The "family wage": some problems for socialists and feminists', *Capital and Class*, no 11, Summer, pp. 51–72.

Barron, R. and G. Norris (1976) 'Sexual divisions and the dual labour market', in Barker and Allen (eds) (1976).

Becker, G. (1981) *A Treatise on the Family*, Cambridge: Harvard University Press.

—— and Barron, R. (1986) 'Altruism and the economic theory of fertility', *Population and Development Review*, vol 12, Supplement, pp. 69–76.

Beechey, V. (1978) 'Women and production: a critical analysis of some sociological theories of women's work', in Kuhn and Wolpe (eds) (1978).

—— (1987) *Unequal Work*, London: Verso.

—— (1988) 'Rethinking the definition of work: gender and work', in Jensen *et al.* (eds) (1988).

—— (1989) 'Women's employment in France and Britain: some problems of comparison', *Work, Employment and Society*, vol 3, no 3, Sept, pp. 369–78.

—— and Perkins, T. (1987) *A Matter of Hours: Women, Part-Time Work and the Labour Market*, London: Polity Press.

Beggs, J. and Chapman, B. (1988) 'The foregone earnings from child-

214

rearing in Australia', *Centre for Economic Policy Research*, Australian National University, Discussion Paper, no 190.

Beller, A. (1982) 'Occupational segregation by sex: determinants and changes', *Journal of Human Resources*, vol XVII, no 3, pp. 371–92.

Beneria, L. and Stimpson, C. (eds) (1987) *Women, Households, and the Economy*, London: Rutgers University Press.

Benn, S. and Gaus, G. (eds) (1983) *Public and Private in Social Life*, London: Croom Helm.

Benston, M. (1969) 'The political economy of women's liberation', *Monthly Review*, vol 21, no 4, Sept, pp. 13–27, reproduced in Malos (ed.) (1982).

Berg, M. (1988) 'Women's work, mechanisation and the early phases of industrialisation in England', in Pahl (ed.) (1988).

Bergmann, B. (1986) *The Economic Emergence of Women*, New York: Basic Books.

Berk, R. and Berk, S. (1983) 'Supply-side sociology of the family: the challenge of the new home economics', *Annual Review of Sociology*, no 9, pp. 375–95.

Bibb, R. and Form, W. (1976/7) 'The effects of industrial, occupational and sex stratification on wages in blue-collar markets', *Social Forces*, pp. 974–96.

Bird, E. and West, J. (1987) 'Interrupted lives: study of women returners', in Allatt *et al.* (eds) (1987).

Bittman, M. and Bryson, L. (1989) 'Persistence and change in the family and gender in Australian society', in Close (ed.) (1989).

Black, C. (ed.) (1983) *Married Women's Work: Being the Report of an Enquiry Undertaken by the Women's Industrial Council*, London: Virago, original of 1915.

Blau, D. and Robins, P. (1988) 'Child-care costs and family labor supply', *Review of Economics and Statistics*, vol LXX, no 3, Aug, pp. 374–81.

Blumenfeld, E. and Mann, S. (1980) 'Domestic labour and the reproduction of labour power: towards an analysis of women, the family and class', in Fox (ed.) (1980).

Bonfield, L. *et al.* (eds) (1986) *The World We Have Gained: Histories of Population and Social Structures*, Oxford: Blackwell.

Bonney, N. (1988) 'Dual earning couples: trends of change in Great Britain', *Work, Employment and Society*, vol 2, no 1, pp. 89–102.

Borman, K. and Frankel, J. (1987) 'Gender inequalities in childhood, social life and adult work life', in Borman *et al.* (eds) (1987).

Borman, K. *et al.* (eds) (1987) *Women in the Workplace: Effects on Families*, New Jersey: Ablex Publishing Corporation.

Borooah, V. and Lee, K. (1988) 'The effect of changes in Britain's industrial structure on female relative pay and employment', *Economic Journal*, vol 98, Sept, pp. 818–32.

Bowlby, S. (1990) 'Women, work and the family: control and constraints', *Geography*, no 326, vol 76, part 1, Jan, pp. 17–26.

Bowlby, S. *et al.* (1986) 'The place of gender in locality studies', *Area*, vol 18, pp. 327–31.

Brackman, H. *et al.* (1988) 'Wedded to the welfare state: women against Reaganite retrenchment', in Jensen *et al.* (eds) (1988).

Bradley, H. (1986) 'Technical change, management strategies, and the development of gender-based job segregation in the labour process', in Knight and Willmott (eds) (1986).

Branca, P. (1978) *Women in Europe since 1750*, London: Croom Helm.

Brannen, J. (1987) 'The resumption of employment after childbirth: a turning point within a life-course perspective', in Allatt *et al.* (eds) (1987).

—— (1989) 'Childbirth and occupational mobility: evidence from a longitudinal study', *Work, Employment and Society*, vol 3, no 2, June, pp. 179–201.

Braverman, H. (1974) *Labour and Monopoly Capital: The Degradation of Work in the Twentieth Century*, New York: Monthly Review Press.

Braybon (1989) *Women Workers in the First World War: The British Experience*, London: Croom Helm.

—— and Summerfield, P. (1987) *Out of the Cage: Women's Experiences in Two World Wars*, London: Pandora.

Brenner, J. and Ramas, M. (1984) 'Rethinking women's oppression', *New Left Review*, 144, Mar/April, pp. 33–71.

Brenner, R. and Glick, M. (1991) 'The regulation school and the west's economic impasse', *New Left Review*, no 188, July/Aug, pp. 45–119.

Bridenthal, R. and Koonz, C. (eds) (1977) *Becoming Visible: Women in European History*, New York: Houghton Mifflin.

Bridges, W. (1980) 'Industry, marginality and female employment: a new appraisal', *American Sociological Review*, vol 45, no 1, pp. 58–75.

—— (1982) 'Sexual segregation of occupation: theories of labor stratification in industry', *American Journal of Sociology*, vol 88, no 2, pp. 270–95.

Briskin, L. (1980) 'Domestic labour: a methodological discussion', in Fox (ed.) (1980).

Brown, C. (1981) 'Mothers, fathers and children: from private to public patriarchy', in Sargent (ed.) (1981).

—— (1982) 'Home production for use in a market economy', in Thorne (ed.) (1982).

—— (1987) 'Consumption norms, work roles and economic growth, 1918–90', in Brown and Pechman (eds) (1987).

—— and Pechman, J. (eds) (1987) *Gender in the Workplace*, Washington, DC: Brookings.

—— and Wilcher, S. (1984) 'Sex-based employment quotas in Sweden' in Reskin (ed) (1984).

Brown, M. (ed.) (1983) *The Structure of Disadvantage*, London: Heinemann.

Bruegel, I. (1979) 'Women as a reserve army of labour: a note on recent British experience', *Feminist Review*, no 3, pp. 12–23.

Bryceson, D. and Vuorela, U. (1984) 'Outside the domestic labor debate: towards a theory of modes of human reproduction', *Review of Radical Political Economics*, vol 16, no 2/3, Summer and Fall, pp. 137–66.

Buchele, R. (1981) 'Sex discrimination and the US labour market', in Wilkinson (ed) (1981).

Buhle, M. (1989) 'Gender and labor history', in Moody and Kessler-Harris (eds) (1989).

REFERENCES

Burchell, B. and Rubery, J. (1989) 'Segmented jobs and segmented workers: an empirical investigation', *SCELI Working Papers*, no 13, Nuffield College, Oxford.

Burman, S. (ed.) (1979) *Fit Work for Women*, London: Croom Helm.

Busfeld, D. (1988) 'Skill and the sexual division of labour in the West Riding', in Jowitt and McIvor (eds) (1988).

Caldwell, J. (1982) *Theory of Fertility Decline*, London: Academic Press.

Cambridge Women's Studies Group (1981) *Women in Society: Interdisciplinary Essays*, London: Virago.

Cantor, M. and B. Laurie (eds) (1977) *Class, Sex, and the Woman Worker*, London: Greenwood Press.

Carter, M. (1975) 'Housework under capitalism', *Revolutionary Communist*, no 2, May, pp. 48–50.

Carter, V. (1987) 'Office technology and relations of control in clerical work organisation', in Wright *et al.* (eds) (1987).

Casey, J. (1989) *The History of the Family: New Perspectives on the Past*, Oxford: Blackwell.

Cass, B. and Whiteford, P. (1989) 'Income support, the labour market and the household', in Ironmonger (ed.) (1989).

Charles, L. (1985) 'Introduction', in Charles and Duffin (eds) (1985).

—— and Duffin, L. (eds) (1985) *Women and Work in Pre-Industrial England*, London: Croom Helm.

Chinn, C. (1988) *They Worked All Their Lives: Women of the Urban Poor in England, 1880–1939*, Manchester: Manchester University Press.

Chiplin, B. and Sloane, P. (1976) *Sex Discrimination in the Labour Market*, London: Macmillan.

—— (1988) 'The effect of Britain's anti-discrimination legislation on relative pay and employment: a comment', *Economic Journal*, vol 98, Sept, pp. 833–8.

Clark, A. (1919) *Working Life of Women in the Seventeenth Century*, London: Routledge.

Close, P. (1989) 'Toward an analytic framework', in Close (ed.) (1989).

—— (ed.) (1989) *Family Divisions and Inequalities in Modern Society*, London: Macmillan.

—— and Collins, R. (1983) 'Domestic labour and patriarchy: implications of a study in the north-east of England', *International Journal of Sociology and Social Policy*, vol 3, no 4, pp. 31–47.

Coale, A. and S. Watkins (eds) (1986) *The Decline of Fertility: The Revised Proceedings of a Conference on the Princeton European Fertility Project*, Princeton: Princeton University Press.

Cockburn, C. (1983) *Brothers: Male Dominance and Technological Change*, London: Pluto.

—— (1985) *Machinery of Dominance*, London: Pluto.

—— (1986) 'The relations of technology: what implications for theories of sex and class', in Crompton and Mann (eds) (1986).

—— (1988) 'The gendering of jobs: workplace relations and the reproduction of sex segregation', in Walby (ed.) (1988).

Cohen, B. (1988) *Caring for Children: Services and Policies for Childcare and*

217

Equal Opportunities in the UK, London: Commission of the European Communities.

Cohn, S. (1985) *The Process of Occupational Sex-Typing: The Feminization of Clerical Labor in Great Britain*, Pennsylvania: Temple University Press.

Collinson, D. (1987) '"Picking women": the recruitment of temporary workers in the mail order business': *Work, Economy and Society*, vol 1, no 3, Sept, pp. 371–87.

—— *et al.* (1990) *Managing to Discriminate*, London: Routledge.

Coltrane, S. (1989) 'Household labor and the routine production of gender', *Social Problems*, vol 36, no 5, Dec, pp. 473–91.

Congdon, P. (1988) 'Occupational mobility and labour market structure: a multivariate Markov model', *Scottish Journal of Political Economy*, vol 35, no 3, Aug, pp. 208–26.

Connell, R. (1987) *Gender and Power: Society, the Person and Sexual Politics*, London: Polity.

Coontz, S. (1988) *The Social Origins of Private Life: A History of American Families, 1600–1900*, London: Verso.

—— and Henderson, P. (eds) (1986) *Women's Work, Men's Property: The Origins of Gender and Class*, London: Verso.

Coulson, M. *et al.* (1975) '"The housewife and her labour under capitalism" a critique', *New Left Review*, no 89, Jan/Feb, pp. 59–71.

Coverman, S. (1983) 'Gender, domestic labor time, and wage inequality', *American Sociological Review*, vol 48, Oct, pp. 623–37.

—— (1985) 'Explaining husband's participation in domestic labor', *Sociological Quarterly*, vol 26, no 1, pp. 81–97.

Cowan, R. (1982) 'The "industrial revolution" in the home: household technology and social change in the twentieth century', in Schlereth (ed.) (1982) reproduced from *Technology and Culture*, vol 17, Jan, 1976, pp 1–23.

—— (1983a) *More Work for Mother: The Ironies of Household Technology from the Open Hearth to the Microwave*, New York: Basic Books.

—— (1983b) 'A case study of technical and social change: the working mother and the working wife', in Brown (ed.) (1983).

Coyle, A. (1982) 'Sex and skill in the organisation of the clothing industry', in West (ed.) (1982).

Crafts, N. (1984a) 'Legitimate fertility in England and Wales, 1911', *Research in Economic History*, vol 19, pp. 89–108.

—— (1984b) 'A time series study of fertility in England and Wales', *Journal of European Economic History*, vol 13, no 3, Winter, pp. 571–90.

—— (1989) 'Duration of marriage, fertility and women's employment opportunities in England and Wales in 1911', *Population Studies*, vol 43, pp. 325–35.

Craig, C. *et al.* (1984) *Payment Structures and Smaller Firms: Women's Employment in Segmented Labour Markets*, Department of Employment, Research Paper no 48.

—— (1985) 'Labour market segmentation and women's employment: a case study from the United Kingdom', *International Labour Review*, vol 124, no 3, May/June, pp. 267–80.

Craven, E. *et al.* (1982) *Family Issues and Public Policy*, Study Commission on the Family, Occasional Paper, no 7.

Creighton, C. (1985) 'The family and capitalism in Marxist theory', in Shaw (ed.) (1985).

Creighton, W. (1979) *Working Women and the Law*, London: Mansell.

Crompton, R. (1988) 'Occupational segregation', *SCELI Working Papers*, no 2, Nuffield College, Oxford.

—— (1989b) 'Women in banking: continuity and change since the Second World War', *Work, Employment and Society*, vol 3, no 2, June, pp. 141–56.

—— (1989a) 'Class theory and gender', *British Journal of Sociology*, vol 40, no 4, pp. 565–87.

—— and Jones, G. (1984) *White-Collar Proletariat: Deskilling and Gender in Clerical Work*, London: Macmillan.

—— and Mann, M. (eds) (1986) *Gender and Stratification*, London: Polity Press.

—— and K. Sanderson (1990) *Gendered Jobs and Social Change*, London: Unwin Hyman.

—— *et al.* (1990) 'Gender relations and employment', *British Journal of Sociology*, vol 41, no 3, pp. 429–49.

Curran, M. (1988) 'Gender and recruitment: people and places in the labour market', *Work, Employment and Society*, vol 2, no 3, Sept, pp. 335–51.

Curtis, B. (1980) 'Capital, the state and the origins of the working-class household', in Fox (ed.) (1980).

Dale, A. (1986) 'The role of theories of labour market segmentation in understanding the position of women in the occupational structure', Occasional Papers in Sociology and Social Policy, no 4, University of Surrey.

—— and Bamford, C. (1988a) 'Flexibility and the peripheral work-force', *Occasional Papers in Sociology and Social Policy*, no 11, University of Surrey.

—— (1988b) 'Temporary workers: cause for concern or complacency', *Work, Employment and Society*, vol 2, no 2, June, pp. 191–209.

—— and Glover, J. (1990) 'An analysis of women's employment patterns in the UK, France and the USA: the value of survey based comparisons', Research Paper no 75, London: Department of Employment.

Dalla Costa, M. and James, S. (1972) *The Power of Women and the Subversion of the Community*, Brighton: Falling Wall Press.

David, P. (1986) 'Comment on Becker and Barro', *Population and Development Review*, vol 12, Supplement, pp. 77–86.

Davidoff, L. (1976) 'The rationalization of housework', in Barker and Allen (eds) (1976).

—— (1979) 'The separation of home and work? Landladies and lodgers in nineteenth and twentieth century England', in Burman (ed.) (1979).

—— and Hall, C. (1987) *Family Fortunes: Men and Women of the English Middle Class, 1780–1850*, London: Hutchinson.

Davies, C. and Rosser, J. (1986) 'Gendered jobs in the health service: a problem for labour process analysis', in Knights and Willmot (eds) (1986).

219

Davies, M. (1982) *Woman's Place is at the Typewriter: Office Work and Office Workers, 1870–1930*, Philadelphia: Temple University Press.

Deacon, D. (1982) 'The employment of women in the Commonwealth public service: the creation and reproduction of a dual labour market', *Australian Journal of Public Administration*, vol XLI, no 3, pp. 232–50.

Deere, C. (1976) 'Rural women's subsistence production in the capitalist periphery', *Review of Radical Political Economics*, vol 8, no 1, Spring, pp. 9–17.

Delphy, C. (1984) *Close to Home: A Materialist Analysis of Women's Oppression*, London: Hutchinson.

Dex, S. (1985) *The Sexual Division of Work: Conceptual Revolutions in the Social Sciences*, Brighton: Wheatsheaf.

—— (1987a) 'Gender and the labour market – a review', University of Keele, Working Paper, no 87–13, Department of Economics and Management Science, University of Keele.

—— (1987b) *Women's Occupational Mobility: a Lifetime Perspective*, London: Macmillan.

—— (1988a) 'Gender and the labour market' in Gallie (ed.) (1988).

—— (1988b) 'Issues of gender and employment', *Social History*, vol 13, pp. 141–50.

—— and Shaw, L. (1986) *British and American Women at Work: Do Equal Opportunities Policies Matter?*, London: Macmillan.

—— and P. Walters (1989) 'Women's occupational status in Britain, France and the USA: explaining the difference', *Industrial Relations Journal*, vol 20, no 2, pp. 203–12.

—— (1990) 'Franco-British comparisons of women's labour supply and the effects of socioeconomic policies', mimeo.

Dey, I. (1989) 'Flexible "parts" and rigid "fulls": the limited revolution in work-time patterns', *Work, Employment and Society*, vol 3, no 4, Dec, pp. 465–90.

Doeringer, P. and M. Piore (1971) *Internal Labor Markets and Manpower Analysis*, Lexington: Heath Lexington Books.

Dohrn, S. (1988) 'Pioneers in a dead-end profession: the first women clerks in banks and insurance companies', in Anderson (ed) (1988).

Dolton, P. and M. Kidd (1990) 'Occupational access and wage discrimination', Discussion Paper 803, Institute for Economic Research, Queen's University, Kingston, Ontario.

—— and G. Makepeace (1987) 'Marital status, child rearing and earnings differentials in the graduate labour market', *Economic Journal*, vol 97, Dec, pp. 897–922.

Dublin, T. (1987) 'Women, work, and protest in the Early Lowell Mills: "The oppressing hand of avarice would enslave us"', in Cantor and Laurie (eds) (1977).

Duchen, C. (1989) 'The family and feminism in France', in Close (ed.) (1989).

Earle, P. (1989) 'The female labour market in London in the late seventeenth and early eighteenth centuries', *Economic History Review*, vol XLII, no 3, pp. 328–53.

Edholm, F. *et al.* (1977) 'Conceptualising women', *Critique of Anthropology*, vol 3, nos 9 and 10, pp. 101–30.

Ehrenreich, B. and English, D. (1978) *For Her Own Good: 150 Years of the Expert's Advice to Women*, New York: Anchor Press.

Eisenstein, Z. (1979) 'Developing a theory of capitalist patriarchy and socialist feminism, in Eisenstein (ed.) (1979).

—— (ed.) (1979) *Capitalist Patriarchy and the Case for Socialist Feminism*, London: Monthly Review Press.

Elbaum, B. and Lazonick, W. (eds) (1986) *The Decline of the British Economy*, London: Oxford University Press.

Elias, P. (1988) 'Family formation, occupational mobility and part-time work', in Hunt (ed.) (1988).

—— and Purcell, K. (1988) 'Women and paid work: prospects for equality', in Hunt (ed.) (1988).

Elliot, R. and Murphy, P. (1987) 'The relative pay of public and private sector employees, 1970–1984', *Cambridge Journal of Economics*, vol 11, pp. 107–32.

Elson, D. (ed.) (1979) *Value: The Representation of Labour in Capitalism*, London: CSE Books.

Emmanuel, A. (1972) *Unequal Exchange: A Study of the Imperialism of Trade*, London: New Left Books.

Engels, F. (1884) *The Origin of the Family, Private Property and the State*, Stuttgart: Dietz.

England, P. (1982) 'The failure of human capital theory to explain occupational sex segregation', *Journal of Human Resources*, vol XVII, no 3, pp. 358–70.

—— (1984) 'Wage appreciation and depreciation: a test of neoclassical economic explanations of occupational sex segregation', *Social Forces*, vol 62, no 3, March, pp. 726–44.

—— (1985) 'Occupational segregation: rejoinder to Polachek', *Journal of Human Resources*, vol XX, no 3, pp. 441–3.

—— and Farkas, G. (1986) *Households, Employment, and Gender: A Social, Economic, and Demographic View*, New York: Aldins.

Enloe, C. (1980) 'The reserve army of army labor', *Review of Radical Political Economics*, vol 12, no 2, Summer, pp. 42–52.

Epstein, T. *et al.* (eds) (1986) *Women, Work and Family in Britain and Germany*, London: Croom Helm.

Ermisch, J. (1983) *The Political Economy of Population Change*, London: Heinemann.

—— (1988) 'Fortunes of birth: the impact of generation size on the relative earnings of young men', *Scottish Journal of Political Economy*, vol 35, no 3, Aug, pp. 266–82.

—— and Wright, R. (1988) 'Differential returns to human capital in full-time and part-time employment: the case of British women', *Birkbeck Discussion Paper*, no 88/14.

—— *et al.* (1990) 'Women's wages in Great Britain', *Birkbeck Discussion Paper*, no 8/90.

Evans, M. and Ungerson, C. (eds) (1983) *Sexual Divisions: Patterns and Processes*, London: Tavistock.

221

Even, W. and MacPherson, D. (1990) 'The gender gap in pensions and wages', *Review of Economics and Statistics*, vol LXXII, no 2, May, pp. 259–65.

Evers, H. (1984) 'Subsistence reproduction: a framework for analysis', in Smith *et al.* (eds) (1984).

Ewen, S. (1976) *Captains of Consciousness: Advertising and the Social Roots of the Consumer Culture*, New York: McGraw-Hill.

Fagnani, J. (1990) 'City size and mothers' labour force participation', *Tijdschrift voor Econ. en Soc. Geografie*, vol 81, no 3, pp. 182–8.

Faulkner, W. and Arnold, E. (eds) (1985) *Smothered by Invention: Technology in Women's Lives*, London: Pluto.

Fee, T. (1976) 'Domestic labour: an analysis of housework and its relation to the production process', *Review of Radical Political Economics*, vol 8, no 1, Spring, pp. 1–8.

Feiner, S. and Roberts, B. (1990) 'Hidden by the invisible hand: neoclassical economic theory and the textbook treatment of race and gender', *Gender and Society*, vol 4, no 2, June, pp. 159–81.

Feldberg, R. and Glenn, E. (1984) 'Male and female: jobs versus gender models in the sociology of work', in Siltanen and Stanworth (eds) (1984).

Ferguson, A. and Folbre, N. (1981) 'The unhappy marriage of patriarchy and capitalism', in Sargent (ed.) (1981).

Finch, J. (1983) *Married to the Job: Wives' Incorporation into Men's Work*, London: Allen and Unwin.

Fine, B. (1987) 'Segmented labour market theory: a critical assessment', *Birkbeck Discussion Paper in Economics*, no 87/12.

—— (1990) 'Segmented labour market theory: a critical assessment', Thames Papers in Political Economy, Spring.

—— and Harris, L. (1979) *Rereading 'Capital'*, London: Macmillan.

—— and Harris, L. (1985) *The Peculiarities of the British Economy*, London: Lawrence & Wishart.

—— and Leopold, E. (1990) 'Consumerism and the Industrial Revolution', *Social History*, vol 15, no 2, May, pp. 151–79.

—— (forthcoming) *Getting and Spending: Food, Fashion and Fallacies in Theories of Consumption*.

Firestone, S. (1970) *The Dialectics of Sex*, New York: Morrow.

Folbre, N. (1980) 'Patriarchy in colonial New England', *Review of Radical Political Economics*, vol 12, no 2, Summer, pp. 4–13.

—— (1982) 'Exploitation comes home: a critique of the Marxian theory of family labour', *Cambridge Journal of Economics*, vol 6, no 4, Dec, pp. 317–29.

—— (1983) 'Of patriarchy born: the political economy of fertility decisions', *Feminist Studies*, vol 9, no 2, Summer, pp. 261–84.

—— (1986) 'Cleaning house: new perspectives on households and economic development', *Journal of Development Economics*, vol 22, pp 5–40.

Ford, J. *et al.* (1984) 'Internal labor market processes', *Industrial Relations Journal*, vol 15, no 2, Summer, pp. 41–50.

Fox, B. (ed.) (1980) *Hidden in the Household: Women's Domestic Labour under Capitalism*, Toronto: The Women's Press.

—— (1980a) 'Introduction', in Fox (ed.) (1980).

—— (1980b) 'Women's double day: twentieth-century change in the reproduction of daily life', in Fox (ed.) (1980).

—— (1990) 'Selling the mechanised household: 70 years of ads in *Ladies Home Journal*', *Gender and Society*, vol 4, no 1, pp. 25–40.

Freifeld, M. (1986) 'Technical change and the "self-acting" mule: a study of skill and the sexual division of labour', *Social History*, vol 11, pp. 319–43.

Friedman, K. (1984) 'Households as income-pooling units', in Smith *et al.* (eds) (1984).

Fuchs, V. (1988) *Women's Quest for Economic Equality*, Cambridge: Harvard University Press.

Gallie, D. (1988a) 'Technological change, gender and skill', *SCELI Working Papers*, no 4, Nuffield College, Oxford.

—— (ed.) (1988b) *Employment in Britain*, Oxford: Blackwell.

Gamarnikow, E. *et al.* (eds) (1983) *The Public and the Private*, London: Heinemann.

Game, A. and Pringle, R (1984) *Gender at Work*, London: Pluto Press.

Gardiner, J. (1975) 'Women's domestic labour, *New Left Review*, no 89, Jan/Feb, pp. 47–58.

—— (1976) 'Political economy of domestic labour', in Barker and Allen (eds) (1976).

—— Himmelweit, S. and Mackintosh, M. (1975) 'Women's domestic labour', *Bulletin of the Conference of Socialist Economists*, vol IV, no 2 (11), June, pp. 1–11.

Garrison, D. (1983) 'The tender technicians: the feminization of public librarianship, 1876–1905', in Hartmann and Banner (eds) (1983).

Gershuny, J. and Miles, I. (1983) *The New Service Economy: The Transformation of Employment in Industrial Societies*, London: Frances Pinter.

Gerstein, I. (1973) 'Domestic work and capitalism', *Radical America*, 7, July/Oct, pp. 101–31.

Gittins, D. (1982) *Fair Sex: Family Size and Structure, 1900–39*, London: Hutchinson.

Glazer, N. (1984) 'Servants to capital: unpaid domestic labour and paid work', *Review of Radical Political Economics*, vol 16, no 1, Spring, pp. 61–87.

Glazer-Molbin, N. (1976) 'Housework', *Signs*, vol 1, no 4, Summer, pp. 905–22.

Glendinning, G. and Millar, J. (eds) (1987) *Women and Poverty in Britain*, Brighton: Wheatsheaf.

Glucksmann, M. (1986) 'In a class of their own? Women and workers in the new industries in inter-war Britain', *Feminist Review*, no 24, Autumn, pp. 7–39.

Goldin, C. (1990) *Understanding the Gender Gap: An Economic History of American Women*, Oxford: Oxford University Press.

Gomulka, J. and N. Stern (1990) 'The employment of married women in the United Kingdom, 1970–83', *Economica*, vol 57, no 226, May, pp. 171–97.

Goodnow, J. (1988) 'Children's household work: its nature and functions', *Psychological Bulletin,* vol 103, no 1, pp. 5–26.

—— (1989) 'Work in households: an overview and three studies', in Ironmonger (ed.) (1989).

Gordon, M. (1988) *Social Security Policies in Industrial Countries: A Comparative Analysis,* Cambridge: Cambridge University Press.

Gough, I. and J. Harrison (1975) 'Unproductive labour and housework again', *Bulletin of the Conference of Socialist Economists,* vol IV, no 1, Feb, pp. 1–7.

Greenhalgh, S. (1990) 'Towards a political economy of fertility: anthropological contributions', *Population and Development Review,* vol 16, March, pp. 85–106.

Gregory, R. and Daly, A. (1990) 'Can economic theory explain why Australian women are so well paid relative to their US counterparts?', Discussion Paper, no 226, Centre for Economic Policy Research, Australian National University.

—— *et al.* (1985) 'Women in the Australian labor force: trends, causes and consequences', in Layard and Mincer (eds) (1985).

—— *et al.* (1989) 'Women's pay in Australia, Great Britain, and the United States: the role of laws, regulations, and human capital', in Michael *et al.* (eds) (1989).

Grieco, M. *et al.* (eds) (1989) *Gender, Transport and Employment: The Impact of Travel Constraints,* Aldershot: Gower.

Griffin, T. (1984) 'Technological change and craft control in the newspaper industry: an international comparison', *Cambridge Journal of Economics,* vol 8, no 1, Mar, pp. 41–62.

Griffiths, D. (1985) 'The exclusion of women from technology', in Faulkner and Arnold (eds) (1985).

Gunderson, M. (1989) 'Male-female wage differentials and policy responses', *Journal of Economic Literature,* vol XXVII, March, pp. 46–72.

Gutek, B. *et al.* (eds) (1988) *Women and Work: An Annual Review,* London: Sage.

Gwartney-Gibbs, P. (1988) 'Women's work experience and the "rusty skills" hypothesis: a reconceptualisation and reevaluation', in Gutek *et al.* (eds) (1988).

Hacker, S. (1989) *Pleasure, Power and Technology: Some Tales of Gender, Engineering and the Cooperative Workplace,* London: Allen & Unwin.

—— (1990) *'Doing It the Hard Way': Investigations of Gender and Technology,* edited by D. Smith and S. Turner, London: Unwin Hyman.

Haddad, C. (1987) 'Technology, industrialisation, and the economic status of women', in Wright *et al.* (eds) (1987).

Haines, M. (1989) 'Social class differentials during fertility decline: England and Wales revisited', *Population Studies,* vol 43, pp. 305–24.

Hakim, C. (1978) 'Sexual divisions within the labour force: occupational segregation', *Employment Gazette,* Nov, pp. 1264–68 and 1278–9.

—— (1981) 'Job segregation: trends in the 1970s', *Employment Gazette,* Dec, pp. 521–9.

—— (1987) 'Home-based work in Britain. A report on the 1981 national homeworking survey and the Department of Employment research programme on homework', *Department of Employment Research Paper*, no 60, May.

Halford, S. (1989) 'Spatial divisions and women's initiatives in British local government', *Geoforum*, vol 20, no 2, pp. 161–74.

Hamilton, K. and L. Jenkins (1989) 'Why women and travel?', in Grieco *et al.* (eds) (1989).

Hardyment, C. (1988) *From Mangle to Microwave: The Mechanisation of Household Work*, London: Polity Press.

Hareven, T. (1982) *Family Time and Industrial Time: The Relationship Between the Family and Work in a New England Community*, Cambridge: Cambridge University Press.

—— (1991) 'The home and the family in historical perspective', *Social Research*, vol 58, no 1, Spring, pp. 253–85.

Harris, C. (1983) *The Family and Industrial Society*, London: Allen & Unwin.

—— and Morris, L. (1986) 'Households, labour markets and the position of women', in Crompton and Mann (eds) (1986).

Harrison, B. (1989) 'Class and gender in modern British labour history', *Past and Present*, no 124, August, pp. 121–58.

Harrison, B. (1990) 'Suffer the working day: women in the "dangerous trades", 1880–1914', *Women's Studies International Forum*, vol 13, nos 1/2, pp. 79–90.

—— and Bluestone, B. (1990) 'Wage polarisation and the "flexibility" debate', *Cambridge Journal of Economics*, vol 14, no 3, Sept, pp. 351–73.

Harrison, J. (1973) 'The political economy of housework', *Bulletin of the Conference of Socialist Economists*, Winter, pp. 35–52.

Hart, N. (1989) 'Gender and the rise and fall of class politics', *New Left Review*, no 175, May/June, pp. 19–47.

Hartmann, H. (1979a) 'The unhappy marriage of Marxism and feminism: towards a more progressive union', *Capital and Class*, no 8, Summer, pp. 1–33.

—— (1979b) 'Capitalism, patriarchy, and job segregation by sex', in Eisenstein (ed) (1979).

—— (1981) 'The family as the locus of gender, class, and political struggle: the example of housework', *Signs*, vol 16, no 3, Spring, pp. 366–94.

—— (1987a) 'Internal labor markets and gender: a case study of promotion', in Brown and Pechman (eds) (1987).

—— (1987b) 'Changes in women's economic and family roles in post-World War II United States', in Beneria and Stimpson (eds) (1987).

—— and Banner, L. (eds) (1983) *Clio's Consciousness Raised: New Perspectives on the History of Women*, New York: Harper and Row.

—— and Markusen, A. (1980) 'Contemporary Marxist theory and practice: a feminist critique', *Review of Radical Political Economics*, vol 12, no 2, Summer, pp. 87–94.

Hay, D. (1987) 'Competition and industrial policies', *Oxford Review of Economic Policy*, vol 3, no 3, pp. 27–40.

Hayden, D. (1982) *The Grand Domestic Revolution: A History of Feminist Designs for American Homes, Neighborhoods, and Cities*, Cambridge: MIT Press.

Hecht, J. (1956) *The Domestic Servant Class in Eighteenth-Century England*, London: Routledge & Kegan Paul.

Heritage, J. (1983) 'Feminisation and unionisation: a case study from banking', in Gamarnikow *et al*. (eds) (1983).

Hewitt, A. (1958) *Wives and Mothers in Victorian Industry*, London: Rickliff.

Higgs, E. (1986) 'Domestic service and household production', in John (ed.) (1986).

—— (1987) 'Women, occupations and work in the nineteenth century censuses', *History Workshop*, no 23, Spring, pp. 59–80.

Hill, B. (1989a) *Women, Work, and Sexual Politics in Eighteenth-Century England*, Oxford: Blackwell.

—— (1989b) 'The marriage age of women and the demographers', *History Workshop Journal*, no 28, Autumn, pp. 129–47.

Himmelweit, S. (1974) 'Domestic labour and the mode of production', *Birkbeck Discussion Paper*, no 33.

—— (1983) 'Production rules OK? Waged work and the family', in Segal (ed.) (1983).

—— (1984a) 'The real dualism of sex and class, *Review of Radical Political Economics*, vol 16, no 1, Spring, pp. 167–83.

—— (1984b) 'Value relations and divisions within the working class' *Science and Society*, vol XLVIII, no 3, pp. 323–43.

—— and Mohun, S. (1977) 'Domestic labour and capital', *Cambridge Journal of Economics*, vol 1, no 1, pp. 15–31.

Holcombe, L. (1973) *Victorian Ladies at Work: Middle-Class Working Women in England and Wales, 1850–1914*, Newton Abbot: David & Charles.

—— (1983) *Wives and Property: Reform of the Married Women's Property Law in Nineteenth-Century England*, Oxford: Martin Robertson.

Holstrom, N. (1981) '"Women's work", the family and capitalism', *Science and Society*, vol XLV, no 2, Summer, pp. 186–211.

Horrell, S. *et al*. (1988) 'Gender and skills?', *SCELI Working Papers*, no 5, Nuffield College, Oxford.

—— (1989) 'Unequal pay or unequal jobs?', *SCELI Working Papers*, no 6, Nuffield College, Oxford.

Huber, J. (1982) 'Toward a sociotechnological theory of the women's movement', in Kahn-Hut *et al*. (eds) (1982).

Hudson, P. and Lee, W. (eds) (1990) *Women's Work and the Family Economy in Historical Perspective*, Manchester: Manchester University Press.

Humphries, J. (1977a) 'Class struggle and the persistence of the working class family', *Cambridge Journal of Economics*, vol 1, no 3, Sept, pp. 241–58.

—— (1977b) 'The working class family, women's liberation and class struggle: the case of nineteenth century British history', *Review of Radical Political Economics*, vol 9, no 3, Autumn, pp. 25–41.

—— (1981) 'Protective legislation, the capitalist state, and working class men: the case of the 1842 Mines Regulation Act', *Feminist Review*, no 7, Spring, pp. 1–34.

—— (1987) ' . . . "The most free from objection . . . " The sexual division of labor and women's work in nineteenth-century England', *Journal of Economic History*, vol XLVII, Dec, pp. 929–49.

—— and Rubery, J. (1984) 'The reconstitution of the supply side of the labour market: the relative autonomy of social reproduction', *Cambridge Journal of Economics*, vol 8, no 4, pp. 331–46.

—— (1988) 'British women in a changing workplace', in Jensen *et al.* (eds) (1988).

—— (1992) 'Women's employment in the 1980s: integration, differentiation and polarisation', in Michie (ed.).

Hunt, A. (ed.) (1988) *Women and Paid Work: Issues of Equality*, London: Macmillan.

Ironmonger, D. (1989) 'Households and the household economy', in Ironmonger (ed.) (1989).

—— (ed.) (1989) *Households Work: Productive Activities, Women and Income in the Household Economy*, London: Allen & Unwin.

—— and Sonius, E. (1989) 'Household productive activities', in Ironmonger (ed.) (1989).

Jacobs, J. (1989a) 'Long term trends in occupational segregation by sex', *American Journal of Sociology*, vol 95, no 1, July, pp. 160–73.

—— (1989b) *Revolving Doors: Sex Segregation and Women's Careers*, Stanford: Stanford University Press.

Jamrozik, A. (1989) 'The household economy and social class', in Ironmonger (ed.) (1989).

Jenkins, R. (1984) 'Acceptability, suitability and the search for the habituated worker: how ethnic minorities and women lose out', *International Journal of Social Economics*, vol 11, no 7, pp. 64–76.

Jensen, A. (1989) 'Reproduction in Norway: an area of non-resposibility', in Close (ed.) (1989).

Jensen, J. (1980) 'Cloth, butter and boarders: women's household production for the market', *Review of Radical Political Economics*, vol 12, no 2, Summer, pp. 14–24.

—— (1988) 'The limit of "and the" discourse', in Jensen *et al.* (eds) (1988).

—— *et al.* (eds) (1988) *Feminization of the Labour Force: Paradoxes and Promises*, London: Polity.

John, A. (1981) Letter Comment on Humphries (1981), *Feminist Review*, no 9, Autumn, pp. 106–9.

—— (1984) *By the Sweat of their Brow*, London: Routledge & Kegan Paul.

—— (ed.) (1986) *Unequal Opportunities: Women's Employment in England, 1800–1918*, Oxford: Blackwell.

Jordan, E. (1989) 'The exclusion of women from industry in nineteenth-century Britain', *Comparative Studies in Society and History*, vol 31, no 2, April, pp. 273–96.

Joseph, G. (1983) *Women at Work*, Oxford: Philip Allan.

Joshi, H. (1984) 'Secondary workers in the employment cycle', *Economica*, vol 48, no 1, pp. 29–44.

—— (1985) 'Motherhood and employment: change and continuity in post-war Britain', in OPCS (1985).

—— (1986) 'Participation in paid work: evidence from the women and employment survey', in Blundell and Walker (eds) (1986).

—— (1987) 'The cost of living', in Glendinning and Millar (eds) (1987).

REFERENCES

—— (1990) 'Sex and motherhood as handicaps in the labour market' in Maclean and Groves (eds) (1990).

—— and Overton, E. (1988) 'Forecasting the female labour force in Britain', *International Journal of Forecasting*, vol 4, pp. 269–85.

—— and Owen, S. (1988) 'Demographic predictors of women's work in postwar Britain', *Research in Population Economics*, vol 6, pp. 401–47.

—— *et al.* (1985) 'Why are more women working in Britain?', in Layard and Mincer (eds) (1985).

Jowitt, J. and McIvor, A. (eds) (1988) *Employers and Labour in the English Textile Industries, 1880–1939*, London: Routledge.

Kahn-Hut, R. *et al.* (eds) (1982) *Women and Work: Problems and Perspectives*, Oxford: Oxford University Press.

Kaluzynska, E. (1980) 'Wiping the floor with theory – a survey of writings on housework', *Feminist Review*, no 6, pp. 27–54.

Kamenka, E. (1983) 'Public/Private in Marxist theory and Marxist practice', in Benn and Gaus (eds) (1983).

Kanter, R. (1982) 'The impact of hierarchical structures on the work behavior of women and men', in Kahn-Hut *et al.* (eds) (1982).

Kendrick, J. (1981) 'Politics and the construction of women as second class workers', in Wilkinson (ed.) (1981).

Kent, D. (1989) 'Ubiquitous but invisible: female domestic servants in mid-eighteenth century London', *History Workshop Journal*, no 28, Autumn, pp. 111–28.

Kessler-Harris, A. (1982a) *Out to Work: A History of the Wage-Earning Women in the United States*, Oxford: Oxford University Press.

—— (1982b) *Women Have Always Worked: A Historical Overview*, New York: The Feminist Press.

—— (1989) 'A new agenda for American labor history: a gendered analysis and the question of class', in Moody and Kessler-Harris (eds) (1989).

—— and Sacks, K. (1987) 'The demise of domesticity in America' in Beneria and Stimpson (eds) (1987).

Kidd, M. (1990) 'Sex discrimination and occupational segregation in the Australian labour market', University of Tasmania, Discussion Paper 1991–01.

Kleinegger, C. (1987) 'Out of the barns and into the kitchens: transformations in farm women's work in the first half of the twentieth century', in B. Wright *et al.* (eds) (1987).

Knights, D. and Willmott, H. (eds) (1986) *Gender and the Labour Process*, Aldershot: Gower.

Korneman, S. and Neumark, D. (1989) 'Is superwoman a myth? Marriage, children, and wages', Federal Reserve Board, Economic Activity Section, Working Paper Series, no 94, Washington.

Kuhn, A. (1978) 'Structures of patriarchy and capital in the family', in Kuhn and Wolpe (eds) (1978).

—— and Wolpe, A. (eds) (1978) *Feminism and Materialism: Women and Modes of Production*, London: Routledge & Kegan Paul.

Land, H. (1980) 'The family wage', *Feminist Review*, no 6, pp. 55–78.

228

Landes, J. (1977/8) 'Women, labor and family life: a theoretical perspective', *Science and Society*, vol XLI, winter, pp. 386–409.

Larwood, L. *et al.* (eds) (1985) *Women and Work, An Annual Review*, vol 1, London: Sage.

Laslett, P. (1971) *The World We Have Lost*, London: Methuen.

—— (1983) *The World We Have Lost: Further Explored*, London: Methuen.

Layard, R and J. Mincer (eds) (1985) *Trends in Women's Work, Education, and Family Building*, special issue of *Journal of Labor Economics*, vol 3, no 1, part 2, Jan.

Lazonick, W. (1986) 'The cotton industry', in Elbaum and Lazonick (eds) (1986).

Leacock, E. *et al.* (eds) (1986) *Women's Work: Development and the Division of Labor by Gender*, South Hadley: Bergin and Garvey Publishers.

Lee, C. (1990) *On the Three Problems of Abstraction, Reduction and Transformation in Marx's Value Theory*, PhD thesis, University of London.

Lehrer, S. (1982) 'Protective labor legislation for women', *Review of Radical Political Economics*, vol 17, no 1/2, Spring and Summer, pp. 187–200.

Leopold, E. (1989) 'Women's employment in the London boroughs of Hackney and Bromley: a report of the findings of the survey of Londoners' living standards', London: Association of London Authorities.

Lerner, G. (1986) *The Creation of Patriarchy*, Oxford: Oxford University Press.

Lesthaeghe, R. (1983) 'A century of demographic and cultural change in western Europe: An exploration of underlying dimensions', *Population and Development Review*, vol 9, no 3, pp. 411–35.

Levine, D. (1985) 'Industrialisation and the proletariat family', *Past and Present*, no 107, pp. 168–203.

—— (1987) *Reproducing Families: The Political Economy of English Population History*, Cambridge: Cambridge University Press.

Lewis, C. and M. O'Brien (eds) (1987) *Reassessing Fatherhood: New Observations on Fathers and the Modern Family*, London: Sage.

Lewis, J. (1984) *Women in England*, Brighton: Wheatsheaf.

—— (1985) 'The debate on sex and class', *New Left Review*, no 149, Jan/Feb, pp. 108–120.

—— and Foord, J. (1984) 'New towns and new gender relations in old industrial regions: women's employment in Peterlee and East Kilbride', *Built Environment*, vol 10, pp. 42–52.

Liff, S. (1986) 'Technical change and occupational sex-typing', in Knights and Willmott (eds) (1986).

Little, J. *et al.* (eds) (1988) *Women in Cities: Gender and the Urban Environment*, London: Macmillan.

Lloyd, C. *et al.* (eds) (1979) *Women in the Labor Market*, New York: Columbia University Press.

Lopata, H. (1971) *Occupation: Housewife*, Oxford: Oxford University Press.

—— *et al.* (1986) *City Women in America: Work, Jobs, Occupations, Careers*, New York: Praeger.

Lown, J. (1983) 'Gender and class during industrialisation', in Gamarnikow *et al.* (eds) (1983).

—— (1990) *Women and Industrialization*, London: Polity Press.

Lupri, E. (ed.) (1983) *The Changing Position of Women in Family and Society: A Cross National Comparison*, Leiden: E. J. Brill.

—— and Mills, D. (1983) 'The changing roles of Canadian women in family and work: an overview', in Lupri (ed.) (1983).

MacBride, T. (1976) *The Domestic Revolution: The Modernisation of Household Service in England and France, 1820–1920*, London: Croom Helm.

—— (1977) 'The long road home: women's work and industrialization', in Bridenthal and Koonz (eds) (1977).

McCrate, E. (1987) 'Trade, merger and employment: economic theory on marriage', *Review of Radical Political Economics*, vol 19, no 1, pp. 73–89.

McDonough, R. and Harrison, R. (1978) 'Patriarchy and relations of production', in Kuhn and Wolpe (eds) (1978).

McDougall, M. (1977) 'Working-class women during the Industrial Revolution, 1870–1914', in Bridenthal and Koonz (eds) (1977).

McIntosh, M. (1979) 'The welfare state and the needs of the dependent family', in Burman (ed.) (1979).

McKee, L. and O'Brien, M. (1983) 'Interviewing man: "Taking gender seriously"', in Gamarnikow (ed.) (1983).

Mackintosh, M. (1977) 'Reproduction and patriarchy', *Capital and Class*, no 2, Summer, pp. 119–27.

—— (1979) 'Domestic labour and the household', in Burman (ed.) (1979).

Maclean, M. and Groves, D. (eds) (1990) *Women's Issues in Social Policy*, London: Routledge.

McNally, F. (1979) *Women for Hire: A Study of the Female Office Worker*, London: Macmillan.

MacNicol, J. (1980) *The Movement for Family Allowances, 1918–1945*, London: Heinemann.

Maconachie, M. (1989) 'Dual-earner couples: factors influencing whether and when white married women join the labour force in South Africa', *South African Journal of Sociology*, vol 20, no 3, pp. 143–51.

Madden, J. (1985) 'The persistence of pay differentials: the economics of sex discrimination', in Larwood *et al.* (eds) (1985).

—— and Chiu, L. (1990) 'The wage effects of residential location and commuting constraints on employed married women', *Urban Studies*, vol 27, no 3, pp. 353–69.

Main, B. (1988) 'Women's hourly earnings: the influence of work histories on rates of pay', in Hunt (ed.) (1988).

Mainardi, P. (1971) *The Politics of Housework*, Agitprop Information.

Mallier, A. and M. Rosser (1987) 'Changes in the industrial distribution of female employment in Great Britain, 1951–1981', *Work, Employment and Society*, vol 1, no 4, pp. 463–86.

Malos, E. (ed.) (1982) *The Politics of Housework*, London: Allison & Busby.

Mann, B. and Elias, P. (1987) 'Women returning to paid employment', *International Review of Applied Economics*, vol 1, no 1, pp. 86–108.

Mark-Lawson, J. and A. Witz (1988) 'From "Family Labour" to "Family Wage"? The case of women's labour in nineteenth-century coalmining', *Social History*, vol 13, pp. 151–74.

Martin, J. and Roberts, C (1984) *Women and Employment: A Lifetime Pespective*, London: HMSO.

Marx, K. (1936) *Letters to Dr Kugelmann*, London: Lawrence & Wishart.

Mathias, P. and Davis, J. (eds) (1989) *The First Industrial Revolutions*, Oxford: Blackwell.

Matthaei, J. (1982) *An Economic History of Women in America: Women's Work, the Sexual Division of Labor and the Development of Capitalism*, Brighton: Harvester.

Mavroudeas, S. (1990) *Regulation Approach: A Critical Assessment*, PhD Thesis, University of London.

Michael, R. *et al.* (eds) (1989) *Pay Equity: Empirical Inquiries*, Washington: National Academy Press.

Michie, J. (ed.) (1992) *1979–1991: The Economic Legacy*, London: Academic Press.

Middleton, C. (1979) 'The sexual division of labour in feudal England', *New Left Review*, 113/4, Jan-Apr, pp. 147–68.

—— (1981a) 'Peasants, patriarchy and the feudal mode of production: a Marxist appraisal: 1. Property and patriarchal relations within the peasantry', *Sociological Review*, vol 29, no 1, pp. 103–35.

—— (1981b) 'Peasants, patriarchy and the feudal mode of production: a Marxist appraisal: 2. Feudal lords and the subordination of peasant women', *Sociological Review*, vol 29, no 1, pp. 137–54.

—— (1985) 'Women's labour and the transition to pre-industrial capitalism', in Charles and Duffin (eds) (1985).

—— (1988) 'Gender divisions and wage labour in English history', in Walby (ed.) (1988).

Mies, M. (1986) *Patriarchy and Accumulation on a World Scale: Women in the International Division of Labour*, London: Zed Press.

Milkman, R. (1972) 'Women's work and economic crisis: some lessons of the Great Depression', *Review of Radical Political Economics*, vol IV, no 3, pp. 73–97.

—— (1983) 'Female factory labor and industrial structure: control and conflict over "women's place" in auto and electrical manufacturing', *Politics and Society*, vol 12, pp. 159–208.

Miller, P. (1987) 'The wage effect of the occupational segregation of women in Britain', *Economic Journal*, vol 97, Dec, pp. 885–96.

Mincer, J. (1985) 'Intercountry comparisons of labor force trends and of related developments: an overview', in Layard and Mincer (eds) (1985).

Minge, W. (1986) 'The Industrial Revolution and the European family: "childhood" as a market for family labor', in Leacock *et al.* (eds) (1986).

Mingione, E. (1985) 'Social reproduction of the surplus labour force: the case of southern Italy', in Redclift and Mingione (eds) (1985).

Mitchell, J. (1975) *Psychoanalysis and Feminism*, Harmondsworth: Pelican.

Mitchison, R. (1977) *British Population Change since 1860*, London: Macmillan.

Molyneux, M. (1979) 'Beyond the domestic labour debate', *New Left Review*, no 116, Jul-Aug, pp. 3–27.

Montgomery, M. (1988) 'On the determinants of employer demand for part-time workers', *Review of Economics and Statistics*, vol LXX, no 1, Feb, pp. 112–17.

Moody, J. and Kessler-Harris, A. (eds) (1989) *Perspectives on American History: The Problems of Synthesis*, DeKalb: Northern Illinois University Press.

Morton, P. (1972) 'A woman's work is never done', in *Women Unite!*, Toronto: The Women's Press.

Moss, P. (1988) *Childcare and Equality of Opportunity: Consolidated Report to the European Commission*, mimeo.

—— (1988/89) 'The indirect cost of parenthood: a neglected issue in social policy', *Critical Social Policy*, no 24, Winter, pp. 20–37.

Murgatoyd, L. (1982) 'Gender and occupational stratification', *Sociological Review*, vol 26, no 5, June, pp. 524–38.

—— et al (eds) (1985) *Localities, Class and Gender*, London: Pinder.

Murphy, M. (1985) 'Demographic and socio-economic influences on recent British marital breakdown patterns', *Population Studies*, vol 39, no 3, pp. 441–60.

Myrdal, A. and Klein, V. (1956) *Women's Two Roles: Home and Work*, London: Routledge & Kegan Paul.

Nazzari, M. (1980) 'The significance of present-day changes in the institution of marriage, *Review of Radical Political Economics*, vol 12, no 2, Summer, pp. 63–75.

Oakley, A. (1974a) *Housewife*, London: Allen Lane.

—— (1974b) *The Sociology of Housework*, London: Allen Lane.

—— (1989) 'Women's studies in British sociology: to end at our beginning', *British Journal of Sociology*, vol 40, no 3, Sept, pp. 442–70.

OECD (1979) *Equal Opportunities For Women*, Paris: OECD.

—— (1980) *Women and Employment: Policies for Equal Opportunities*, Paris: OECD.

OEEC (1985) *The Integration of Women into the Economy*, Paris: OECD.

O'Neill, J. (1985) 'Role differentiation and the gender gap in wage rates', in Larwood *et al.* (eds) (1985).

OPCS (1985) *Measuring Socio-Demographic Change*, OPCS Occasional Paper, no 34, London: HMSO.

Osterud, N. (1986) 'Gender divisions and the organisation of work in the Leicester hosiery industry', in John (ed.) (1986).

—— (1989) 'Gender relations in the process of capitalist industrialization: toward a bifocal perspective', *Bulletin of the Society for the Study of Labour History*, vol 54, no 1, Spring, pp. 10–12.

Owen, S. and Joshi, H. (1987) 'Does elastic retract? The effect of recession on women's labour force participation', *British Journal of Industrial Relations*, vol 25, no 1, pp. 125–43.

Pahl, R. (1984) *Divisions of Labour*, Oxford: Blackwell.

—— (ed.) (1988) *On Work: Historical, Comparative and Historical Approaches*, Oxford: Blackwell.

Pallister, D. *et al.* (1987) *South Africa Incorporated: The Oppenheimer Empire*, London: Lowry.

Pennington, S. and Westover, B. (1989) *A Hidden Workforce: Homeworkers in England, 1850–1985*, London: Macmillan.

REFERENCES

Perkin, J. (1989) *Women and Marriage in Nineteenth Century England*, London: Routledge.

Perkins, T. (1983) 'A new form of employment', in Evans and Ungerson (eds) (1983).

Perman, L. and Stevens, B. (1989) 'Industrial segregation and the gender distribution of fringe benefits', *Gender and Society*, vol 3, no 3, Sept, pp. 388–404.

Phillips, A. and Taylor, B. (1980) 'Sex and skill: notes towards a feminist economics', *Feminist Review*, no 6, pp. 79–88.

Phipps, S. (1990) 'Gender wage differences in Australia, Sweden, and the United States', *Review of Income and Wealth*, vol 36, no 4, Dec, pp. 365–80.

Pickup, L. (1984) 'Women's gender-role and its influence on travel behaviour', *Built Environment*, vol 10, pp. 61–8.

—— (1988) 'Hard to get around: a study of women's travel mobility', in Little *et al.* (eds) (1988).

—— (1989) 'Women's travel requirements: employment with domestic constraints', in Grieco *et al.* (eds) (1989).

Pinchbeck, I. (1969) *Women Workers and the Industrial Revolution, 1750–1850*, London: Cass & Company, first published 1939.

Polachek, S. (1979) 'Occupational segregation among women: theory, evidence, and a prognosis' in Lloyd *et al.* (eds) (1979).

—— (1985a) 'Occupational segregation: a defense of human capital predictions', *Journal of Human Resources*, vol XX, no 3, pp. 437–40.

—— (1985b) 'Occupational segregation: reply to England', *Journal of Human Resources*, vol XX, no 3, p. 444.

Pollert, A. (1988) 'The "flexible firm": fixation or fact?', *Work, Employment and Society*, vol 2, no 3, pp. 281–316.

Popenoe, D. (1987) 'Beyond the nuclear family: a statistical portrait of the changing family in Sweden', *Journal of Marriage and the Family*, vol 49, no 1, Feb, pp. 173–83.

Power, M. (1983) 'From home production to wage labor: women as a reserve army of labor', *Review of Radical Political Economics*, vol 15, no 1, Spring, pp 71–91.

Pratt, G. and Hanson, S. (1991) 'On the links between home and work: family-household strategies in a buoyant labour market', *International Journal of Urban and Regional Research*, vol 15, no 1, Mar, pp. 55–74.

Probert, B. (1989) *Working Life: Arguments about Work in Australian Society*, Melbourne: McPhee Gribble.

Prus, M. (1990) 'Mechanization and the gender-based division of labour in the US cigar industry', *Cambridge Journal of Economics*, vol 14, no 1, March, pp. 63–79.

Purcell, K. (1979) 'Militancy and acquiescence amongst women workers', in Burman (1979).

—— (1984) 'Militancy and acquiescence among women workers', in Siltanen and Stanworth (1984).

—— et al (eds) (1986) *The Changing Experience of Employment: Restructuring and Recession*, London: Macmillan.

Quick, P. (1972) 'Women's work', *Review of Radical Political Economics*, vol 4, no 3, July, pp. 2–19.

Redclift, N. (1985) 'The contested domain: gender, accumulation and the labour process', in Redclift and Mingione (eds) (1985).

—— and Mingione, E. (eds) (1985) *Beyond Employment: Household, Gender and Subsistence*, Oxford, Blackwell.

Rees, G. and Rees, T. (eds) (1980) *Poverty and Social Inequality in Wales*, London: Croom Helm.

Reilly, B. (1991) 'Occupational segregation and selectivity bias in occupational wage equations: an empirical analysis using Irish data', *Applied Economics*, vol 23, no 1A, Jan, pp. 1–7.

Reskin, B. (ed.) (1984) *Sex Segregation in the Workplace: Trends, Explanations, Remedies*, Washington DC: National Academic Press.

—— and H. Hartmann (eds) (1986) *Women's Work, Men's Work: Sex Segregation on the Job*, Washington DC: National Academic Press.

Richards, E. (1974) 'Women in the British economy since about 1770: an interpretation', *History*, vol 59, pp. 337–57.

Roberts, E. (1977) 'Working class standards of living in Barrow and Lancaster, 1840–1914', *Economic History Review*, vol xxxx, no 2, pp. 306–21.

—— (1988) *Women's Work, 1840–1940*, London: Macmillan.

Robinson, J. and McIlwee, J. (1989) 'Women in engineering: a promise unfulfilled?', *Social Problems*, vol 36, no 5, Dec, 1989, pp. 455–73.

Robinson, O. (1988) 'The changing labour market: growth of part-time and labour market segmentation in Britain', in Walby (ed.) (1988).

Rockeis-Strugl, E. (1983) 'The position of Austrian women in the family: many queries and a few interpretations', in Lupri (ed.) (1983).

Rose, S. (1986) '"Gender at Work": Sex, class and industrial capitalism', *History Workshop Journal*, no 21, Spring, pp. 113–31.

—— (1988) 'Gender antagonisms and class conflict: exclusionary strategies of male trade unionists in nineteenth-century Britain', *Social History*, vol 13, pp. 191–208.

Rothschild, J. (1983) 'Technology, housework, and women's liberation: a theoretical analysis', in Rothschild (ed.) (1983).

—— (ed.) (1983) *Machina ex Dea: Feminist Perspectives on Technology*, Oxford: Pergamon Press.

Rothwell, S. (1980) 'United Kingdom', in Yohalem (ed) (1980).

Rowbotham, S. (1973) *Hidden From History: 300 Years of Women's Oppression and the Fight Against It*, London: Pluto Press.

—— (1981) 'The Trouble with "patriarchy"', in Samuel (ed.) (1981).

Rowntree, M. and Rowntree, J. (1970) 'More on the political economy of women's liberation', *Monthly Review*, vol 21, no 8, Jan, pp. 88–103.

Rowthorn, B. (1974) 'Skilled labour in the Marxist system', *Bulletin of the Conference of Socialist Economists*, Spring, pp. 25–45, reproduced in Rowthorn (1980).

—— (1980) *Capitalism, Conflict and Inflation: Essays in Political Economy*, London: Lawrence and Wishart.

Rowthorn, R. and Wells, J. (1987) *De-industrialization and Foreign Trade*, Cambridge: Cambridge University Press.

Rozen, F. (1987) 'Technical advances and increasing militance: flight attendant unions in the jet age', in Wright *et al.* (eds) (1987).

Rubery, J. (ed.) (1988) *Women and Recession*, London: Routledge & Kegan Paul.

Ruggie, M. (1984) *The State and Working Women: A Comparative Study of Britain and Sweden*, Princeton: Princeton University Press.

Samuel, R. (ed.) (1981) *People's History and Socialist Theory*, London: Routledge & Kegan Paul.

Sandquist, K. (1987) 'Swedish family policy and the attempt to change paternal roles', in Lewis and O'Brien (eds) (1987).

Sargent, L. (ed.) (1981) *Women and Revolution: A Discussion of the Unhappy Marriage of Marxism and Feminism*, London: Pluto.

Sarsby, J. (1985) 'Sexual segregation in the pottery industry', *Feminist Review*, no 21, Winter, pp. 49–68.

Savage, M. (1988) 'Trade unionism, sex segregation, and the state: women's employment in "new industries" in inter-war Britain', *Social History*, vol 13, no 2, May, pp. 209–30.

Schlereth, T. (ed) (1982) *Material Studies in America*, Nashville: The American Association of State and Local History.

Schoer, K. (1987) 'Part-time employment: Britain and West Germany', *Cambridge Journal of Economics*, vol 11, no 1, March, pp. 83–94.

Schofield, R. (1986) 'Did the mothers really die? Three centuries of maternal mortality in "the world we have lost"', in Bonfield *et al.* (eds) (1983).

Schreiner (1911) *Women and Labour*, London: Virago, reprint of 1978.

Scott, H. (1984) *Working Your Way to the Bottom: The Feminization of Poverty*, London: Pandora Press.

Scott, J. (1983) 'Women in history: The modern period', *Past and Present*, vol 101, pp. 141–57.

—— (1986) 'Gender: a useful category of historical analysis', *American Historical Review*, vol 91, no 5, Dec, pp. 1053–75.

—— (1988) *Gender and the Politics of History*, New York: Columbia University Press.

Seccombe, W. (1974) 'The housewife and her labour under capitalism', *New Left Review*, no 83, Jan/Feb, pp. 3–24.

—— (1975) 'Domestic labour: reply to critics, *New Left Review*, no 94, Nov/Dec, pp. 85–96.

—— (1980a) 'Domestic labour and the working-class household' in Fox (ed.) (1980).

—— (1980b) 'The expanded reproduction cycle of labour power in twentieth-century capitalism', in Fox (ed.) (1980).

—— (1983) 'Marxism and demography', *New Left Review*, no 137, Jan/Feb, pp. 22–47.

—— (1986) 'Patriarchy stabilized: the construction of the male breadwinner wage norm in nineteenth century Britain', *Social History*, vol 11, pp. 53–76.

Segal, L. (ed.) (1983) *What Is To Be Done about the Family?*, Harmondsworth: Penguin.

Select Committee (1982) *Voluntary Part-Time Work*, House of Lords Select

REFERENCES

Committee on the European Communities, 19th Report, 1981/2 (216), London: HMSO.

Sen, G. (1980) 'The sexual division of labor and the working class family: towards a conceptual synthesis of class relations and the subordination of women', *Review of Radical Political Economics*, vol 12, no 2, Summer, pp. 76–86.

Shah, A. (1990) 'The returns to industrial training in the graduate labour market', *The Manchester School*, vol LVIII, June, pp. 128–41.

Shammas, C. (1990) *The Pre-Industrial Consumer in England and America*, Oxford: Clarendon Press.

Shaw, M. (ed.) (1985) *Marxist Sociology Revisited: Critical Assessments*, London: Macmillan.

Shelton, B. and Firestone, J. (1989) 'Household labor time and the gender gap in earnings', *Gender and Society*, vol 3, no 1, March, pp. 105–112.

Showstack Sassoon, A. (ed.) (1987) *Women and the State: The Shifting Boundaries of Public and Private*, London: Hutchinson.

Siltanen, J. (1981) 'A commentary on theories of female wage labour', in Cambridge Women's Studies Group (1981).

—— (1986) 'Domestic responsibilities and the structuring of employment', in Crompton and Mann (eds) (1986).

—— and Stanworth, M. (eds) (1984) *Women and the Public Sphere: A Critique of Sociology and Politics*, London: Hutchinson.

Silverstone, R. (1976) 'Office work for women: an historical review', *Business History*, vol XVIII, no 1, Jan, pp. 98–110.

Smith, J. (1984) 'Non-wage labor and subsistence', in Smith *et al.* (eds) (1984).

—— *et al.* (eds) (1984) *Households and the World Economy*, London: Sage.

Smith, P. (1978) 'Domestic labour and Marx's theory of value', in Kuhn and Wolpe (eds) (1978).

Snell, K. (1985) *Annals of the Labouring Poor: Social Change and Agrarian England, 1660–1900*, Cambridge: Cambridge University Press.

Snyder, D. *et al.* (1978) 'The location of change in the sexual structure of occupations 1950–1970: insights from labour market segmentation theory', *American Journal of Sociology*, vol 84, no 3, pp. 706–17.

Sokoloff, N. (1980) *Between Money and Love: The Dialectics of Women's Home and Market Work*, New York: Praeger.

Sprague, A. (1988) 'Post-war fertility and female labour force participation rates', *Economic Journal*, vol 98, Sept, pp. 682–700.

Stacey, M. (1981) 'The division of labour revisited, or overcoming the two Adams', in Abrams *et al.* (eds) (1981).

Steadman *et al.* (1981) *The Value Controversy*, London: Verso.

Strober, M. (1984) 'Toward a general theory of occupational segregation: the case of public school teaching', in Reskin (ed.) (1984).

—— and Arnold, C. (1987) 'Occupational segregation among bank tellers', in Brown and Pechman (eds) (1987).

Summerfield, P. (1984) *Women Workers in the Second World War: Production and Patriarchy in Conflict*, London: Croom Helm.

Summers, A. (1979) 'A home from home – women's philanthropic work in the nineteenth century', in Burman (ed.) (1979).

Teitelbaum, M. (1984) *The British Fertility Decline*, Princeton: Princeton University Press.
—— and Winter, J. (1985) *The Fear of Population Decline*, London: Academic Press.
Thom, D. (1986) 'The bundle of sticks: women trade unionists and collective organisation before 1918', in John (ed.) (1986).
Thompson, F. (1988) *The Rise of Respectable Society: A Social History of Victorian Britain, 1830–1900*, London: Fontana.
Thorne, B. (ed.) (1982) *Rethinking the Family: Some Feminists' Questions*, New York: Longman.
Tienda, M. *et al.* (1987) 'Industrial restructuring, gender segregation, and sex differences in earnings', *American Sociological Review*, vol 52, no 2, April, pp. 195–210.
Tijdens, K. *et al.* (eds) (1989) *Women, Work and Computerization: Forming New Alliances*, Amsterdam: North-Holland.
Tilly, L. (1986) 'Paths of proletarianization: organization of production, sexual division of labor, and women's collective action', in Leacock *et al.* (1986).
—— and Scott J. (1978) *Women, Work and the Family*, New York: Holt, Rinehart and Winston.
Titmuss, R. (1963) 'The position of women: some vital statistics', in Titmuss (1963).
—— (1963) *Essays on 'the Welfare State'*, London: Unwin.
Turbin, C. (1984) 'Reconceptualizing family, work and labor organizing: working women in Troy, 1860–1890', *Review of Radical Political Economics*, vol 16, no 1, Spring, pp. 1–16.
Valverde, M. (1987/8) '"Giving the females a domestic turn": the social, legal and moral regulation of women's work in British cotton mills, 1820–50', *Journal of Social History*, vol 21, no 4, pp. 619–34.
Vanek, J. (1980) 'Time spent in housework', in Amsden (ed.) (1980), reproduced from *Scientific American*, vol 231, November, 1974, pp. 116–20.
Van Horn, S. (1988) *Women, Work, and Fertility, 1900–1986*, New York: University Press.
Vann, R. (1977) 'Toward a new lifestyle: women in pre-industrial capitalism', in Bridenthal and Koonz (eds) (1977).
Vogel, L. (1977) 'Hearts to feel and tongues to speak: New England mill women in the early nineteenth century', in Cantor and Laurie (eds) (1977).
—— (1981) 'Marxism and feminism: unhappy marriage, trial separation or something else?', in Sargent (ed.) (1981).
Wajcman, J. (1981) 'Work and the family: who gets "the best of both worlds"', in Cambridge Women's Studies Group (1981).
Walby, S. (1985) 'Spatial and historical variations in women's unemployment and employment', in Murgatoyd *et al.* (eds) (1985).
—— (1986) *Patriarchy at Work: Patriarchal and Capitalist Relations in Employment*, London: Polity.
—— (ed.) (1988) *Gender Segregation at Work*, Milton Keynes: Open University Press.

—— (1988a) 'Segregation in employment in social and economic theory', in Walby (ed.) (1988).

—— (1988b) 'Gender politics and social theory', *Sociology*, vol 22, no 2, May, pp. 215–32.

—— (1990) 'From private to public patriarchy: the periodisation of British history', *Women's Studies International Forum*, vol 13, nos 1/2, pp. 91–104.

—— (1990) *Theorizing Patriarchy*, Oxford: Basil Blackwell.

Wallace, J. (1985) *An Examination of the Influence of Labour Demand on the Growth of Part-Time Employment in Great Britain*, University of Bath PhD.

Wallerstein, I. (1984) 'Household structures and the world-economy', in Smith *et al*. (eds) (1984).

Walsh, M. (1989) 'Working women in the United States', *Bulletin of the Society for the Study of Labour History*, vol 54, no 1, Spring, pp. 37–53.

Wandersee, W. (1981) *Women's Work and Family Values, 1920–1940*, Cambridge: Harvard University Press.

Ward, K. (1988) 'Women in the global economy', in Gutek *et al*. (eds) (1988).

Webster, J. (1986) 'Word processing and the secretarial labour process', in Purcell *et al*. (eds) (1986).

—— (1989) 'Influencing the content of women's work in automated offices', in Tijdens *et al*. (eds) (1989).

—— (1990) *Office Automation: The Labour Process and Women's Work in Britain*, London: Wheatsheaf.

West, J. (ed.) (1982) *Work, Women and the Labour Market*, London: Routledge and Kegan Paul.

Whipp, R. and Grieco, M. (1989) 'Time, task and travel: budgeting for interdependencies', in Grieco *et al*. (eds) (1989).

White, L. and Brinkerhoff, D. (1981a) 'Children's work in the family: its significance and meaning', *Journal of Marriage and the Family*, Nov, pp. 789–98.

—— (1981b) 'The sexual division of labor: evidence from childhood', *Social Forces*, vol 60, no 1, Sept, pp. 170–81.

Wilkinson, F. (ed.) (1981) *The Dynamics of Labour Market Segmentation*, with Introduction, London: Athlone Press.

Williams, C. (1988) *Examining the Nature of Domestic Labour*, Aldershot: Avebury.

—— (1989) *Gender Differences at Work: Women and Men in Non-traditional Occupations*, Berkeley: University of California Press.

Wills, J. (1987) 'Women and the economy: issues for the states', in Beneria and Stimpson (eds) (1987).

Wilson, E. (1977) *Women and the Welfare State*, London: Tavistock.

Winter, J. (1979) 'Infant mortality, maternal mortality and public health in Britain in the 1930s', *Journal of European Economic History*, vol 8, no 2, Fall, pp. 439–62.

—— (1982) 'The decline of mortality in Britain 1870–1950', in Barker and Drake (eds) (1982).

Wolpe, H. (1972) 'Capitalism and cheap labour power in South Africa: from segregation to apartheid', *Economy and Society*, vol 1, no 4, pp. 425–56.

—— (ed.) (1980) *The Articulation of Modes of Production: Essays from "Economy and Society"*, London: Routledge & Kegan Paul.

Wood, S. (ed.) (1982) *The Degradation of Work: Skill, Deskilling and the Labour Process*, London: Hutchinson.

Woods, R. (1989) 'Population growth and economic change in the eighteenth and nineteenth centuries', in Mathias and Davis (eds) (1989).

—— and Woodward, J. (eds) (1984) *Urban Disease and Mortality*, London: Batsford Academic.

Wray, K. (1984) 'Labour market operation, recruitment strategies and workforce structures', *International Journal of Social Economics*, vol 11, no 7, pp. 6–31.

Wright, B. *et al.* (eds) (1987) *Women, Work, and Technology: Transformations*, Ann Arbor: University of Michigan Press.

Wright, R. and Ermisch, J. (1990) 'Male–female wage differentials in Great Britain', *Birkbeck Discussion Paper*, no 10/90.

Wrigley, E. (1969) *Population and History*, London: McGraw Hill.

—— and Schofield, R. (1981) *The Population History of England, 1541–1871*, London: Edward Arnold.

Yanagisako, S. (1979) 'Family and household: the analysis of domestic groups', *Annual Review of Anthropology*, vol 18, pp. 161–205.

Yanz, L. and Smith, D. (1983) 'Women as a reserve army of labour: a critique', *Review of Radical Political Economics*, vol 15, no 1, Spring, pp. 92–106.

Yohalem, A. (ed.) (1980) *Women Returning to Work: Policies and Progress in Five Countries*, London: Pinter.

Young, I. (1981) 'Beyond the unhappy marriage: a critique of the dual systems theory', in Sargent (ed.) (1981).

Young, K. (1978) 'Modes of appropriation and the sexual division of labour: a case study from Oaxaca, Mexico', in Kuhn and Wolpe (eds) (1978).

Young, M. and Willmott, P. (1973) *The Symmetrical Family: A Study of Work and Leisure in the London Region*, London: Routledge & Kegan Paul.

Zabalza, A. and Tzannatos, Z. (1985) *Women and Equal Pay: The Effects of Legislation on Female Employment and Wages in Britain*, Cambridge: Cambridge University Press.

—— (1988) 'Reply to the comments on the effects of Britain's anti-discrimination legislation on relative pay and employment', *Economic Journal*, vol 98, Sept, pp. 839–43.

Zaretsky, E. (1976) *Capitalism, the Family and Personal Life*, London: Pluto.

—— (1985) 'The place of the family in the origins of the Welfare State', in Shaw (ed.) (1985).

Zeitlin, J. (1989) 'Theories of women's work and occupational segregation', *Bulletin of the Society for the Study of Labour History*, vol 54, no 1, Spring, pp. 6–10.

Zelizer, V. (1985) *Pricing the Priceless Child*, New York: Basic Books.

NAME INDEX

SUBJECT INDEX